FRIEND OR FOE

Columbia Studies in Middle East Politics

COLUMBIA STUDIES IN MIDDLE EAST POLITICS
Marc Lynch, Series Editor

Columbia Studies in Middle East Politics presents academically rigorous, well-written, relevant, and accessible books on the rapidly transforming politics of the Middle East for an interested academic and policy audience.

The Arab Uprisings Explained: New Contentious Politics in the Middle East, edited by Marc Lynch

Sectarian Politics in the Gulf: From the Iraq War to the Arab Uprisings, Frederic M. Wehrey

From Resilience to Revolution: How Foreign Interventions Destabilize the Middle East, Sean L. Yom

Protection Amid Chaos: The Creation of Property Rights in Palestinian Refugee Camps, Nadya Hajj

Religious Statecraft: The Politics of Islam in Iran, Mohammad Ayatollahi Tabaar

Local Politics in Jordan and Morocco: Strategies of Centralization and Decentralization, Janine A. Clark

Jordan and the Arab Uprisings: Regime Survival and Politics Beyond the State, Curtis Ryan

Friend or Foe

MILITIA INTELLIGENCE AND ETHNIC VIOLENCE IN THE LEBANESE CIVIL WAR

Nils Hägerdal

Columbia University Press
New York

Columbia University Press
Publishers Since 1893
New York   Chichester, West Sussex
cup.columbia.edu
Copyright © 2021 Columbia University Press
All rights reserved

Library of Congress Cataloging-in-Publication Data
Names: Hägerdal, Nils, author.
Title: Friend or foe : militia intelligence and ethnic violence in the Lebanese civil war / Nils Hägerdal.
Description: New York : Columbia University Press, 2021. | Series: Columbia studies in Middle East politics | Includes bibliographical references and index.
Identifiers: LCCN 2020046086 (print) | LCCN 2020046087 (ebook) | ISBN 9780231200646 (hardback) | ISBN 9780231200653 (trade paperback) | ISBN 9780231553728 (ebook)
Subjects: LCSH: Ethnic conflict—Lebanon. | Lebanon—History—Civil War, 1975-1990. | Lebanon—Ethnic relations.
Classification: LCC DS87.5 .H326 2021 (print) | LCC DS87.5 (ebook) | DDC 956.9204/4—dc23
LC record available at https://lccn.loc.gov/2020046086
LC ebook record available at https://lccn.loc.gov/2020046087

Cover image: Photo, central Beirut, December 2013, by author
Cover design: Chang Jae Lee

For Laura

Contents

Acknowledgments ix

Introduction 1

I   Ethnic Violence in Non-Separatist Wars 16

II The Lebanese Civil War, 1975–1990 40

III Demographics, Migration, and Violence 65

IV Lebanon's Christian Militias 93

V   Palestinian, Muslim, and Left-Wing Armed Groups 121

Conclusion 149

Notes 163
References 187
Index 201

Acknowledgments

Every author incurs debts of gratitude, intellectual and otherwise, in the course of writing a book; mine span across more than a decade and extend across multiple continents.

This research project began its life many years ago as a master's thesis in the Committee on International Relations at the University of Chicago. My thesis advisors, John Schuessler and Matthias Staisch, read and commented on the very first words I ever put on paper about the Lebanese civil war. At Chicago I also first met Sarah Parkinson, who has provided important feedback at several steps of the project and continuously encouraged me to treat this complex case study with great respect. The University of Chicago provided a remarkable intellectual community with benefits that extended far beyond the short time I spent there. John Mearsheimer's colorful seminars and Charlie Glaser's analytical precision strikes shaped my thinking on international security, and their letters of recommendation took me to my next destination.

At Harvard I am grateful for the things I learned from my formal advisors—Bob Bates, Melani Cammett, Monica Toft, and Steve Walt—as well as from many other members of the Government Department and the Kennedy School, including Kara Ross Camarena, Volha Charnysh, Ishac Diwan, Raissa Fabregas, Julie Faller, Nilesh Fernando, Jeff Friedman, Tara Grillos, Shelby Grossman, Alicia Harley, Dan Honig, Torben Iversen, Josh Kertzer, Dominika Kruszewska, Akos Lada, John Marshall, Dan

Masterson, Tarek Masoud, Rich Nielsen, Rob Schub, Trisha Shrum, Beth Simmons, George Yin, and Yuri Zhukov. Harvard attracts an amazing array of visiting scholars, and I was particularly fortunate to meet Peter Krause, Vera Mironova, Lama Mourad, Amanda Rizkallah, and Jonah Schulhofer-Wohl during their time in residence at the Belfer Center. Nearby MIT provided great resources as well, including coursework on ethnic politics with Roger Petersen and Fotini Christia. Another memorable experience of graduate school was the annual Harvard-Yale-MIT Conference on Political Violence, which provided wonderful opportunities to solicit feedback from scholars at other universities, including Zeynep Bulutgil, Stathis Kalyvas, Matt Kocher, Steven Wilkinson, and Libby Wood. During the last two years of the doctoral program the Weatherhead Center for International Affairs provided office space and financial support as I finished my dissertation, which also allowed me to attend the Peace Science Society International conference and the Middle East Studies Association meeting to present my work. Finally, I am grateful to Nicole Tateosian at Harvard Kennedy School who saved me from its administrative dysfunction on multiple occasions.

During graduate school I also began the adventure of learning Arabic, a journey guided by Bill Granara and facilitated by the incredible Feryal Hijazi. Her first-year Arabic class enabled me to bypass second-year coursework altogether at Middlebury Summer Arabic School, where I completed third-year college-level Arabic in eight weeks of intensive classes, which included a "language pledge" prohibiting all communication in other languages. At this program I met fellow political scientists Rick McAlexander and Gerasimos Tsourapas, with whom I have luckily been allowed to speak English on our subsequent encounters. An Arabic Language Grant from Hilary Rantisi at the Middle East Initiative of Harvard Kennedy School helped me attend this unique summer program, as did generous financial aid from Middlebury College. The following summer I was grateful to receive the David S. Dodge Award covering tuition and housing costs for the summer Arabic program at American University of Beirut.

The most precious part of doctoral research was the opportunity to spend the 2013–2014 academic year in Lebanon as affiliated researcher at the Center for Arab and Middle Eastern Studies at the American University of Beirut, enabled by a generous research grant from Sixten Gemzéus Stiftelse in Stockholm. In Lebanon, my primary debt stands to the men and

Contents

Acknowledgments ix

Introduction 1

I Ethnic Violence in Non-Separatist Wars 16

II The Lebanese Civil War, 1975–1990 40

III Demographics, Migration, and Violence 65

IV Lebanon's Christian Militias 93

V Palestinian, Muslim, and Left-Wing Armed Groups 121

Conclusion 149

Notes 163
References 187
Index 201

Acknowledgments

Every author incurs debts of gratitude, intellectual and otherwise, in the course of writing a book; mine span across more than a decade and extend across multiple continents.

This research project began its life many years ago as a master's thesis in the Committee on International Relations at the University of Chicago. My thesis advisors, John Schuessler and Matthias Staisch, read and commented on the very first words I ever put on paper about the Lebanese civil war. At Chicago I also first met Sarah Parkinson, who has provided important feedback at several steps of the project and continuously encouraged me to treat this complex case study with great respect. The University of Chicago provided a remarkable intellectual community with benefits that extended far beyond the short time I spent there. John Mearsheimer's colorful seminars and Charlie Glaser's analytical precision strikes shaped my thinking on international security, and their letters of recommendation took me to my next destination.

At Harvard I am grateful for the things I learned from my formal advisors—Bob Bates, Melani Cammett, Monica Toft, and Steve Walt—as well as from many other members of the Government Department and the Kennedy School, including Kara Ross Camarena, Volha Charnysh, Ishac Diwan, Raissa Fabregas, Julie Faller, Nilesh Fernando, Jeff Friedman, Tara Grillos, Shelby Grossman, Alicia Harley, Dan Honig, Torben Iversen, Josh Kertzer, Dominika Kruszewska, Akos Lada, John Marshall, Dan

Masterson, Tarek Masoud, Rich Nielsen, Rob Schub, Trisha Shrum, Beth Simmons, George Yin, and Yuri Zhukov. Harvard attracts an amazing array of visiting scholars, and I was particularly fortunate to meet Peter Krause, Vera Mironova, Lama Mourad, Amanda Rizkallah, and Jonah Schulhofer-Wohl during their time in residence at the Belfer Center. Nearby MIT provided great resources as well, including coursework on ethnic politics with Roger Petersen and Fotini Christia. Another memorable experience of graduate school was the annual Harvard-Yale-MIT Conference on Political Violence, which provided wonderful opportunities to solicit feedback from scholars at other universities, including Zeynep Bulutgil, Stathis Kalyvas, Matt Kocher, Steven Wilkinson, and Libby Wood. During the last two years of the doctoral program the Weatherhead Center for International Affairs provided office space and financial support as I finished my dissertation, which also allowed me to attend the Peace Science Society International conference and the Middle East Studies Association meeting to present my work. Finally, I am grateful to Nicole Tateosian at Harvard Kennedy School who saved me from its administrative dysfunction on multiple occasions.

During graduate school I also began the adventure of learning Arabic, a journey guided by Bill Granara and facilitated by the incredible Feryal Hijazi. Her first-year Arabic class enabled me to bypass second-year coursework altogether at Middlebury Summer Arabic School, where I completed third-year college-level Arabic in eight weeks of intensive classes, which included a "language pledge" prohibiting all communication in other languages. At this program I met fellow political scientists Rick McAlexander and Gerasimos Tsourapas, with whom I have luckily been allowed to speak English on our subsequent encounters. An Arabic Language Grant from Hilary Rantisi at the Middle East Initiative of Harvard Kennedy School helped me attend this unique summer program, as did generous financial aid from Middlebury College. The following summer I was grateful to receive the David S. Dodge Award covering tuition and housing costs for the summer Arabic program at American University of Beirut.

The most precious part of doctoral research was the opportunity to spend the 2013–2014 academic year in Lebanon as affiliated researcher at the Center for Arab and Middle Eastern Studies at the American University of Beirut, enabled by a generous research grant from Sixten Gemzéus Stiftelse in Stockholm. In Lebanon, my primary debt stands to the men and women I interviewed and who shared their personal experiences and insights. Almost without exception, the people I contacted not only made time to talk to me but insisted on treating me to coffee or other sustenance sometimes on multiple occasions. Pertinence prohibits me from mentioning names, but several individuals also went above and beyond to facilitate further contacts or access to other resources to help me with my research. Without their tremendous generosity there would be no empirical material to base this book upon. Beyond my interlocutors I am also grateful to Youssef Shatila and his entire extended family, my landlords who became good friends, for providing a comfortable home in Beirut, where I have since returned to stay multiple times. For their friendship, camaraderie, and advice during my fieldwork I thank Dylan, Magnus, Maja, May, Lina, Alexandra, Mostafa, Soman, Welmoed, Konstantin, and Angela. In Lebanon I also first met Kelly Stedem, at the time a staff member at UMAM Documentation & Research, who subsequently became a valuable colleague in the Boston area. Yosra Al Ahmad taught me Syrian Arabic through her idiosyncratic but extremely effective program; I hope that Berlin provides her and her children with a life that Beirut could not, and that she no longer writes sad poems about the sea.

After defending my dissertation I moved to Princeton for a year as a postdoctoral researcher at the Niehaus Center, located in what was then known as the Woodrow Wilson School. I am grateful to all of my fellow fellows in this fantastic program—and in particular to Nikhar Gaikwad, Josh Kertzer, and Lauren Peritz—who saw multiple iterations of my presentation and provided valuable and constructive feedback. Helen Milner was extremely generous with the center's resources, including by providing funding for two month-long trips to Lebanon. Beyond the Niehaus Center I enjoyed the wider Politics Department community and learned many things from Carles Boix, Killian Clarke, Sharan Grewal, Amaney Jamal, Melissa Lee, Steve Monroe, Jake Shapiro, Dan Tavana, and Manuel Vogt. During this year I also met Dan Corstange and Abbey Steele, both of whom have been highly supportive and provided useful feedback. Finally, I had the pleasure of being invited to give a talk at the Program on Order, Conflict and Violence at Yale; I am grateful to Stathis Kalyvas and Libby Wood for inviting me and to Consuelo Amat and Stephen Moncrief for organizing the visit.

The next step of the journey brought me back to Boston and the Crown Center for Middle East Studies at Brandeis, where I spent a year as junior research fellow. At the end of this year Eva Bellin generously organized a book conference for my project, and I am grateful to her and to Shai Feldman, David Siddhartha Patel, Roger Petersen, and Jonah Schulhofer-Wohl for reading and commenting on my work. Their comments revealed great interest in the project but also forced me to redesign and rewrite several chapters. On a related note, I later realized that most colleagues know down to the dollar how much it cost to organize their book conferences; in honest testament to Eva's support for junior scholars, I have no idea what expenses mine incurred.

Most of the final manuscript subsequently emerged during a spell of unemployment. After I filed my Green Card application, I spent almost five months in the United States in formal applicant status but without work or travel permits. For most of this time I spent my days squatting in empty office space at the Middle East Initiative in Mount Auburn Street. I thank Raissa Fabregas, Daniel Velez-Lopez, Avery Schmidt, and the MEI staff for their pleasant company and for sharing their printer and coffee maker. The Harvard Library issued me an alumni card that let me into the library buildings to browse and read, while my spousal library card at Boston College also came with thirty-day borrowing privileges. I am grateful to both institutions as I could not have completed the manuscript without access to their collections.

Once endowed with the legal right to work—as a freshly anointed permanent resident of the United States of America—I started a new postdoctoral position at the Center for Strategic Studies at the Fletcher School of Tufts. I am deeply grateful to Monica Toft for hosting me at the center, in various capacities over multiple years, and to her and Ivan for inviting the whole team into their home every semester. My research has benefited from input by all members of this vibrant community but I am particularly grateful to Thomas Cavanna, Bridget Coggins, Ben Denison, Karim Elkady, and Sidita Kushi for extensive comments on multiple projects and presentations. I also thank the center for finding room in its budget to pay for indexing this book.

Marc Lynch quickly took an interest in my manuscript when I contacted him, and I am honored to have it included among the other titles in Columbia Studies in Middle East Politics. A whole generation of political scientists studying the Middle East is indebted to Marc for his support of this community through the Project on Middle East Political Science. The editorial team at Columbia University Press, Caelyn Cobb and Monique

Briones, run a smooth and professional operation, and kindly enabled me to use a photograph I took during fieldwork (while walking along the infamous "Green Line" that divided Beirut during the war) as cover art for the book. Two anonymous reviewers combined a close and perceptive reading of the manuscript with a generous spirit, a constructive tone, and insightful recommendations that helped make the final product stronger, tighter, and more readable. I am grateful to all of them for their support and assistance in completing this project. Some of the material in the book previously appeared in "Ethnic Cleansing and the Politics of Restraint: Violence and Coexistence in the Lebanese Civil War," *Journal of Conflict Resolution* 63, no. 1 (2019); and "Toxic Waste Dumping in Conflict Zones: Evidence from 1980s Lebanon," *Mediterranean Politics* 26, no. 2 (2021), and I thank the publishers for permission to reuse relevant sections.

Among debts of gratitude, my family is like a revolving credit line. I owe so many things to my parents, Görel and Magnus, who inspired my path to academic research; to Måns, Erik, and Astrid and her family in the Malmö-Lund area; to Martin and his family in Stockholm; and to Eglal and David in Northampton. Without their support and encouragement there would be no book. Yet my deepest gratitude goes to my wife, Laura, who supported me in innumerable ways through some rather challenging times while being the first to celebrate every moment of joy or triumph along the journey. This book is dedicated to her.

FRIEND OR FOE

Introduction

In January 1976 Christian forces attacked the Karantina neighborhood in Beirut, a slum area that housed thousands of poor residents who worked as day laborers in the nearby port facilities. While home to a mix of mostly Lebanese Sunni and Shia Muslims and a few Palestinians and stateless Kurds, the area was located in East Beirut, which is otherwise the predominantly Christian side of the city. After facing light military resistance, the militias entered the neighborhood and proceeded to systematically raze it. Most residents survived the attack but were not allowed to stay. Instead, they were placed on trucks and buses and transported to the front lines. Christian leaders telephoned Palestine Liberation Organization (PLO) chairman Yasser Arafat in advance, and at a prearranged time the combatants observed a brief cease-fire so that the civilians from Karantina could cross the front lines on foot and enter permanent exile in Palestinian-controlled territory. During the attack on Karantina, Christian militias thus intentionally and forcibly displaced all Muslim residents, based on their sectarian identity rather than their individual or personal characteristics.[1] This behavior is the textbook definition of ethnic cleansing.[2]

Nearby Sunni residents in the Baydoun area, named for its eponymous mosque and located no more than a ten-minute drive from Karantina, somehow escaped this treatment. The area was controlled by the same Christian militia groups and hosted several thousand Sunni residents who lived intermingled with a larger Christian population. This area is just as close to the front lines as Karantina and commands a strategic location at the heart of East Beirut. A small number of Muslim residents left Baydoun during the first two years of the war because of political and security issues, possibly including active threats that involved coercion but stopped short of bloodshed.[3] However, an overwhelming majority of Sunni families remained in place during the civil war. The local mosque stayed open for Friday prayers every single week throughout fifteen years of civil war, and local Muslims attended without hiding themselves or their identity. The mosque remains in operation to the present and was packed from wall to wall with worshippers when I visited during Friday prayers on a warm, sunny spring day in 2014.[4] Unlike in Karantina, it appears that Christian militias in Baydoun forced only select Muslim individuals to leave while permitting the majority to stay. The fact that these Sunni residents remained in place shows not only that militia forces permitted them to stay but also that the Sunnis felt sufficiently safe to choose not to move to Sunni-dominated West Beirut, located only a few kilometers away. Why would members of the same sectarian community, residents of two different neighborhoods in close geographic proximity, experience such radically different fates?

This book explores the role of ethnicity in civil war violence. In plural societies, political mobilization typically occurs along ethnic lines, such as through ethnic political parties contesting peaceful elections.[5] Whenever political conflict evolves into armed hostilities, it is therefore quite common to find that its combatants generally hail from separate ethnic communities. As the fog of war thickens during chaotic circumstances, where the ability to separate friend from foe is a matter of life and death, many participants rely on ethnicity as an informational shortcut and start to view non-coethnics in general with suspicion.[6] Ethnicity thereby serves as an informational cue or a heuristic device that signals an individual's likely political loyalties and potential hostility. Some armed groups engage in ethnic cleansing—comprehensive forced displacement of entire civilian communities based on their ethnic identity. In armed conflicts fought across an ethnic divide, ethnic cleansing may become a rational military strategy because if all hostile militants are non-coethnics then the full set of non-coethnics contains the full set of hostile militants. Even extensive patterns of prewar interethnic trust can rapidly break down and yield ethnic separation, as militants displace non-coethnics and civilians elect to flee from areas where they no longer feel safe.[7]

Sometimes the military-strategic incentives for ethnic cleansing are compounded by political incentives to cause ethnic separation and create homogenous nation states. There is a large body of work on separatist conflict in political science and on how those conflicts generate political incentives for ethnic cleansing.[8] Many nationalist ideologies contain narratives of how certain territory forms part of an ancestral homeland that should be reserved for members of a particular group only.[9] Bosnian Serb forces employed ethnic cleansing against Muslim Bosniaks in East Bosnia in the mid-1990s because, by rendering the area homogenously Serbian, they hoped to fold this territory into the neighboring state of Serbia; their compatriots tried the same dirty trick against Albanians in Kosovo only a few years later.[10] Partition between Greece and Turkey or India and Pakistan generated millions of refugees who needed to leave their original homes in order to form mono-confessional new polities.[11]

Yet in non-separatist ethnic conflicts, contestants generally have political incentives to act with some degree of moderation and to avoid causing permanent ethnic separation.[12] In such conflicts combatants may regard non-coethnics as enemies but often still view them as fellow citizens; the armed struggle concerns how to govern multiethnic countries, not how to partition them. Combatants have incentives to exercise restraint because even if they succeed on the battlefield, they will need to rule a large population of non-coethnics after the war ends. For instance, national leaders in multiethnic countries like Cote d'Ivoire, Mali, and Senegal have consistently backed away from the precipice of ethnic mass killings to avoid spirals of escalating violence and to keep their plural societies intact.[13] While these leaders did not deny the existence of ethnic differences, they genuinely viewed different ethnic communities as full members of a diverse society. In fact, research shows that somewhere between one-third and one-half of all civil wars fought across an ethnic cleavage since 1945 feature non-separatist political goals.[14] Aside from Lebanon, which fought non-separatist civil wars along sectarian lines in 1958 as well as in 1975–1990, some other important cases include Jordan (1970–1971), Angola (1975–1991), Chad (1980–1994), and Tajikistan (1992–1997). Interestingly, I show that non-separatist ethnic wars have predominantly occurred in the Arab world and sub-Saharan Africa.

My first contribution in this book is to systematically explore the dynamics of violence in non-separatist ethnic civil wars. Using ethnicity as a proxy for political allegiance is easy. What is more difficult—for those armed groups that do not seek ethnic separation as a political goal—is to correctly identify non-coethnics who are politically loyal, neutral, or apathetic and who do not pose any military threat. How can militants discriminate among neutral and hostile non-coethnics? What kind of information helps them accomplish this task? Under what conditions will they choose to use ethnicity as an informational shortcut, and when might they prefer to make decisions based on other kinds of intelligence? The classic problem of counterinsurgency is how to identify militant fish hiding in a civilian sea.[15] Conversely, in a way, the problem I study is how militants can identify friendly non-coethnics in a setting where any non-coethnic could be a hostile militant, and where participants increasingly conflate ethnic identity with political loyalties. My argument considers how armed groups behave when they face divergent political and military incentives regarding forced displacement of non-coethnics, and when ethnic cleansing as a result becomes a reluctant last resort rather than a primary political goal.

The issue of how militants discriminate among non-coethnics raises the larger question of how they collect and process intelligence during armed conflict. This question forms a central puzzle in the literatures on civil war violence and forced displacement.[16] The most influential approach to micro-level variation in wartime violence centers on how armed groups strive to pacify military resistance in areas they control and how access to information drives their choice between various forms of selective and indiscriminate violence to accomplish this goal. This literature shows that consensual provision of information by local residents usually constitutes the best source of intelligence, as local residents have better knowledge of their social and geographical environs than outside militants do. Civilians have agency over their own actions, and models of civil war violence usually center on what conditions enable militants to induce local civilians to collaborate or otherwise reveal information. Violence emerges as a joint product of militant organizations and civilians, each participating for their own purposes that often deviate from whatever macro-level political cleavages ostensibly animate the armed conflict they endure.

However, we also know from the literature on industrial organization of violence that many armed groups have deep ties to residents in areas where they operate because they mobilize volunteers in the community to create and sustain their military fighting force.[17] Constructing a military organization requires great efforts of both recruitment and logistics. Many armed groups solve these problems by mobilizing preexisting social and political organizations, such as political parties, and rely on volunteer efforts by local residents. Community members may participate in a range of differentiated military and nonmilitary roles, ranging from frontline combat to cooking food. For instance, insurgents in El Salvador could count on as much as one-third of the civilian population in some areas where they operated to contribute material support for their struggle by making *tamale* sandwiches for fighters.[18] Large numbers of Ugandan villagers willingly provided rebel groups with simple meals—perhaps peasant staples like cassava, yams, and porridge thickened with cornmeal—to enable the insurgency to fight government forces in their geographic vicinity.[19] Malayan and Vietnamese insurgents operated mostly in areas where locals served them fragrant steamed rice.[20]

My second contribution in the book is to explore militia intelligence capabilities. I show that when a significant share of community members actively aid an armed group in ways large and small, and when most individuals who aid the militia contribute to the war effort in their own residential location, then the group can also use these extensive support networks to access local intelligence. Simply put, militias gain tremendous intelligence capabilities in areas where their active and loyal supporters live. When the residents who possess valuable local knowledge are the very same individuals who are local volunteers for the militia, the entire problem of how to solicit collaboration disappears. While much of the literature focuses on cases where armed groups were particularly poorly informed about their surroundings, including counterinsurgents fighting foreign wars of occupation, many other armed groups are comparatively well informed about their theater of operations. When armed groups operate in areas where they have local supporters, they can use this support to tap into local networks deeply embedded in particular local communities.

In wars fought across an ethnic divide, most armed groups have predominantly coethnic supporters, while enemy operatives tend to be non-coethnics. This ethnic divide complicates intelligence collection. When and how can armed groups rely on coethnic supporters to provide intelligence about non-coethnics? To study this problem, I focus on the role of prewar demographic intermixing in allowing information to cross ethnic boundaries. In intermixed locations, where residents from different ethnic groups live in dense and intermingled social space, local militia coethnics will likely know intimate details about non-coethnic community members—such as overt political sympathies, formal party membership, or history of activism—that may indicate hostile political loyalties. If an armed group can access this kind of detailed information from local sympathizers, militia operatives may be able to assess which individual non-coethnics pose a military risk. Equally important, local militia coethnics might also vouch for their non-coethnic friends who they trust and want the militia to leave in peace. Since this kind of information is generally more accurate than using ethnicity as a proxy for political loyalties, the armed group does not need to rely on heuristic devices in those situations.

Conversely, when the very same armed group operates in local areas where they have little support, they may have no feasible alternative to using ethnic identity as an informational cue, as obtaining more reliable information could be prohibitively costly. The same group might operate simultaneously across both high- and low-information settings; sometimes merely crossing the street from one neighborhood to the next could mean switching from one type of information environment to another. Homogenous non-coethnic enclaves are particularly difficult environments to collect intelligence for militias that primarily command support among coethnics. Militias might learn whether such an area hosts hostile militants, for instance if nearby coethnics report overt signs of political or military activity such as the presence of a political party headquarters accompanied by flags, posters, and armed men. However, militias generally find it much harder to discern who those individual hostile militants are. Gathering more detailed intelligence often requires huge expenses of time and labor. As a result, the militia may perceive of few effective remedies to the threat of local militancy beyond ethnic cleansing. My central empirical prediction is therefore that the demographic configuration of a village or neighborhood heavily influences the ability of militias to collect local intelligence, which in turn influences the strategies of violence they employ if they decide that they need to pacify opposition forces in a particular location.

My argument thus has two key parts. First, I argue that some armed groups find themselves in a strategic dilemma because while they have military incentives to perpetrate ethnic cleansing, they have political incentives to abstain. Under these conditions, armed groups should use ethnic cleansing because it remains a powerful military tool, but only as a last resort in situations when they perceive no other recourse. The key to resolve this dilemma, which sits at the heart of non-separatist ethnic civil wars, is to obtain more detailed information to better discriminate among neutral and hostile non-coethnics. Second, I argue that whenever and wherever militias mobilize community volunteers into wartime service, they can also draw on their ties to those local communities to collect intelligence. Armed groups in ethnic wars gain powerful intelligence capabilities in areas where they have coethnic residents, and in intermixed areas they can often cheaply gather detailed intelligence about local non-coethnics. As a result, they are more likely to perpetrate selective violence in intermixed areas while homogenous non-coethnic enclaves are more prone to ethnic cleansing.

This argument adds complexity to debates over the role of ethnicity in civil war violence, which remain dominated by two opposite extremes. One school of thought holds that ethnic identities are visible, sticky, and uniquely predictive of political loyalties and behavior.[21] The alternative view is that ethnic identities not only intersect with cross-cutting political cleavages and material interests but are themselves shaped by violence and even somewhat endogenous to conflict.[22] The former view sees ethnicity as the central defining aspect of conflict and violence, while the latter argues that ethnic cleavages are often inconsequential to micro-level outcomes. Prior explanations of ethnic cleansing in the Lebanese civil war tend to follow the former perspective, emphasizing the role of hardened identity cleavages in explaining violence and forced displacement along ethnic and sectarian lines.[23] Other scholars have written about the historical origins of this "culture of sectarianism," which divides the Lebanese into several distinct and identifiable sectarian groups each ostensibly represented by political elites that claim to speak for their community.[24]

In contrast, my argument shows that the role of ethnicity can vary even within the same conflict. Ethnicity is one kind of information: in situations where armed groups possess detailed information about individual non-coethnics, they need not rely on such crude proxies, but in other situations the very same organization may have no other option but to use ethnic identity as an indicator of political loyalties. Collecting information is expensive, and ethnicity is a cheap source of an expensive good. With reference to the specific case of Lebanon, my work thus follows others who have shown that the practice of sectarian politics often takes surprising and counterintuitive shapes. For instance, sectarian political parties frequently both neglect the welfare of their coreligionists and court out-group voters for strategic purposes.[25] Sectarian politics ensured that the Lebanese civil war broke out across a sectarian divide, and the fact that the sectarian identity of a person remained a somewhat reliable predictor of their loyalties generated military incentives for ethnic cleansing. Yet sectarian politics also contained a mutual covenant that inextricably bound sectarian communities together in a national identity. Lebanese nationalism had genuine meaning to participants in its civil war, even if they conceived of this nation in quite different ways and sought to impose their own vision through armed struggle. Paradoxically, the kaleidoscopic mosaic of Lebanese sectarianism simultaneously provided the key incentives for both violence and restraint.

This dynamic teaches us an important general lesson about ethnic violence in non-separatist wars. For instance, armed groups in Angola and Tajikistan recruited almost exclusively along linguistic lines, while Chadian militia membership was mostly defined by religion and tribal affiliation.[26] All three conflicts witnessed forced displacement or massacres of civilians along identity lines precisely because social identity was a fairly reliable indicator of political allegiance. However, like Lebanon, none of those three countries experienced comprehensive ethnic separation between different communities. Armed groups generally fought for control of the central state, which would allow them to impose their ideological vision for the country as well as to reap material rewards, but no militia had separatist goals or other ideological incentives to perpetrate ethnic cleansing. As I show in this book, this general conflict dynamic has been fairly common in the Middle East and sub-Saharan Africa but hitherto has eluded systematic study by social scientists.

Empirical Evidence

To assess my argument, I use the Lebanese civil war of 1975–1990 as a case study. Lebanon has a dizzying mosaic of social diversity. Its citizenry consists mostly of Muslim and Christian speakers of Arabic but also contains a modest share of Armenians and a small number of Kurds.[27] Christian speakers of Arabic further divide into Maronite Catholics, Greek Orthodox, Greek Catholic, and a large number of very small minority communities. Muslims divide into the Sunni, Shia, and Alawi communities, while the Druze sect also caucuses with Muslims in Lebanon's consociational parliament.[28] Parliament maintains set quotas for eleven sectarian groups, including "Christian minorities" that amalgamate several minor confessions.[29] As there has not been a census in almost a century, the true demographic balance in Lebanon remains highly contested, but for the sake of a rough approximation we can think of contemporary Lebanon as dominated by three demographic blocs of comparable magnitude: Maronite Catholics and Sunni and Shia Muslims.[30] Armenians, Druze, Greek Orthodox, and Greek Catholics constitute meaningful population shares while other communities are very small. Ever since the war of 1948 Lebanon also hosts a large community of Palestinian refugees, most of whom are Sunni Muslims with a small minority of Christians. Almost none of these refugees were ever granted Lebanese citizenship, and the community still resides mostly in squalid UN-administered refugee camps that have grown into urban shantytowns.[31] Today the country also hosts over one million Syrian refugees who have arrived in waves after the outbreak of the Syrian civil war in 2011.[32]

My empirical work focuses on the first two years of the war, known as the Two Years' War (Harb Sanateyn), which pitted a set of allied Christian militia forces against the Palestinian national movement and its left-wing, Muslim, and Druze Lebanese allies.[33] The former militias had almost exclusively Christian fighters, whereas the second set of forces had almost universal appeal among Palestinians and Sunni and Druze Lebanese. For these reasons, the war had strong sectarian undertones from its inception. My quantitative empirical work focuses on the Muslim–Christian cleavage, which is the most relevant identity cleavage for understanding the early civil war years. Fighters on both sides committed horrific acts of sectarian violence. Yet some Christians sympathized with left-wing and pro-Palestinian parties, and a very small number of Muslims—mostly Shia—found comfort in the Lebanese nationalist visions associated with Christian militia forces. The role of sectarian identities in this conflict and its violence is very complex, which makes it a fecund case study. The political salience of these identities has changed over time, however; today, arguably the most important cleavage is the Sunni–Shia divide, which did not play as important of a role in 1970s Lebanon.[34]

Between early summer 2013 and late summer 2014, I spent fourteen months in Lebanon partly to identify, approach, and interview individuals with deep knowledge about various aspects of the Lebanese civil war and its militias. In 2017 I returned for two additional month-long trips. During most of this time I had the pleasure of being an affiliated researcher at the Center for Arab and Middle Eastern Studies at American University of Beirut. In total, I interviewed about seventy individuals during these spells of fieldwork. About 30 percent of interviews were conducted in Arabic and the rest in English; I did not work with a translator. Having an introduction was usually critical to secure an interview, and many individuals I interviewed suggested others for me to talk to as well. As a result, the majority of interviews were obtained through this method, known as snowball sampling. However, for the Christian forces in particular, I was also able to use multiple points of entry, which gave added perspective on disagreements and factional splits. About a third of the people I interviewed were at some point affiliated with a wartime militia, and many of those served in mid-level or senior leadership positions. The other interviewees represent a broad spectrum of positions in academia, media, think tanks, nongovernment organizations, the private sector, and clergy from some of Lebanon's eighteen officially recognized confessional communities. Some of the individuals in this second category have very strong political ties to a party or militia, and in these instances, I try to indicate these relationships throughout the text. Interviews were semistructured with certain recurring questions to allow comparisons across individuals, organizations, and locations.

I can barely imagine any question one might ask about the Lebanese civil war that would not broach a sensitive topic. After the war, parliament passed a general amnesty law that absolved all perpetrators of wartime abuse from legal proceedings.[35] Consequently, government agencies generally abstained from systematic efforts to document and prosecute wartime abuse. Because of the sensitive and controversial nature of the topic, the civil war is not taught in public schools.[36] Youths largely learn about the war from their parents or other family members, community elders, and media sources often operated by the very same sectarian political parties that contested the war.[37] As a result, different sectarian communities tend to perpetuate separate narratives of events, suffering, and guilt. The literature on the anthropology of violence teaches several valuable practices in how to capture the lived experience of both victims and perpetrators in politically sensitive contexts. With perpetrators in particular we need to be mindful that interview evidence only represents the perpetrator's current understanding of their own past actions and must walk a fine line between accurately capturing their personal experience without succumbing to "ethnographic seduction" and inadvertently "humanizing the inhumane."[38]

While the general amnesty law is a travesty from the perspective of transitional justice, it had fortunate consequences for ethnographic fieldwork.

Wartime military leaders and other perpetrators of violence mostly returned to ordinary civilian life after the war ended, and they can at present speak their mind without facing legal consequences. It was not difficult to find interview subjects. On the contrary, the persons I contacted were usually eager to explain "what really happened." Many Lebanese invited me into their homes, and I drank many cups of Turkish coffee while admiring intricate Oriental rugs and lamps. Others preferred to meet in coffee shops, and my most common interview location remains the Starbucks coffee shop in ABC Mall of East Beirut. Somewhat unexpectedly, the former military commander of the Lebanese Communist Party asked to meet in Dunkin Donuts on Hamra Street. It appears that fifteen years of bitter bloodshed, mixed with the sweet glazing of American donuts, has taken a toll on the Marxist faith of his youth. In general, sifting through contradictory narratives from self-interested sources presented some problems, but a dearth of evidence was not one of them.

The second purpose of my fieldwork was to collect systematic microlevel data on wartime demographics, migration, and violence. Quantitative data is a rare commodity in Lebanon, where the last census occurred in 1932 and where the general amnesty law ensures that there is limited systematic documentation of wartime abuse. In my quest for data sources, I spent considerable time interviewing academics, staff at survey companies, government officials, think tank leaders, religious functionaries, and even an economist at the Lebanese central bank who, ironically, connected me to a network of wartime Communist activists. In addition, during a few weeks in the library at the Institut français du Proche-Orient, I accessed the small but highly competent academic literature on Lebanese demographics and wartime migration mostly published by Lebanese academics writing in French.[39] The librarians at American University of Beirut and Université Saint-Joseph also helped me obtain some data, such as prewar election results, that are available from public sources.

My stack of hard copy materials in English, French, and Arabic slowly grew into a respectable pile. One breakthrough during my fieldwork came when I discovered a copy of the voter registration rolls that register individuals by both sect and location, thereby providing nationwide village-level demographic data. This data comes from the same central registry—maintained by the Ministry of Interior—used to track births, deaths, and marriages and to apply for things like a driver's license, thus covering all Lebanese. The register does not cover Palestinians, who are not Lebanese citizens, and I therefore complement it with statistics and surveys from the United Nations Relief and Works Agency. Another important step came when a sympathetic nongovernmental organization staffer gave me a copy of a recent report about wartime abuse of civilians by the International Center for Transitional Justice, whose researchers had combed through a wealth of publicly available sources in multiple languages, including the entire universe of wartime reporting in the two largest national newspapers, and arranged the results in a chronological report available in English. My third major source of quantitative data is a systematic report on forced displacement by the Ministry of the Displaced (1996), which a helpful employee gifted me as we sipped strong coffee on one of my multiple visits to the ministry. Through these endeavors this book introduces a nationwide dataset that covers over 1,400 rural villages or urban neighborhoods and presents the first available statistical modeling of wartime violence in Lebanon.

Chapter Roadmap

Chapter 1 presents my theoretical argument. I discuss the most important political and military incentives for and against ethnic cleansing and explain why armed groups in non-separatist ethnic wars face a strategic dilemma because of contradictions between their political and military incentives. Non-separatist ethnic wars are an understudied category of conflicts, and I briefly theorize why some conflicts are more likely to obtain these characteristics based on what we know about their incidence. Subsequently, I discuss the strategic calculus facing armed groups in these conflicts and why they should generally opt for ethnic cleansing as a last resort when they cannot use other options such as selective violence against hostile individuals only. Finally, I delve into the topic of how militias collect intelligence. One key factor is that armed organizations are better able to collect intelligence in areas where they have loyal supporters, particularly in the locations their fighters and other operatives themselves hail from. The second key insight about intelligence collection concerns the role of ethnic intermixing during peacetime civilian life in allowing information to transcend ethnic boundaries, frequently permitting wartime militias to discriminate among non-coethnic individuals in such areas.

Chapter 2 introduces the reader to the Lebanese civil war. After Lebanon gained independence in 1943, the country adopted a rigid consociational power-sharing model with a privileged position for the Christian community. Over time, Muslim leaders and secular political parties demanded institutional reform especially as the Christian population share shrank below its pre-independence majority status. This domestic conflict interacted with the regional Arab–Israeli conflict. Lebanon hosts many Palestinian refugees ever since the war of 1948, and after the civil war in Jordan in 1970–1971, the Palestinian national movement and its military forces relocated to Lebanon, its last regional sanctuary. Christian political parties eventually began to arm their supporters as well, and in 1975 civil war broke out largely across the Muslim–Christian sectarian divide. During the first two years of the war, both sides engaged in appalling episodes of ethnic cleansing. However, forced displacement was not comprehensive: about half of Muslims remained in the Christian enclave throughout the war, and about half of Christians remained in Muslim-dominated territory as well. Neither side had political incentives to cause ethnic separation as both coalitions strove to conquer and rule this small country in its entirety.

Chapter 3 addresses data and quantitative methods. The chapter explains how I construct a nationwide data set at the village or neighborhood level and shows how the data reveals several strong and robust findings. First, my statistical models show that—conditional on violence taking place—selective violence was more common in intermixed locations while ethnic cleansing was more likely when an armed group had fewer coethnics in a location. Second, I use electoral returns from the last prewar election in May 1972 to estimate how violence correlates with political loyalties. These models show that violence was more likely in Palestinian- and Muslim-controlled areas that had strong prewar electoral support for those Christian political parties that subsequently developed into wartime militias. The first set of results provides evidence that militias chose different kinds of violence in locations with different demographic configurations (according to my argument, because demographic configuration influences access to intelligence). The second set shows that armed groups were more likely to use any form of violence—whether selective violence or ethnic cleansing—in areas where their political enemies had geographic concentrations of loyal supporters. These findings conform to my argument that militias targeted political and military enemies rather than all non-coethnics.

The following two chapters rely on qualitative methods to provide evidence for my claim that the link between demographics and violence takes place through an information transmission mechanism. Chapter 4 chronicles the origins and operations of Lebanon's Christian militias. These armed groups had deep roots in prewar politics as political parties with nationwide organizations and significant parliamentary representation, which turned their peacetime social and political organizational infrastructure into militia forces by further mobilizing sympathetic community members. Because of these origins, the militias commanded deep loyalties within broad segments of the Christian community—especially among Maronite Catholics and Greek Catholics—and drew on this support to gather intelligence. Many fighters fought in their own neighborhoods, and the very distinction between civilian and militant is not always clear, such as in cases where individuals aided militias with simple logistical services like cooking meals for fighters. In demographically intermixed residential areas, militia supporters reported suspicious activities but also vouched for the neutrality of Muslim friends, neighbors, and colleagues they trusted. In contrast, Christian forces cleansed several predominantly Muslim slum areas and shantytowns that they knew hosted pro-Palestinian militants but where they had no local sympathizers to provide information.

Chapter 5 mirrors its predecessor but focuses on the Palestinian, Muslim, and left-wing armed groups. Several wartime militias, such as the Lebanese Communist Party and the Progressive Socialist Party, had deep pockets of communal support going back decades before the war broke out. The Palestinian factions have different origins as they only migrated to Lebanon starting in the late 1960s. Yet they had a non-trivial share of Lebanese members, especially Sunni Muslims, and they also received intelligence from their Lebanese allies with whom they shared territory. This coalition had particularly deep support across the Sunni and Druze communities but also had some Christian supporters with left-wing political views. In intermixed areas, many Christians used their social and political connections to credibly signal their neutral or pro-Palestinian views, which enabled them to stay even as many other Christians left—or were forced out of—the same location. Conversely, militias had very limited abilities to collect intelligence in many homogenous Christian enclaves where they had no local supporters. The Palestinian factions and their Lebanese allies responded in kind to Christian attacks, such as the assault on Karantina, by ethnically cleansing Christian towns and villages that were known to have a strong presence of hostile political parties that had distributed arms among their supporters.

The final chapter discusses theoretical implications and avenues for future research and specifies policy implications. The book shows that ethnic separation during the Lebanese civil war was less comprehensive than commonly imagined. My explanation centers on political loyalties: the Christian militias were trying to destroy the PLO and its allies, who responded in kind, but neither side had separatist ambitions or other political reasons to kill or displace their non-coethnic community in its entirety. As a result, their ability to collect reliable military intelligence played a major role in when and how they employed violence. I use these results to discuss future directions in research on conflict and violence. While we generally have a good understanding of why armed groups use violence and forced displacement against civilians, we lack a unified conceptual framework for thinking about their intelligence capabilities even though we know that access to information is the single most important variable that affects whether armed groups use selective or indiscriminate forms of violence. Furthermore, while we understand the processes that generate forced migration, we have a much less sophisticated understanding of how displaced persons behave. This shortcoming is unfortunate in a world with at least 65 million displaced persons at present and has important policy implications for how to provide humanitarian aid, prevent radicalization, and encourage return migration. Finally, thinking about the Lebanese experience as a non-separatist conflict provides several policy implications for issues including peacekeeping missions, postwar reconstruction, and the prospects of partition with relevance for conflicts elsewhere, and especially in the contemporary Arab world.

CHAPTER 1

Ethnic Violence in Non-Separatist Wars

> What do we mean by the defeat of the enemy? Simply the destruction of his forces, whether by death, injury, or any other means—either completely or enough to make him stop fighting.
> —CARL VON CLAUSEWITZ, ON WAR

One of the most famous insights about warfare, attributed to Prussian strategist Carl von Clausewitz, holds that war is merely the continuation of politics by other means.[1] No war has only military objectives: on the contrary, all military objectives arise because they ultimately serve some political goal. As a result, wartime leaders often face difficult tradeoffs between their political and military objectives. This chapter explores how some armed groups contesting civil wars face a strategic dilemma because they have military incentives to engage in extensive ethnic cleansing but political incentives to minimize harm to non-coethnics. Ethnic cleansing serves the narrow military objective of defeating enemy forces, much as sacking Atlanta did for General Sherman or leveling Aleppo for Syrian president Bashar al-Assad.[2] Yet, at the same time, this brutal practice can undermine the ultimate political objective of ruling a stable united country, much as the federal government struggled to regain legitimacy among Whites in the American South during Reconstruction and Bashar al-Assad does among large swathes of Syrian Sunnis at present. I argue that military organizations facing this strategic dilemma should employ ethnic cleansing only as a last resort, in areas where they do not perceive other viable options. If most existing studies conceive of ethnic cleansing as a constrained optimization problem where militants try to maximize displacement of non-coethnics subject to finite military capabilities, the strategic dilemma I describe rather entails that armed groups should minimize displacement of civilians subject to the constraint that they need to secure territorial control.

War is a process where two opposing military organizations try to achieve victory by systematically destroying each other's forces. This process is more complicated in civil wars than in international ones because civilians and militants are so closely intertwined. This intermingling pertains both in the physical sense that civilians and fighters occupy the same geographic space and in the conceptual sense that many supporters aid militias with logistics or information in ways that make them difficult to classify according to a simple civilian–militant dichotomy. The comingling of enemy combatants with innocent civilians creates the central problem of how to identify political and military opponents. Militants in ethnic conflicts sometimes solve this problem by using ethnicity as a heuristic device to indicate individual loyalties and indiscriminately target members of other ethnic communities. Yet ethnic identity is often a poor predictor of both preferences and behavior, and excessive violence carries risks and costs as well. Any military organization that indiscriminately attacks members of another ethnic community—regardless of how rational it may be in some instances to use ethnicity as an informational cue—maims and kills innocent civilians in cold blood.

Armed groups in non-separatist wars normally have some political incentives to moderate violence against non-coethnics. But how do combatants distinguish between hostile and neutral individuals in areas where they operate? Most existing work on civil war violence studies armed organizations that are very poorly informed about local conditions in their theater of operations. The brutality of Russian counterinsurgency stems precisely from its inability to distinguish civilians from militants; the image of American farm boys navigating Iraqi tribal politics would be comical if not for the gravity of the situation. Ignorance, frustration, fear, and desperation can cause men and women in uniform to descend to the most savage forms of violence. The history of civil wars, insurgencies, colonial wars, and foreign occupations bursts with examples of ethnic cleansing, forced resettlement, arbitrary imprisonment, and torture. Liberal democracies show no particular mercy: American forces in Iraq resorted to torture out of perceived necessity, much like the French had done before them in Algeria, the British in Kenya and Northern Ireland, and Israel in the West Bank and Lebanon.

In contrast, I study militias that were particularly well-informed about their surroundings because they primarily operated in areas where they counted on local residents to participate in their operations. For these militias, community volunteers provided everything from frontline fighters to logistics. Locals cooked lunch for fighters, brought them tea in the afternoon, and gave them a ride if they needed transportation at the end of a long day. When individuals participate in militia logistics in their own residential community, they transgress the boundary between local resident and militia soldier. Many fighters also contested the civil war in their own residential neighborhoods and were themselves simultaneously frontline fighters and well-informed locals. Armed groups gain powerful intelligence capabilities in areas where they have loyal supporters. In such areas, military organizations easily collect a wealth of intelligence that allows them to make relatively detailed inferences about the individuals who live there, including about local non-coethnic residents. Conversely, in areas where armed organizations operate without local supporters, they face much greater challenges when it comes to collecting intelligence. In those situations, when local intelligence is costly and time-consuming to gather and process, militants with limited resources face the enticing temptation to simply rely on ethnicity as an informational shortcut and treat all non-coethnics as hostile enemies.

The first section of the chapter outlines the strategic incentives that arise from common political and military objectives and describes how these incentives can produce a strategic dilemma. The second section explains how these strategic dilemmas form in non-separatist ethnic wars, describes the case universe of such conflicts, and provides a few salient observations about regional variation in its incidence. The third section discusses strategic behavior within such a dilemma and shows why militants should prefer both to minimize violence and to substitute selective violence for ethnic cleansing whenever possible. Detailed and reliable local intelligence is the critical variable that allows militants to accomplish these goals. The fourth section focuses on how militias gather intelligence. The section explains why some armed groups have deep roots within their coethnic communities in many areas where they operate and how those ties to local residents allows the armed group to collect detailed intelligence in such locations. The fifth section contrasts how ethnic intermixing produces interethnic ties in intermixed local communities with how homogenous non-coethnic enclaves serve as barriers to information and make intelligence gathering very costly. As a result, armed groups are better positioned to collect intelligence in the former than the latter. The sixth section specifies the have a strong presence of hostile political parties that had distributed arms among their supporters.

The final chapter discusses theoretical implications and avenues for future research and specifies policy implications. The book shows that ethnic separation during the Lebanese civil war was less comprehensive than commonly imagined. My explanation centers on political loyalties: the Christian militias were trying to destroy the PLO and its allies, who responded in kind, but neither side had separatist ambitions or other political reasons to kill or displace their non-coethnic community in its entirety. As a result, their ability to collect reliable military intelligence played a major role in when and how they employed violence. I use these results to discuss future directions in research on conflict and violence. While we generally have a good understanding of why armed groups use violence and forced displacement against civilians, we lack a unified conceptual framework for thinking about their intelligence capabilities even though we know that access to information is the single most important variable that affects whether armed groups use selective or indiscriminate forms of violence. Furthermore, while we understand the processes that generate forced migration, we have a much less sophisticated understanding of how displaced persons behave. This shortcoming is unfortunate in a world with at least 65 million displaced persons at present and has important policy implications for how to provide humanitarian aid, prevent radicalization, and encourage return migration. Finally, thinking about the Lebanese experience as a non-separatist conflict provides several policy implications for issues including peacekeeping missions, postwar reconstruction, and the prospects of partition with relevance for conflicts elsewhere, and especially in the contemporary Arab world.

CHAPTER 1

Ethnic Violence in Non-Separatist Wars

> What do we mean by the defeat of the enemy? Simply the destruction of his forces, whether by death, injury, or any other means—either completely or enough to make him stop fighting.
>
> —CARL VON CLAUSEWITZ, ON WAR

One of the most famous insights about warfare, attributed to Prussian strategist Carl von Clausewitz, holds that war is merely the continuation of politics by other means.[1] No war has only military objectives: on the contrary, all military objectives arise because they ultimately serve some political goal. As a result, wartime leaders often face difficult tradeoffs between their political and military objectives. This chapter explores how some armed groups contesting civil wars face a strategic dilemma because they have military incentives to engage in extensive ethnic cleansing but political incentives to minimize harm to non-coethnics. Ethnic cleansing serves the narrow military objective of defeating enemy forces, much as sacking Atlanta did for General Sherman or leveling Aleppo for Syrian president Bashar al-Assad.[2] Yet, at the same time, this brutal practice can undermine the ultimate political objective of ruling a stable united country, much as the federal government struggled to regain legitimacy among Whites in the American South during Reconstruction and Bashar al-Assad does among large swathes of Syrian Sunnis at present. I argue that military organizations facing this strategic dilemma should employ ethnic cleansing only as a last resort, in areas where they do not perceive other viable options. If most existing studies conceive of ethnic cleansing as a constrained optimization problem where militants try to maximize displacement of non-coethnics subject to finite military capabilities, the strategic dilemma I describe rather entails that armed groups should minimize displacement of civilians subject to the constraint that they need to secure territorial control.

War is a process where two opposing military organizations try to achieve victory by systematically destroying each other's forces. This process is more complicated in civil wars than in international ones because civilians and militants are so closely intertwined. This intermingling pertains both in the physical sense that civilians and fighters occupy the same geographic space and in the conceptual sense that many supporters aid militias with logistics or information in ways that make them difficult to classify according to a simple civilian–militant dichotomy. The comingling of enemy combatants with innocent civilians creates the central problem of how to identify political and military opponents. Militants in ethnic conflicts sometimes solve this problem by using ethnicity as a heuristic device to indicate individual loyalties and indiscriminately target members of other ethnic communities. Yet ethnic identity is often a poor predictor of both preferences and behavior, and excessive violence carries risks and costs as well. Any military organization that indiscriminately attacks members of another ethnic community—regardless of how rational it may be in some instances to use ethnicity as an informational cue—maims and kills innocent civilians in cold blood.

Armed groups in non-separatist wars normally have some political incentives to moderate violence against non-coethnics. But how do combatants distinguish between hostile and neutral individuals in areas where they operate? Most existing work on civil war violence studies armed organizations that are very poorly informed about local conditions in their theater of operations. The brutality of Russian counterinsurgency stems precisely from its inability to distinguish civilians from militants; the image of American farm boys navigating Iraqi tribal politics would be comical if not for the gravity of the situation. Ignorance, frustration, fear, and desperation can cause men and women in uniform to descend to the most savage forms of violence. The history of civil wars, insurgencies, colonial wars, and foreign occupations bursts with examples of ethnic cleansing, forced resettlement, arbitrary imprisonment, and torture. Liberal democracies show no particular mercy: American forces in Iraq resorted to torture out of perceived necessity, much like the French had done before them in Algeria, the British in Kenya and Northern Ireland, and Israel in the West Bank and Lebanon.

In contrast, I study militias that were particularly well-informed about their surroundings because they primarily operated in areas where they counted on local residents to participate in their operations. For these militias, community volunteers provided everything from frontline fighters to logistics. Locals cooked lunch for fighters, brought them tea in the afternoon, and gave them a ride if they needed transportation at the end of a long day. When individuals participate in militia logistics in their own residential community, they transgress the boundary between local resident and militia soldier. Many fighters also contested the civil war in their own residential neighborhoods and were themselves simultaneously frontline fighters and well-informed locals. Armed groups gain powerful intelligence capabilities in areas where they have loyal supporters. In such areas, military organizations easily collect a wealth of intelligence that allows them to make relatively detailed inferences about the individuals who live there, including about local non-coethnic residents. Conversely, in areas where armed organizations operate without local supporters, they face much greater challenges when it comes to collecting intelligence. In those situations, when local intelligence is costly and time-consuming to gather and process, militants with limited resources face the enticing temptation to simply rely on ethnicity as an informational shortcut and treat all non-coethnics as hostile enemies.

The first section of the chapter outlines the strategic incentives that arise from common political and military objectives and describes how these incentives can produce a strategic dilemma. The second section explains how these strategic dilemmas form in non-separatist ethnic wars, describes the case universe of such conflicts, and provides a few salient observations about regional variation in its incidence. The third section discusses strategic behavior within such a dilemma and shows why militants should prefer both to minimize violence and to substitute selective violence for ethnic cleansing whenever possible. Detailed and reliable local intelligence is the critical variable that allows militants to accomplish these goals. The fourth section focuses on how militias gather intelligence. The section explains why some armed groups have deep roots within their coethnic communities in many areas where they operate and how those ties to local residents allows the armed group to collect detailed intelligence in such locations. The fifth section contrasts how ethnic intermixing produces interethnic ties in intermixed local communities with how homogenous non-coethnic enclaves serve as barriers to information and make intelligence gathering very costly. As a result, armed groups are better positioned to collect intelligence in the former than the latter. The sixth section specifies the empirical implications of my argument, both in terms of geographic variation in violence and of the scope for change over time.

Strategic Incentives for and Against Ethnic Cleansing

To understand the strategic incentives behind ethnic cleansing, we need to consider the practice in comparison to other modes of violence during civil wars. A large literature on civil war violence studies armed groups that try to secure military victory in substate conflicts and how they quash hostile militants in areas they control using some combination of selective and indiscriminate violence.[3] Selective violence can take the shape of threats, physical abuse, material destruction, kidnappings, or lethal violence and can target either all militants or some subset believed to serve in leadership roles.[4] Either way, the key requirement of selective violence is information: the armed group that wants to selectively target enemy combatants must have detailed and reliable information about who the combatants are. In civil wars it is often difficult to obtain this information because combatants hide among the general population and are difficult to distinguish from innocent civilians. The strategy of hiding among civilians is the very definition of insurgency warfare and the central problem of counterinsurgents everywhere.[5]

The alternative to selective violence is various kinds of indiscriminate violence. The key premise of indiscriminate violence is that when armed groups know that some particular community shields militants but they do not know who the individual militants within this community are, the armed group can attack members of the community in an indiscriminate fashion. For instance, the armed group can use violence against randomly selected members of a local community as collective punishment.[6] Indiscriminate violence can take other shapes besides physical violence against individuals or groups; in particular, indiscriminate violence can also consist of forced displacement.[7] The logic of forced displacement is that by displacing an entire community that shields militants, all of those militants will also be displaced by necessity. Tactics of indiscriminate violence still vary somewhat in their level of discrimination. One extreme example is Soviet counterinsurgency operations that used extensive resettlement campaigns to effectively resettle entire ethnic groups from one location to another within its empire.[8] On the other end of the spectrum, Colombian counterinsurgents could discriminate among different villages because they relied on prewar election results as an indicator of which villages had particularly strong concentrations of Communist sympathizers.[9]

Ethnic cleansing is a variation of indiscriminate tactics whereby armed groups use ethnicity as a proxy for political loyalties, viewing all members of a particular ethnic group as potential enemies based solely on the heuristic of their group membership. If recruitment in a war occurs predominantly along ethnic lines, then displacing all members of the opposing community is a potent strategy that follows the logic of "catching the fish by draining the sea."[10] Armed groups may rely on ethnicity in situations where they have insufficient access to intelligence, or insufficient resources to gather more detailed intelligence, and therefore cannot make accurate assessments about particular individuals.[11] Ethnicity is rarely a perfect indicator of preferences or loyalties, as some individuals may cross ethnic lines because of cross-cutting cleavages such as material interests or secular ideology.[12] However, in general, ethnicity is a cheap and easily available source of information compared to discerning someone's ideological beliefs or political loyalties.[13] Compared to most other feasible alternatives for controlling a population, ethnic cleansing stands out as a particularly effective military strategy, albeit one that comes at a high cost in terms of bloodshed. It requires less time and resources (and fewer and less disciplined troops) than controlling a population through surveillance or "winning hearts and minds" by service provision.[14] By displacing all members of another community from a location, the armed group removes both currently active militants and the threat of future mobilization among potentially hostile non-coethnics.[15] Unlike collective punishment, there is no uncertainty over its effects.[16]

Some armed groups also face political incentives to engage in ethnic cleansing because they have a nationalist ideology—usually connected to separatist conflict and struggles over national self-determination—whereby they want to make certain territory ethnically homogenous.[17] Even territory of dubious material value can become perceived as invaluable when linked to nationalist identity politics.[18] Desires for national self-determination involve a refusal to be politically or socially dominated by other ethnic groups.[19] Political incentives of this nature have fueled campaigns of ethnic cleansing, partition, and population resettlement in contexts ranging from the separation of Greece and Turkey and the partition of India and Pakistan to the civil war in Bosnia.[20] Note, however, that

I view ethnic cleansing as conceptually distinct from certain other forms of mass killings such as genocide.[21] Genocide is a process that aims to exterminate another ethnic or religious community in its entirety; since the end goal of ethnic cleansing is primarily about displacement, there is more variation in the amount of lethal violence employed.[22]

Yet nationalist ideology can also produce powerful political incentives for armed groups contesting civil wars in plural societies to moderate their behavior, exercise restraint, and abstain from ethnic cleansing.[23] Consider a combatant whose ideological goal is to rule a united country rather than to secede from, or partition, a plural society. Such an actor might genuinely view members of all ethnic communities as their compatriots and may sincerely wish to minimize the death and destruction they cause innocent civilians regardless of their ethnicity. The content of nationalist ideology can emphasize unity across ethnic lines in a plural citizenry just as well as separation. If a leader with the former motivation defeats their enemy in a decisive military victory, they still have to reach a political settlement with their non-coethnics and ensure at least a minimal level of compliance with a future regime. A leader who wishes to govern a plural society may wish to promote an inclusive national identity and to act with magnanimity toward members of other groups. Even a vicious despot like Saddam Hussein, who used indiscriminate violence against Shia and Kurds, only resorted to this behavior in the late 1980s after having spent the entire 1970s quite successfully co-opting these groups through material inducement.[24] While you can rule through fear alone, doing so should not be the first choice for any prince.[25]

Aside from political-ideological incentives for restraint, armed groups may also face military-strategic incentives to abstain from ethnic cleansing. For instance, if both parties to a conflict have the option to engage in extensive ethnic violence, then they face a situation analogous to mutual hostage-taking.[26] If one side escalates violence against non-coethnics, it faces the risk that its opponent will escalate violence against coethnics in enemy zones to mete out revenge. Both sides may exercise restraint, partly to avoid setting off a spiral of violence that either side would be powerless to stop. Under these circumstances, moderating violence against non-coethnics becomes a rational strategy to protect coethnics. This dynamic should be particularly salient if neither party has secessionist aims. Violence and migration could destroy an intermixed society and create two new homogenous ones; any combatant who wants to avoid this outcome then has an incentive to moderate violence against civilians. This process is somewhat analogous to nuclear strategy, where two rivals may engage in tacit bargaining and coordination to keep a limited war from escalating into mutual annihilation.[27]

Several other military-strategic sources of restraint could also incentivize combatants to moderate their behavior. For instance, the international community has strong norms against ethnic cleansing, and those who perpetrate it may provoke international intervention either on behalf of the enemy or for humanitarian reasons. There are also economic incentives to moderate displacement. Whether armed groups secure wartime funding using taxes or predation, they should prefer to maintain as large, stable, and productive of a civilian tax base as possible.[28] Even in cases of widespread abuse, there is often restraint in areas of firm military control so as not to destroy the economic base of production.[29] However, it is hard to generalize on the economic value of non-coethnics. In some societies dominant groups relegate minorities to low-status jobs or reduced pay, but in other situations minorities use tight networks, in-group trust, and resource pooling to dominate lucrative trades or product markets.[30] In addition, valuable skills and valuable assets provide different incentives: if non-coethnics possess valuable skills, then armed groups need to keep the community intact and induce it to produce taxable economic activity, whereas valuable assets can be expropriated. Economic incentives may therefore impact armed group behavior, but it will not always be a salient concern.

Finally, regardless of what strategic goals an armed group possesses, implementing their preferred strategy usually requires considerable military capabilities. Not all armed groups possess the resources to produce their favored outcome. Some armed groups may have insufficient manpower to ethnically cleanse all the territories they want to dominate, either because their forces are too small or because their objectives are too extensive.[31] One example is the Janjaweed militias in Darfur, which tried to control an enormous desert area while restricted to traveling on camelback. Other military organizations face the opposite dilemma and fail to exercise restraint because commanders lack the institutional tools to control the behavior of rank-and-file soldiers.[32] Amelia Hoover Green (2018) elaborates on the "commander's dilemma" whereby commanders of military organizations face a dilemma between, on the one hand, creating organizations capable of producing vast amounts of violence and, on the other hand, retaining effective command-and-control of these sprawling and unruly entities. Some create elaborate internal disciplinary instruments to keep soldiers accountable to their superiors. Other non-state armed groups respond to this dilemma by investing in political education to infuse their frontline soldiers with the same ideology, worldview, and values of senior commanders. The latter practice has been particularly common among Marxist-Leninist groups.

Non-Separatist Ethnic Civil Wars

My argument differs from the existing literature because I study organizations that have the option of engaging in ethnic cleansing but nevertheless prefer to abstain because of political and ideological incentives. In terms of scope conditions, this argument thus applies primarily to armed groups in non-separatist ethnic civil wars. Some armed groups in separatist wars could also behave in the same manner, but they are much more likely to have political incentives to perpetrate ethnic cleansing so as to establish demographic domination over whatever territory they seek to turn into a national homeland.[33] In wars that do not feature salient national, ethnic, religious, or other social identity–based cleavages, armed groups have no identity-based heuristic to use as a proxy for hostile loyalties and cannot engage in ethnic cleansing.[34]

What do we know about non-separatist ethnic wars? When and where are they most likely to occur? How do they relate to other kinds of warfare? While providing a full causal argument and empirical test is beyond the current endeavor, table 1.1 uses data on civil wars from 1945 to 2005 provided by Monica Toft (2010) that allows us to classify wars into three categories across five continents. The three categories are wars that do not primarily revolve around salient identity cleavages; civil wars based on salient identity cleavages where one or more parties fight for national self-determination; and identity-based wars where no party seeks national self-determination, or non-separatist ethnic wars. To ensure that the cases are as comparable as possible, I remove anticolonial wars of national liberation from the data.[35] Based on these descriptive statistics, we can make a few observations about these different types of wars as well as some political factors that affect the nature of warfare in different regions of the world.

A cursory perusal of the data reveals that the most common type of non–identity war is a left-wing insurgency based on secular ideology. This type

TABLE 1.1
Civil wars 1945–2005 organized by region and political goals

	Wars not based on identity cleavages	Identity-based wars for national self-determination	Non-separatist wars with an identity cleavage
Latin America	14	0	0
Asia	17	21	2
MENA	7	6	7
Eurasia	1	13	1
Africa	10	8	15

Source: Toft 2010.

of war has been particularly common in Latin America; in fact, every single Latin American conflict in the aforementioned data set is coded as not primarily based on identity cleavages. Most of these wars revolve around some combination of conflict over the material distribution of resources within society, especially arable land, and relations with the United States. Examples include the conflicts in Cuba (1956–1959), Nicaragua (1978–1990), and El Salvador (1979–1992). The data also contains a sizable number of left-wing insurgencies and coups in Asia and sub-Saharan Africa during this time period and a couple in the Middle East and North Africa. A few non–identity wars—mostly in Africa in the 1990s—appear essentially kleptocratic in nature, such as the war in Sierra Leone (1991–2002).[36]

There are several identity-based wars for national self-determination in Africa during this time period—including cases such as Katanga, Biafra, and Eritrea—and a few in the Middle East, a majority of which involve the Kurds. However, wars for national self-determination have been more common in Eurasia—mostly relating to the implosion of the Soviet Union and Yugoslavia—and particularly so in Asia. A majority of the cases in Asia concern South Asia and have occurred in India, Pakistan, Bangladesh, Burma, and Sri Lanka. In addition, Indonesia and the Philippines also feature multiple cases each of rebels fighting for national self-determination, such as the Aceh revolt and the Moro conflict. Why are there so many cases of wars for national self-determination in this relatively small set of countries? The simplest explanation would be that they are all both very populous and very diverse. India, Pakistan, Bangladesh, Indonesia, and the Philippines all rank among the fifteen most populous countries in the world, according to the CIA World Factbook. They also have more internal linguistic diversity than other populous countries like China, Russia, and the United States, according to the Ethnologue database, which catalogs all 7,100 known languages worldwide.[37]

Finally, the data shows that non-separatist ethnic wars have occurred almost exclusively in the Middle East and Africa.[38] Why does this type of conflict show such a remarkable geographic clustering effect? The answer most likely lies in the regional politics of Africa and the Arab world. Most countries in sub-Saharan Africa did not gain independence until after 1945, and their leaders subsequently struggled to manage the legacy of colonialism.[39] On the one hand, they were firm in their anti-imperialist beliefs and regarded colonial structures as illegitimate. On the other hand, they realized that endlessly redrawing political boundaries would open up a Pandora's box of challenges that would risk undermining political stability across the continent. Consequently, the first generation of post-independence leaders agreed to keep African borders intact and resist the temptation to redraw the map. The majority of subsequent ethnic civil wars in Africa have concerned a desire among select groups or elites to capture the central government or otherwise extract more resources, rather than claims to national self-determination. Examples include the wars in Chad (1965–1997), Angola (1975–1994), and several bouts of violence in Burundi during the 1980s and 1990s.

The other major cluster of non-separatist ethnic wars have occurred in the Arab world, including sectarian wars along Muslim–Christian lines that broke out in Lebanon in 1958 and 1975; the contestation between the Palestinian national movement and East Bank Jordanians in 1970–1971; and the Shia uprising against Saddam Hussein in 1991–1993. One important factor in all of those conflicts is that while violence generally followed a social identity cleavage, the groups involved still shared important aspects of culture and identity such as the Arabic language and—with the exception of some Lebanese Christians—Arab identity. In general, the dominant regional political trend in Arab countries in the early post-independence era concerned Arab unity rather than substate separatism.[40] For instance, the Arab League was founded in 1945 ostensibly to facilitate inter-Arab cooperation; pan-Arab nationalism and concern for the Palestinian cause were dominant ideological currents; and Egypt and Syria briefly merged as the United Arab Republic in 1958, only to split in 1961.

Ethnic Cleansing with Incentives for Restraint

How will armed groups behave if they face contradictory political and military incentives such that ethnic cleansing is an effective military strategy but remains a second-best option because of political objectives? My argument is that armed groups facing such conditions should treat ethnic cleansing as a last resort when they have exhausted all other options. First, armed groups in this situation will prefer to use violence only against non-coethnics in situations where they perceive that non-coethnics actually pose some form of military threat. Second, whenever possible, they will try to limit themselves to using selective violence instead of indiscriminate violence such as ethnic cleansing. Ethnic cleansing remains a final option reserved for areas where the armed group faces a military threat but knows only that those who pose this threat belong to a particular ethnic group. With no further information to act upon and a clear military threat that needs to be addressed, there are few options other than to simply rely on ethnicity as a proxy for political loyalties, attacking and displacing all local members of that community based solely on their ethnic identity.

Figure 1.1 illustrates my argument as a simple decision tree. Consider an armed group that controls areas with non-coethnic residents; militants are a subset of non-coethnics while the rest are neutral, and the armed group wants to pacify all militants while minimizing violence against neutral non-coethnics. The armed group scans for indications of militant activity among non-coethnics, but in areas where there is no indication of such activity (or where the armed group perceives some other strong and credible signal of neutrality), it leaves non-coethnics in peace. This is the left side of the decision tree. If the armed group notices militant activity—the right side of the decision tree—it responds using violence, but the kind of violence it employs is a function of its access to intelligence in the area.

If the armed group can access detailed intelligence in an area such that it can distinguish militant non-coethnics from neutral ones, it can respond using selective violence to target militants only. If the armed group can correctly identify neutral non-coethnics, it can choose to leave them in

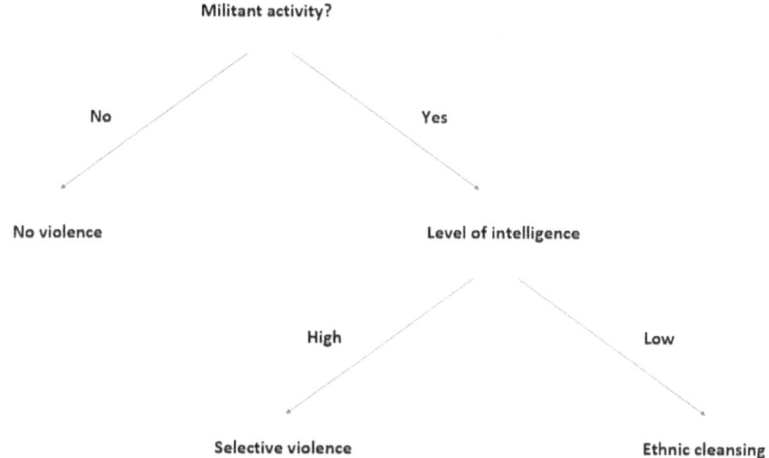

Figure 1.1 Ethnic violence with incentives for restraint

peace. However, if the armed group notices militant activity among non-coethnics in a location where it cannot easily access detailed intelligence, it might have few options beyond ethnic cleansing. Note that the decision to act with restraint is a macro-level strategic condition; it does not vary across locations. Rather, it is variation in access to local intelligence that determines whether an armed group can pacify militants using selective violence, which is a more restrained option, or whether it will perpetrate ethnic cleansing. In places where the armed group knows only that some non-coethnics engage in militant activity, it may view every non-coethnic as a potential militant; under those conditions ethnicity serves as a heuristic device or an informational cue and as a proxy for political loyalties and militant actions. This situation is different from areas where the armed group can access high-quality intelligence because in the latter areas the group can make decisions about how to treat individuals based on their individual characteristics and behavior, and it does not need to use ethnicity as an indicator of political loyalties.

My argument is complementary to explanations of ethnic violence that focus on the military-strategic value of territory. Armed groups generally try to conquer and pacify territory with the greatest strategic value and may therefore be more likely to perpetrate ethnic violence in areas of greater strategic value or during periods of territorial contestation.[41] There are many aspects of territory that can increase its strategic value: geographic factors such as elevation, rough terrain, and the presence of rivers or other natural obstacles to movement; infrastructure such as roads, port facilities, and other transportation hubs; and social factors such as the presence of large populations and other features of urban centers. Military-strategic value may determine *what* territory an armed group is prepared to expend resources to conquer or defend and adds urgency to ensuring its pacification. My argument concerns *how* armed groups pacify territory, not *what* territory they set their sights on.

How do armed groups define and experience threats? Why are some areas, individuals, or political affiliations perceived as threats? What makes someone or something threatening? Some work on civil wars evades this question by neatly delineating a sharp boundary between "civilians" and "militants," where the former are entirely disconnected from combat operations and the latter encompasses individuals engaged in either frontline combat or insurgent or terrorist tactics. In this case, it is conceptually easy to determine what non-coethnics are neutral or trustworthy: it is simply all of those who are not active militants. However, as we will see in more detail later in this chapter, more recent work problematizes this simple distinction because individuals can contribute to a war effort in many different functional forms. For instance, an individual who relays intelligence about the armed group in control of their residential location to a military enemy may cause untold damage despite not technically engaging in violence or militancy.[42] Non-coethnics can be a threat even if they are not active militants. Threats are often subtle, shifting, and subjective experiences; multiple complex indicators may interact to determine why some individuals, areas, or organizations become perceived as a threat beyond the obvious factors such as frontline wartime military service.

Coethnics as a Source of Intelligence

Access to intelligence is the main variable that drives variation in how armed organizations employ ethnic violence, which raises several important concomitant questions. Why would some armed groups have better access to intelligence than others? And why would a group have better access to intelligence in some areas than in others? Intelligence comes in many forms, including geospatial intelligence, signal intelligence, open-source intelligence, and human intelligence.[43] Geospatial intelligence relies on material and technological prowess. Where ancient armies rushed sentries to observe surrounding landscapes from hills and treetops, modern armies use drones and satellites to gather visible signs of enemy movements. Signal intelligence deals with intercepting enemy communications, whether they be messenger pigeons or encrypted radio signals. Open-source intelligence comes, as the name implies, from open sources such as newspapers or other unclassified print material in public circulation. But military organizations frequently find that the most important source of intelligence is human intelligence, which is a general term that involves gathering reports and assessments from human beings, whether by recruiting professional spies, interrogating captured enemy fighters, or other forms of human interaction.

Military organizations often receive their most useful intelligence through consensual provision by ordinary local residents in areas where they operate, as local residents are usually the most knowledgeable sources about political loyalties and military activity in their immediate social and geographical vicinity.[44] Local residents often have clues, suspicions, or firm knowledge about political and military activism among their neighbors, friends, coworkers, former classmates from school, and other members of their local community, particularly among those who have lived in the same location for a long time. Information of this kind allows armed groups to target those individuals using selective violence. Aside from the literature on civil war violence, recent scholarship on state repression also shows that domestic security services can implement more selective and narrowly targeted modes of repression the further they are embedded in local areas, with access to networks of informants and channels for receiving a continuous flow of detailed intelligence.[45]

Civilians have agency over their own actions, and they may or may not want to share their private information with militants that operate in their location.[46] Micro-level actions by local actors, including civilians, often deviate significantly from the macro-level cleavages ostensibly animating civil wars. Many local collaborators aid militants by providing information for self-interested reasons unrelated to the political macro-level cleavages of war, such as targeting a personal or professional rival either for private gain or as revenge for past misdeeds. Armed groups have developed a range of creative ways to solicit collaboration among local residents in areas where they exert dominant military control, including exploiting local conflicts and cleavages to gather intelligence in areas where they operate. Patterns of violence emerge as a joint product of armed groups seeking to identify local enemies and local civilians often pursuing self-interested agendas that may be unrelated to the macro-level issues of civil war. One problem for armed groups in this process is how to verify the information they receive, as local residents may report others for mendacious reasons—such as framing a personal or professional rival—by making a false denunciation.

Military organizations systematically differ in the kinds of relationships they develop with local residents and, thus, how easily they collect intelligence. For instance, foreign military occupations or other counterinsurgency forces generally have only weak ties to local civilians and struggle to acquire even the simplest kind of local intelligence without spending resources on surveillance, policing, or soliciting collaboration. National armies defending homeland territories against a foreign invasion sit at the opposite end of the spectrum: they often use not only the full range of institutional resources endowed in a sovereign and independent state but also wholehearted support from their entire community in the areas where they operate. Military forces in civil wars exhibit great variation in the kind of ties they possess to local residents, depending on how they mount and sustain their war effort. Some armed groups operate under circumstances that closely resemble foreign occupations, while others engage in armed struggles more reminiscent of homeland defense.

There are two major strategies for rapidly creating an effective military fighting force: economic predation and community participation. These two pathways produce different organizational modes exhibiting radically different characteristics and behavior.[47] Creating an effective military fighting force is a huge enterprise involving recruiting, training, equipping, supplying, motivating, directing, and disciplining a large and complex organization. We would normally expect this enterprise to require considerable time and energy, yet we typically observe that instigators of civil war somehow solve all of these problems in a surprisingly short period of time as war breaks out.[48] Some organizations primarily rely on various forms of predation both to recruit and motivate fighters and to fund logistics and military operations.[49] In particularly brutal cases, armed groups may staff their ranks with involuntary recruits conscripted through press-ganging, kidnapping, or inducting child soldiers.[50] As a consequence of this mode of organizing forces, militaries of this kind generally do not have strong or affectionate ties to local civilians in areas where they operate, regardless of whether locals agree with their stated macro-level political objectives.

Other organizations use the opposite strategy as they mount and sustain their military operations by mobilizing preexisting social organizations, institutions, and networks in communities where they enjoy widespread public support.[51] Armed organizations that rely on community participation assemble a military fighting force by building on organizational foundations such as political parties, religious organizations, private businesses, and other mundane institutions of everyday civilian life. The militia typically recruits individuals into military service through social ties such as family members, neighbors, workplace colleagues, fellow parishioners, political connections, or classmates from schools and universities. When whole segments of a community are mobilized into military service, a large number of individuals make costly private sacrifices to create, support, and sustain the armed organization across a range of differentiated military and nonmilitary roles. Systematic overlap between the military organization and its underlying social base of support can become so comprehensive that it is sometimes difficult to separate the two analytically. As a result, it is sometimes difficult conceptually to distinguish civilians from militants because many individuals serve in such roles as logistics, intelligence, finance, and political relations that are critical for sustaining an armed organization and form an integral part of its operations without involving combat duties.

My central argument about militia intelligence capabilities is that, for some military organizations, the very same local residents who possess valuable local intelligence are the very individuals who volunteer as local supporters of the militia and contribute to its operations. Local support helps armed groups solve four specific problems related to intelligence collection and verification. First, local networks of supporters provide a powerful channel through which armed groups can access local intelligence from a vast number of sources. Local intelligence can inform the armed group about which non-coethnics engage in militancy and therefore pose a military threat. However, loyal supporters can also play an important role when local non-coethnic residents attempt to signal neutrality to a militia. By informing the militia about which non-coethnics they know well, trust, perceive as neutral, and want the militia to leave in place, loyal supporters enable the militia to discriminate among non-coethnics and use selective violence instead of indiscriminate tactics. Armed groups benefit from credible information not only about militancy but also about neutrality.

Second, when local residents support the militia, they—and the intelligence that they provide—gain credibility with the armed group, and the armed group is more likely to trust the information they provide. Any local who makes costly private sacrifices to further the war effort—whether by incurring risks as frontline soldiers or by contributing to a range of differentiated nonmilitary functions including finance and logistics—gains credibility as a loyal supporter. When military organizations operate in areas where they have widespread social support, networks of trusted loyalists provide an extremely powerful tool for collecting and processing local intelligence. Many models of civil war violence begin from the premise that militants need to coax intelligence from self-interested civilians by either bitter repression or sweet bribery. But in areas where local residents want to provide intelligence to a militia they support, and where the militia trusts the locals and the intelligence they supply, the problem of how to solicit collaboration disappears.

Third, even armed groups with wide social support face various challenges in gathering and processing intelligence. Rumors, noisy signals, and simple misunderstandings can reduce the quality of information. Even loyal civilians might be tempted to report mendaciously for private gain and frame a personal, political, or business rival by making a false denunciation. Armed groups with extensive ties to local residents in areas where they operate are therefore still likely to sometimes incorrectly classify non-coethnic individuals. However, organizations with broad support have a multitude of sources, and they may sometimes be able to use this extensive volume of information to judge the quality and accuracy of individual reports. This is particularly true of the problem of false denunciations, where a larger volume of sources may quickly reveal that only a small number of self-interested actors stand by a certain allegation, making it significantly less credible than if it is echoed widely within a community. In contrast, a larger volume of sources need not help against misclassifying non-coethnics due to rumors or noisy signals and in theory could even make the problem worse: consider, for instance, how conformism and mass hysteria tend to characterize witch trials throughout the ages.

Fourth, extensive ties to local residents make it particularly easy to police disloyal coethnics. Cross-cutting cleavages mean not only that non-coethnics can be neutral but also that not all coethnics will be loyal supporters of a militia that poses as their communal guardian. However, even politically disloyal coethnics will be embedded in the kind of coethnic networks and structures based on family, faith, school, community, and professional life that some armed organizations mobilize to create a military fighting force. As a result, armed organizations with very extensive community ties should find it relatively easy to identify disloyal coethnics. This fact does not mean they will always use violence against such individuals, precisely because they come from the same ethnic community. Militias might go to great lengths to use threats and other inducements to get disloyal coethnics to refrain from political and militant activities, particularly if those hostile individuals have friends and family members who are loyal contributors to the armed struggle. Nevertheless, militias with extensive community support should find it much easier to pacify disloyal coethnics than disloyal non-coethnics.

The Effects of Social Intermixing

Armed groups in ethnic wars tend to receive their best intelligence from coethnics, but the most valuable content of this information will be intelligence about non-coethnics: Who poses a security risk and who is neutral? When will loyal coethnics possess the kind of detailed and reliable intelligence about non-coethnics that enable armed groups to discriminate between neutral and hostile non-coethnics? After all, if all the information that loyal coethnics can accurately and credibly relay is that they do not know very much about non-coethnics, then their information is not particularly useful. This section addresses the question of when and how members of different ethnic groups learn detailed information about each other. Ethnic militias have more opportunities to collect detailed information about local non-coethnics in intermixed villages or neighborhoods because when members of different ethnic groups mix in prewar society, they learn about each other's political sympathies and activities. Conversely, in homogenous non-coethnic enclaves, it will generally be more difficult for armed groups to solicit local information because they typically have few, if any, local supporters in such areas.

For members of different ethnic groups to learn about each other as individuals, it is not sufficient merely to live in close physical proximity, but they need to intermingle through social processes that involve ethnic intermixing. The literature on ethnic politics shows that individuals often self-segregate along ethnic lines, even in cases where different ethnic groups technically live in close physical proximity in the same location.[52] A general lack of informal contacts and connections across ethnic lines, which allow individuals to learn about each other and hold each other accountable in social and economic transactions, is a common impediment to intergroup cooperation. Yet we know that there are several ways for individuals to connect across ethnic boundaries. For instance, members of different ethnic groups learn about each other when intermingling socially as neighbors. Those who live in close physical proximity might mix further through academic and social life in integrated schools.[53] Professional and business life opens up an array of opportunities for interethnic contact.[54] The more extensively and frequently that members of different ethnic communities intermingle, the more they learn about individuals from other ethnic groups in their social and geographic proximity. Recent work emphasizes that it is frequently the instrumentality of ethnicity, rather than its ideological content, that sustains intra-ethnic cooperation and indirectly causes segregation.[55] If intra-ethnic cooperation is driven more by extensive in-group social capital than by ideology, then there is plenty of scope for interethnic cooperation and contact given the right institutional framework.

As a result, coethnics of a militia will often hold important clues about the political loyalties and activities of individual non-coethnics who are their neighbors, their friends, their former class mates from schools and universities, and their workplace colleagues. They might know what political party a non-coethnic supports, who they voted for in the last election, whether they consume media sources with a particular political affiliation or outlook, whether they have any formal party membership or other ties, and what they genuinely think about the militia that is now in control of their village or neighborhood. They know who is an ideological firebrand, a true believer in the enemy cause, and who has a history of political activism. These effects will be stronger in locations where members of different groups live side by side as neighbors and attend the same schools than if they live on opposite sides of a highway with a segregated school system. Two communities on equal socioeconomic footing will mix more densely in professional and community life than two groups entrenched in a strict status hierarchy.[56] Finally, the amount of time that a community has been intermixed also matters: if a community is mixed because members of a second ethnic group have only recently moved into the area, then members of the two groups might not yet have established many cross-ethnic relationships.

Equally important, local residents may also know non-coethnics in their community who are politically apathetic or maintain neutral positions, who have no desire to engage with the politics of civil war, and who desire nothing more than to avoid becoming entangled in the conflict. When loyal coethnics transmit this information to a militia, the militia may choose to trust this information and leave those non-coethnics—who are widely perceived by other locals as neutral—in peace. Loyal coethnic civilians generally have an incentive to truthfully report not only signs of hostile activity but also their private beliefs about neutrality. Coethnics of the militia who value their local non-coethnic friends, neighbors, classmates, colleagues, customers, shopkeepers, or other community members have an incentive to report the neutrality of these individuals to the militia in control of the area so that those non-coethnics may remain in place. Information from local militia supporters, whose loyalty is credible because of their contributions to the war effort, is therefore both the main way for the militia to learn about non-coethnics, and the main way for non-coethnics to signal their neutrality to the militia.

In sum, ethnic intermixing provides information. Information allows militants to moderate their behavior, should they have incentives to do so; if their goal is to maximize displacement or fatalities, then amicable prewar ethnic relations are hardly sufficient in their own right to induce restraint. For instance, one harrowing feature of the wars in Bosnia and Rwanda is that the perpetrators of violence were often prewar neighbors and sometimes even personal friends of their victims.[57] Furthermore, information obviously does not cause moderation if the content of the information is that all non-coethnics in a particular location are irredeemably hostile enemy partisans. Finally, one caveat is that social intermixing across ethnic lines likely has other effects beyond providing a flow of information about individuals. Intermixing might change preferences, for instance, by increasing tolerance of non-coethnics among those who live in the intermixed space. Through increasing tolerance and interethnic contact, intermixing could also increase the social value that members of one community place on members of another and increase their willingness and desire for communal mixing. Intermixing could also lead to greater economic exchange, linkages, and interdependencies, thus introducing or strengthening economic incentives for intercommunal peace.[58] There could also be a selection effect at work: perhaps more tolerant individuals are more likely to choose to live in intermixed settings in the first place. If intermixing is both a cause and an effect of individual tolerance, then intermixed and homogenous areas could become quite different in nature. Empirical work needs to tread carefully in disentangling these causal mechanisms.

Non-coethnic enclaves follow the opposite logic as militants will normally struggle to find local sympathizers to provide detailed information. Without access to local sources, intelligence gathering must focus on crude indicators of whether the location hosts political or armed opposition. Coethnics in nearby locations might notice and report overt signs of militant activity, such as the presence of arms and fighters, rudimentary fortifications and manned checkpoints, regular patrols of uniformed personnel, or other similar indicators, such as the presence of a local branch of a political party. Intelligence of this kind allows an armed organization to choose whether to target a particular village or neighborhood with violence but not to do so in a selective manner. If an armed organization chooses to attack a village or neighborhood based on such crude indicators as the presence of a party headquarters, flags, posters, and armed guards, then it will most likely be unable to discriminate among the individuals who live there. Armed groups facing these circumstances may therefore decide that they have little choice but to engage in ethnic cleansing of such locations.

My argument adds nuance to our understanding of the role of ethnicity in civil war violence. Prior work on this topic tends to view ethnicity as a variable that either completely dominates conflict dynamics, or that is largely irrelevant to understanding micro-level patterns of violence.[59] Of course, armed conflicts differ widely in their characteristics, and some civil wars may more closely approximate one model or the other. The two perspectives are perhaps not so much rival arguments as they are models that describe different types of conflicts. Nevertheless, in contrast to these two opposite frameworks, my argument shows that the role of ethnicity in civil war violence can vary even within the same conflict. In situations where militants possess detailed information about individuals in an area, they may have powerful tools that help them discriminate among neutral and hostile individuals based on personal characteristics and behavior. In such areas the militants therefore do not need to rely on crude indicators such as ethnic identity when making judgments about individual loyalties. Conversely, in areas where militants have very limited information about the individuals who live there, they may not have any reliable clues to help them discriminate among neutral and hostile individuals. In such low-information settings militants may have little choice but to use ethnic identity as a proxy for political loyalties.

Finally, displacement outcomes depend not only on how the militia behaves but also on how local non-coethnics act. If we observe that non-coethnics remain in an area dominated by a particular militia, then the militia must have chosen not to displace them, but these non-coethnics must also have chosen to remain in the area instead of relocating to other territories. Most people might prefer not to relocate from their homes, their jobs, and their local social and community lives, but non-coethnics who fear for their own physical security are highly likely to relocate.[60] Why would non-coethnics of an armed group perpetrating ethnic cleansing feel safe in territory that this armed group controls? They must believe two things: that the armed group in control of their area discriminates among neutral and hostile residents, and that the armed group accurately perceives their own personal neutrality. My general answer is that linkages, ties, relationships, and other forms of intergroup contacts in prewar social, political, and economic life help neutral non-coethnics form such beliefs during wartime.[61] If the armed group has deep roots in its coethnic community and in prewar institutions such as political parties, religious groups, or private businesses, then it is also likely that some non-coethnics have a history of interaction with those prewar institutions and their members. Non-coethnics may have interacted with those institutions through political alliances, business transactions, and community life for extended periods of time and may have formed norms and expectations of tolerance, exchange, and reciprocity. During wars, strong prewar relationships of trust and cooperation may sometimes survive and allow some non-coethnics to feel sufficiently safe to remain as residents in their original areas.

Empirical Implications and Change over Time

I study rural villages or urban neighborhoods as the geographic unit of analysis rather than more aggregated units, such as regions or electoral districts, or more disaggregated ones, such as streets or apartment buildings. A region can be intermixed even if it only contains homogenous villages, while an intermixed village could consistently contain homogenous streets or apartment buildings. Nevertheless, I find individual villages or neighborhoods to be the most appropriate unit of analysis since residents usually encounter others through the regular flow of daily life and quotidian activities. These types of mundane everyday activities in prewar community life form a central component of my theoretical argument.

My argument has two central empirical predictions. First, armed groups will use violence in response to political and militant opposition among non-coethnics; second, the type of violence armed groups employ will differ among locations with different demographic composition. Highly intermixed locations are most susceptible to selective violence, whereas ethnic cleansing tends to afflict relatively homogenous non-coethnic enclaves. Demographic intermixing creates areas of contact between individuals from different ethnic groups and allows local residents to learn about the personal characteristics, loyalties, and activities of individual non-coethnics. If the armed group can count on coethnics in intermixed areas to transmit detailed information about local non-coethnics, then the armed group can use this intelligence to discriminate on an individual basis. If local coethnics are willing to vouch for the neutrality of particular non-coethnics, the armed group can choose to trust their assessment and leave those individuals in peace. Consequently, I predict that intermixed and segregated locations will tend to face divergent outcomes.

What are the prospects for change during the course of a war? The processes I outline suggest that when a plural country descends into civil war, armed groups will rapidly gather whatever information it can easily obtain on non-coethnics and use a combination of selective violence and ethnic cleansing to pacify its domains. The argument also suggests that those non-coethnics who are deemed to be neutral and not to pose a threat, and who are not displaced, may well be able to remain in their homes even if the civil war evolves into a prolonged military conflict of significant duration. However, conditions do change during war, and patterns of displacement might not remain static or stable as wars evolve. While it is of course possible in theory that an armed group could become better at processing intelligence and develop stronger trust in non-coethnics, the more likely outcome is, regrettably, that change will involve breakdowns in trust, renewed violence, and further displacement. Two processes in particular could cause this outcome. One is if there is a major shift in the military front lines such that an armed group comes to control new areas with non-coethnics whom it struggles to collect intelligence about. The second is if an armed group faces mobilization among previously placid non-coethnics in some area; renewed mobilization might render previous intelligence estimates useless. In either case, armed groups that had previously abstained from ethnic cleansing might be compelled to change their course. Change over time is thus likely to involve previously stable patterns of interethnic trust and peaceful coexistence breaking down, causing further ethnic separation.

When armed substate conflicts occur across an ethnic cleavage, then violence tends to do so as well, but political loyalties rarely overlap completely with ethnic identities. Some armed groups have political incentives to act with restraint, and those who want to distinguish neutral civilians from political enemies need access to intelligence. There is consensus in the literature that the best source of intelligence is local residents with intimate knowledge about friends, neighbors, classmates, colleagues, and community members in their social and geographic proximity. Militants use a range of tactics to solicit collaboration, but we have not sufficiently explored the simplest explanation of all: civilians might truthfully provide militants with information because they believe in their cause and want them to succeed militarily and win the war. Sometimes the same local civilians who are friends, neighbors, and colleagues of disloyal individuals are the same local civilians who are housing, feeding, and transporting militia fighters. My argument thereby also shows how the role of ethnicity can vary from one location to the next, even within the same civil war. Gathering information is a costly process, and ethnicity is a cheap source of an expensive good. In areas where militants have strong ties to local communities, the militia can tap into these local networks of supporters to access detailed information and may avoid discriminating based on ethnic identity. However, if local residents tell fighters only that "the Muslims" from a nearby village are coming to kill them, making decisions based on ethnicity alone becomes a vital necessity.

CHAPTER II

The Lebanese Civil War, 1975–1990

> Over here is the Baydoun mosque. It was open for Friday prayers every single week throughout the civil war. We would take foreign journalists there sometimes to show them that we weren't at war with Islam or Muslims. They usually didn't listen.
> —INTERVIEW WITH A CHRISTIAN POLITICIAN, APRIL 2014

On December 6, 1975, a group of Christian men set up improvised checkpoints on a busy highway near the port district of Beirut. They stopped motorists and asked to see their national identity card, which at the time contained an indicator of sectarian identity. Muslim motorists were asked to step out of their vehicles and lead afield to attend a routine inspection, but as soon as they were out of sight from the highway, hooded men grabbed them and slit their throats on the spot. Countless mutilated bodies were later found in a nearby garbage dump. One of the instigators behind the event, known in Lebanon as "Black Saturday," later stated openly that he sought revenge for his son, whose dead body had been discovered the previous day after an incident widely blamed on Palestinian militants.[1] Black Saturday is noteworthy because its perpetrators had only one goal: to inflict death and suffering on members of the other sectarian community, regardless of the political loyalties or activities of individual victims. In response to Black Saturday, Muslim militants perpetrated similar massacres in West Beirut as well, and the phenomenon has subsequently become known as "ID card killings" after how militants identified their victims. The ID card killings have become one of the most canonical and widely known acts in the repertoire of violence during the civil war and rightfully gained notoriety for its gruesome cruelty, although there are only a handful of documented episodes.[2]

There is no question that Lebanon witnessed savage ethnic violence between Christians and Muslims during its fifteen years of civil war, or that some of this violence had the primary intention of hurting members of a different ethnic or sectarian community. Aside from the ID card killings, there were many instances of snipers firing at civilians across neighborhoods in cities like Beirut and Tripoli. As the war progressed, kidnappings became increasingly common and were often countered by more kidnappings with the intention of arranging prisoner swaps.[3] Some individuals engaged in private vendettas by targeting the life or property of innocent members of different communities in retaliation for their own loss and suffering at the hands of unidentified assailants. Many people surely experienced—and acted upon—feelings of resentment or hatred. Both military coalitions engaged in acts of de facto ethnic cleansing of entire villages and neighborhoods, which were sanctioned all the way at the top by the most senior leaders on both sides.

Yet the Lebanese civil war represents something much more complicated than a communal war of Muslims versus Christians. The fault lines that produced armed conflict in 1975 had deep roots both in domestic Lebanese politics and in the regional Arab–Israeli struggle. To a certain extent these conflicts did pit sectarian communities against each other. One of the two military alliances that contested the war in 1975 had Christian fighters almost exclusively, while the other had nearly universal support among Druze and Sunni Muslims. Most Sunni Muslims viewed the Palestinian community as ethnic brethren fighting injustice and oppression, while many Christians—especially Maronite Catholics—believed that the Palestinian armed forces on Lebanese soil constituted a foreign military occupation. However, smaller numbers of Christians were swayed by left-wing ideologies and fought for radical change to the sectarian Lebanese political system in a tight alliance with the Palestinian national movement. Even those Christian militias that opposed the armed Palestinian presence nevertheless realized that Lebanon would always remain an intermixed country and that any postwar settlement they could ever hope to impose, even if militarily victorious, would need to elicit some minimum level of acceptance in Muslim communities. As the war ground on, new actors entered the fray, including not only the regular armed forces of Syria and Israel but also new nonstate groups such as the Shia Muslim group Hezbollah sponsored by Iran. Some previously allied groups within both alliances eventually fell out and turned into bitter enemies.

This chapter introduces readers to Lebanese history and tries to do justice to the full complexity of its sectarian cleavages and how the culture of sectarianism contributed to the outbreak of civil war. Toward the end of the chapter I also provide a very brief introduction to the main phases of the war. My goal is to make this material accessible to readers who are not familiar with Lebanese history rather than to provide a comprehensive literature review or extensive historiographical discussion. There are many excellent books about why the civil war broke out—and perhaps Salibi (1976), Hanf (1993), and El-Khazen (2000) stand out as particularly strong—but they are lengthy, dense, and not always readily accessible to a lay reader. There are relatively few accessible introductions to this topic.[4] Readers who want a quick overview of military and political developments during the war itself could consult Makdisi and Sadaka (2003) or the vignettes to each section in the report by the International Center for Transitional Justice (2013) on wartime abuse against civilians, which includes an extensive bibliography for each period. I see no need to reproduce this material here. While I do highlight some salient and persistent historiographical controversies, this chapter aims to provide an introduction comprehensible to the uninitiated.

The chapter begins with an introduction to the origins of sectarian politics in Mount Lebanon during the nineteenth century. The second section explains how political tensions over the post-independence Lebanese sectarian political regime intensified in the decades after independence, particularly between Maronite Catholics and Sunni Muslims, and how domestic Lebanese conflicts became intertwined with the regional Arab–Israeli conflict. The third section describes the two coalitions whose uncompromising stances yielded an armed confrontation in 1975: the Lebanese National Movement, dominated by Sunni Muslim and left-wing groups in close alliance with the Palestinian national movement, and the Lebanese Front with almost exclusively Christian adherents. The fourth section provides a very brief overview of the main phases of the civil war that raged from 1975 to 1990. This section also describes briefly why I choose empirical material related to the first phase of the war, the Two Years' War of 1975–76, to test my theoretical argument and how this period relates to subsequent developments in the conflict.

How Muslims and Christians Created Lebanon

Historians date the emergence of sectarian politics in Lebanon to political developments in the mid-nineteenth century.[5] In Ottoman times, the area that we know today as Lebanon had been a sleepy backwater controlled by a series of mostly unremarkable emirs formally administering local affairs on behalf of the Sublime Porte in Constantinople.[6] While the area contained both Muslims and Christians, politics followed a typical feudal pattern of conflict primarily between and among lords and peasants. Two sets of political developments shattered this old model. First, the Tanzimat reforms launched by the Ottoman sultan in 1839 sought to modernize the empire by, among other things, elevating the status of non-Muslim subjects. Second, Britain and France were looking for local allies as they competed for influence in the Eastern Mediterranean. In response, a new set of leaders emerged in Lebanon that for the first time claimed legitimacy as political representatives for their sectarian communities. As new leaders fought for influence and old leaders defended their privileges, Mount Lebanon entered a period of political instability and violence that culminated in a brutal Druze–Maronite civil war of 1860, rife with massacres of civilians. Ever since this period, politics in Lebanon revolves around sectarian communities and the leaders who claim to represent them.

In the aftermath of World War I, the French government created Lebanon as a French mandate within its present-day borders.[7] After the Ottoman Empire took the fateful decision to join the war on the German side, Britain and France launched a major military campaign in 1915 to conquer its Middle East domains. In late 1917 British forces gained the upper hand, and when the war ended in 1918 European forces had conquered all Arab lands of the Ottoman Empire. Intense negotiations and diplomatic summits followed the war as neither Britain nor France had planned in detail for how to govern this territory. The two Great Powers rapidly split the region into spheres of influence—mostly in accordance with the hastily drawn up Sykes–Picot Agreement—to avoid costly security competition, but it took years of deliberations and conflict to turn those spheres of influence into units of governance. French leaders created Lebanon in accordance with two contradictory principles. On the one hand, they wanted a Christian-dominated mandate based on the Ottoman administrative unit (*mutasarrifiyya*) of Mount Lebanon because they believed that such a unit would form a natural ally in this strategic region. On the other hand, the mountainous Christian heartlands were poor and prone to periodic starvation, so French imperial planners also added fertile Muslim-dominated agricultural land to its east, north, and south. Lebanon was thus an artificial construction that did not quite correspond to any historical unit of governance.

Most Christians rejoiced in the creation of Lebanon.[8] After almost a century of political conflict revolving around sectarian hierarchies, both in Lebanon and elsewhere in the region, they saw in mandate Lebanon the precursor of a Christian-dominated state. With the massacres of 1860 in fresh memory, they considered a Christian-dominated state to be the best guarantor of communal security. Furthermore, as Christians constituted a demographic majority in Mount Lebanon, it was natural to them that these lands should be governed by Christians. Finally, some Lebanese Christians do not consider themselves to be Arabs but claim that their community hails back to ancient Phoenicia or other non-Arab origins. Based on this belief, regardless of its historical accuracy, they therefore rejected inclusion into Arab countries like Syria on ideological grounds. These sentiments were particularly widespread among Maronite Catholics, which is the largest Christian denomination in Lebanon, but extensive among other confessional communities such as Greek Catholics as well.

These sentiments were not universal, as some Christians rejected sectarian discourses in favor of various stripes of secular and left-wing doctrines.[9] The Lebanese Communist Party, founded in 1924, always had a strong contingent of Christians especially among its senior leaders. Furthermore, while support for Lebanese nationalism was widespread among Maronite Catholics and Greek Catholics, the sentiment was not as widely shared by Greek Orthodox. One reason is that the Greek Orthodox constitute the largest Christian community across the Arab world but only a small share in Lebanon. While Lebanon represented a unified homeland for almost all Maronite Catholics, it divided Greek Orthodox from their religious compatriots in Syria, Palestine, Iraq, and elsewhere. Many Greek Orthodox eschewed Christian-dominated Lebanese nationalist parties and eventually placed their faith in the mythological visions of the Syrian Social Nationalist Party. This far-right nationalist party, founded in 1932, espouses a mythical, pre-Islamic Syrian nationalism and wants to unify Lebanon with other territories such as Syria, Jordan, Palestine, Cyprus, and parts of Iraq that supposedly form part of "Natural Syria."[10]

Lebanese Sunnis massively opposed the creation of Lebanon as a separate mandate.[11] The Sunni community almost universally considered Lebanon to be an integral part of Greater Syria (Bilad Al-Sham) that comprises present-day Syria, Lebanon, Jordan, and Palestine.[12] Sunnis wanted Greater Syria to remain intact not only because of ideological desires but also because of practical concerns as many had extended family or tribal links across the region. There was also an economic dimension to this sentiment; for instance, the Sunni-dominated port city of Tripoli connected Western markets to a hinterland that stretched deep into present-day Syria, including cities like Hama and Homs. Its merchants correctly anticipated that new international borders would rupture their trade flows. In later years the Lebanese Sunni community was to become among the strongest proponents of Arab unity and pan-Arab nationalism in the whole region; admiration for Egyptian president Gamal Abdel Nasser was widespread, and concern for Palestine was almost universal. We see remnants of those sentiments today in the Sunni community's staunch support for the Sunni-dominated uprising against the Assad regime in Syria as well as in the many Lebanese Sunnis who have crossed international borders to fight for Islamist groups in Syria and Iraq.[13]

The penchant for pan-Arab daydreams was less true of Shia Muslims and Druze.[14] The Shia at the time were a very poor and heavily marginalized community of mostly rural sharecroppers. Its elites played only a marginal role in the struggle for independence, and its masses received very limited privileges in the political system despite their significant population share. While some Shia played an important role in left-wing groups like the Lebanese Communist Party, Shia sectarian leaders only gained prominence with the growth of the Amal Movement in the late 1970s. Its current dominance of the political system stems from the rise of Hezbollah, founded after the Israeli invasion in 1982 and little but a set of disorganized terrorist cells until Iran decided to fuse them into the major regional military power that we know today.[15] As for the Druze, this sect represents only a few percent of the Lebanese population, and its leaders have always been more committed to the welfare of their community than to any abstract principles of governance.

During the 1930s Christian political and intellectual leaders grew increasingly vociferous and organized around the goal of Lebanese independence. Sunni leaders found themselves in a difficult situation as they also wanted independence from European domination but did not want

Lebanon to be separated from the rest of Greater Syria. Many Sunni leaders had a background as deputies in the Ottoman Parliament in Constantinople, and had extensive ties to Sunni elites in other formerly Ottoman Arab lands.[16] It merely seemed natural to these elite figures that Sunni Arabs across the Fertile Crescent merited some form of political unity.[17] Eventually, however, they decided that they could not fight both Lebanese Christians and European powers at the same time and chose to embrace Lebanese independence in a tight alliance with Christian elites. The strategic thought behind this alliance was that it was better to use all feasible allies to put an end to European domination first and then subsequently look for alliances in the wider region to reintegrate Lebanon with the Arab world at a later time. The 1930s subsequently saw fierce political activity as both Christian and Muslim leaders organized youth movements, labor unions, and media outlets to fight for independence through demonstrations, strikes, petitions, and other organized political activities.

The pressures of World War II caused the French Republic to disintegrate into Vichy and Free French factions and severely limited its ability to control its colonial possessions. Lebanon eventually gained independence in 1943, and its elites negotiated an agreement, known as the National Pact, which specified an explicit model for sectarian power sharing in the newly independent republic.[18] The National Pact had no legal status, but in letter and spirit it shaped the new institutions that would govern the nation. Geographic realities most likely influenced elite willingness to reach a compromise over institutional power sharing as well. Lebanon is a tiny country: with just over ten thousand square kilometers, it is smaller than all U.S. states except Delaware and Rhode Island, or less than half the size of New Hampshire or Vermont.[19] The country adopted a consociational parliamentary democracy and a free press and was for a time widely regarded as a model case of how to foster tolerance and peaceful power sharing in multiethnic states.[20] However, the political system operated under a rigid sectarian formula, and power was concentrated in the presidency, an office perpetually reserved for a Maronite Catholic. The Sunni and Shia communities retained the offices of prime minister and speaker of Parliament, respectively, although those posts held significantly less power. Seats in Parliament were divided at a ratio of six Christian seats for every five Muslim parliamentarians, with set quotas for all major sectarian communities.

On the one hand, the National Pact represents a triumphal political success whereby all stakeholders in an extremely diverse country managed to implement a stable power-sharing agreement and transition to democracy. On the other hand, the National Pact cemented certain political cleavages and hierarchies whose inflexible nature eventually produced disastrous consequences. Its inherent political tensions first erupted in major violence as a brief civil war in 1958.[21] The immediate cause involved the formal state merger that year of Egypt and Syria into the United Arab Republic (UAR), a move applauded by many Lebanese Sunnis who wanted Lebanon to also join this new entity and participate in fundamentally redrawing the political boundaries of the region.[22] In response to these developments, term-limited Maronite Catholic Lebanese president Camille Chamoun decided to seek another term as president in flagrant violation of constitutional law, ostensibly to prevent another president from merging Lebanon with the UAR. Outraged Sunni and Druze leaders mounted an armed challenge to bring down the president, and street battles in various parts of the country produced significant casualties. Chamoun appealed to U.S. president Dwight Eisenhower, who rapidly landed a large force of Marines in Beirut under the recently promulgated Eisenhower Doctrine of aiding non-Communist governments in the Middle East. In the presence of the Marines, U.S. diplomats successfully mediated between the two sides, and Chamoun was eventually replaced as president by army commander Fouad Chehab, a consensus candidate palatable to both sides.

During the 1960s Lebanon experienced what is widely regarded as its golden era. Many outside visitors found Lebanon's bewildering sectarian diversity to be perhaps its most important national treasure. Its social diversity fused cultural links and historic ties to East and West and produced a natural hub for regional trade and banking, particularly the growing financial flows as Western motorists enriched Gulf Arab oil producers. Beirut earned the moniker "Paris of the Middle East," conveniently wedged between Mediterranean beaches and the Swiss-designed ski resort at Faraya Mzaar. As a series of despotic tyrants turned most of the Arab world into repressive dictatorships, freedom of the press made Beirut the regional capital of print media and the base of operations for both Western journalists and Arab intellectuals. Social scientists gushed over its consociational system as a model of institutional design for other plural societies to emulate and as a blueprint for turning every diverse country into a local Switzerland.[23] It seemed as if its diversity was the very cornerstone of Lebanese economic and cultural success.

From Independence to Civil War

Despite the successful transition to peaceful power sharing after independence in 1943, Lebanon descended into civil war in 1975 because of domestic political conflicts that interacted with the Arab–Israeli regional conflict and the politics of Palestinian dispossession.[24] After independence three issues—political inequality, economic inequality, and Palestinian refugees—gradually polarized the Lebanese into two camps. To understand the two resultant political coalitions, their ethnic and sectarian composition, and why their differences evolved into civil war it helps to understand the three aforementioned dimensions of political conflict.

The first issue was growing Muslim frustration over the political inequality entrenched in a system dominated by Christians. The sectarian regime was supposed to distribute power in accordance with each group's share of the population but instead relied on the 1932 census as the sole criterion to determine what those shares were. According to this census, Christians were a slim majority and Maronite Catholics a plurality of the population. However, regardless of whether this census painted a fair and accurate picture of the demographic balance in 1932, virtually all observers agree that the Muslim share of the population has grown since then, in particular from the 1930s until the 1980s.[25] During this period Christians had lower fertility rates and higher emigration rates, both of which served to increase the share of Muslims in the population. As a result, Muslim elites and masses believed they were entitled to more political power within any sectarian framework of governance. The offices of prime minister and speaker of Parliament barely appeared as consolation prizes in comparison to the magnificent powers concentrated in the presidency. Parliament served little independent function in legislative matters.[26]

Second, ideological demands for secular governance and economic equality fueled reformist and radical left-wing political movements that sought to abolish the sectarian system altogether.[27] Lebanon was not, contrary to some perceptions, a free-market economy, as various regulations—including legal monopolies in commercial agriculture—limited many economic opportunities to the privileged few with political connections. In rural areas, old feudal bonds often remained intact after independence as local landowners dominated agricultural communities. Most citizens accessed economic opportunities, social welfare, and government services through clientelistic ties to local political families, and elections rarely produced real change as the same families tended to win in the same districts every time. Christians generally had higher standards of living than Muslims, especially since the Shia Muslim community mostly lived in a stage of significant economic underdevelopment in rural areas.[28] However, far from all members of the Maronite Catholic community were better off in economic terms under this kleptocratic regime, even though the powerful presidency was reserved for a member of its ranks. Beirut had historically been a city divided between Sunni Muslim and Greek Orthodox residents, and many of its traditional business elites hailed from these communities while the Maronite heartlands were the farmers and craftsmen of Mount Lebanon.[29] Left-wing movements recruited members from all sectarian communities.

Sectarian and economic tensions eventually became intertwined with the Palestinian refugee problem.[30] Hundreds of thousands of Palestinian refugees reside in Lebanon since the 1948 war, and this community, lacking work permits and citizenship rights, mostly subsists in squalid UN Relief Works Agency–run refugee camps with limited prospects for socioeconomic advancement. In its early days the Arab–Israeli conflict was largely perceived as an international conflict between Israel and Arab states, but in the 1960s new Palestinian political parties emerged that demanded recognition as the sole legitimate representatives of Palestinian national aspirations. Those parties emerged in all jurisdictions where Palestinian refugees resided, and in the late 1960s created the PLO as an official umbrella organization. Yasser Arafat's party, Fatah, grew in significance during the 1960s and eventually propelled Arafat to the chair of the entire PLO organization. The 1974 Arab League summit in Rabat, Morocco, unanimously declared the PLO to be the sole legitimate representative of the Palestinian people.

Lebanon eventually became the center of most Palestinian political and military activity across the region. After the 1967 war, Palestinian militants began building up conventional military forces, mostly in Jordan, but both King Hussein of Jordan and President Hafez al-Assad of Syria feared the long-term consequences for their regimes of an armed Palestinian presence. King Hussein quashed the militants in a brief civil war in 1970–1971, and Hafez al-Assad effectively relocated the bulk of Palestinian military forces to Lebanon by allowing transit through Syrian territory but denying them a base of operations. After 1971 all major armed Palestinian groups conducted their operations from Lebanese soil. Palestinian armed groups developed considerable conventional military capabilities and staged commando raids into Israel that provoked Israeli retaliation deep into Lebanese territory, with terrible consequences for local communities. The Lebanese army tried to contain these operations and intermittently clashed with the militants. Clashes escalated in the 1970s and spread from the south into the Palestinian refugee camps elsewhere, including in Beirut, partly as different factions pushed for political dominance of the Palestinian community.

The Palestinian struggle, Muslim frustrations, and secular left-wing currents formed a powerful informal alliance in Lebanon during the 1960s. Sunni and Druze leaders considered the PLO natural allies in their struggle to radically reform the Lebanese state and saw the Lebanese state as a natural ally in the Palestinian struggle against Israel. However, many Lebanese Christians perceived the armed Palestinian groups as akin to a foreign military occupation, in violation of Lebanese independence and sovereignty, and followed developments with increasing alarm. During a particularly dramatic encounter in 1973, the army failed to subdue Palestinian militants despite a two-week campaign, which underscored that the army lacked both the military muscle and the political backing of Muslim parliamentary leaders to decisively control Palestinian armed groups. After 1973 the army suffered from political paralysis and defections and played only a minor role for the rest of the decade.[31] Prior to these events a few nationalist parties with an overwhelmingly Christian following had organized minor paramilitary training sessions through ad hoc local initiatives, mostly by university students, and, while somewhat encouraged, they were not formally sanctioned by senior leadership.[32] There was no central military organization, and the parties and their supporters had limited access to arms and ammunition. In 1973 several Christian politicians and political parties began procuring arms and organizing military training for their supporters.

Parties and Militias of the Civil War

The civil war was contested at its outset by two coalitions, one of which comprised a number of Palestinian, Sunni-dominated, Druze-dominated, and left-wing political parties and armed factions while the other had almost exclusively Christian followers. This section outlines the membership and political goals of each coalition and then briefly discusses one of the most salient remaining historiographical debates, accounting for why the civil war broke out.

The Palestinian Movement, Muslim Parties, and Left-Wing Groups

On one side of the political divide were several Arab nationalist, progressive, and radical Lebanese political parties in a coalition known as the Lebanese National Movement (LNM), allied to the Palestinian national movement and senior PLO leadership.[33] While some of these parties had supporters among Christians with an ideological commitment to secular government, particularly among the Greek Orthodox, in absolute numbers the largest constituency of LNM supporters was Sunni Muslims. The LNM consisted of many different Lebanese political parties and other elites, and over the years this coalition has been described by various observers as "the Left," "the Progressives," "the Muslims" and various other monikers. The LNM generally described itself as an alliance of secular, progressive, and radical political parties. By its own description, it was a nonconfessional alliance opposed to the status quo of entrenched political and economic privilege and in favor of social and political change including abolishing the sectarian political system. Several of its members were political parties committed to various stripes of left-wing ideology, such as the Lebanese Communist Party, but the alliance also contained most of the traditional Sunni Muslim elites. To a large extent, the LNM was united more by its opposition to the status quo than agreement on any coherent or shared alternative political platform.

While in theory there is an obvious difference between secular and sectarian parties, it can in practice be difficult to classify individual cases. One example of how sectarian and left-wing ambitions fused in this time period is the Progressive Socialist Party and its leader, Kamal Joumblatt.[34] The Joumblatt family had for centuries held a leadership position within the Druze community based partly on their semifeudal origins as major landholders in the Mount Lebanon region where most Druze live. After independence Kamal Joumblatt founded the party with a plurality of Druze members but a healthy representation of all sectarian communities. On the one hand, Joumblatt likely believed that secular, progressive social democracy was the best regime for the newly independent country when he founded the party in 1949. On the other hand, he also acted as a communal guardian for the Druze: secular democracy with nonconfessional elections was most likely the best institutional framework for furthering the interests of this small community, which was doomed to a marginal role under a sectarian framework. Finally, the party was a vehicle for his personal ambitions to obtain the highest office in the country, which required constitutional reform to amend the requirement that the president be a Maronite Catholic. As a result, sectarian and other parochial interests thus aligned with the secular doctrines of social democracy.

As for the Palestinian national movement, the PLO is an umbrella organization with about a dozen constituent member political parties.[35] The largest political party within this group is Fatah, a secular Palestinian nationalist party founded by Yasser Arafat in the 1950s. Its ideological platform centers on secular Palestinian nationalism and the struggle for national self-determination. The second largest group, the Popular Front for the Liberation of Palestine, is a radical left-wing group that links the Palestinian struggles to left-wing themes such as Marxism and anti-imperialism. The third largest faction, the Democratic Front for the Liberation of Palestine, is a Marxist-Leninist outfit that prides itself more on doctrinal purity than military ability. Other smaller members of the PLO were defined largely by their individual leaders and their foreign sponsors, including groups tightly allied to—if not outright controlled by—the Syrian and Iraqi Baath parties and their respective security services. In 1975 Yasser Arafat served both as the chairman of Fatah, a PLO constituent party, as well as chairman of the executive committee of the PLO itself; he was at the time the undisputed political leader of the Palestinian national movement.

The main goal of the Palestinian movement in Lebanon was to use sanctuary space in the south of the country to build up both a state-in-exile and sufficient military capabilities to mount a military threat to Israel.[36] By 1971 the entire political and military organization of the Palestinian national movement was located on Lebanese soil, and they were not welcome anywhere else in the region. Having already been dislodged from the West Bank and Jordan and denied a base of operations in Syria, Lebanon was the only site left where Arafat could build up military capabilities next to the Israeli border. His Lebanese allies knew both that the Palestinians would have no choice but to fight in case political conflict precipitated civil war and that Palestinian forces would easily outgun anything the Christian parties could muster. As a result the LNM pushed hard for political reform with little room for compromise in the belief that Christian leaders would come to the same realization and therefore back down.

Some small extremist Muslim groups engaged in gratuitous violence against Christians, such as the obscure Shia gang Knights of Ali, based in the Bashoura neighborhood of West Beirut.[37] While they were small and lacked importance at the strategic level, these crimes obviously caused great suffering for their victims. In addition, some Sunni Lebanese rank-and-file soldiers, who included many teenagers with limited education, may not have been able to explain the finer ideological distinctions of how Arab nationalism differs from Sunni supremacy. Finally, large swathes of the country was in practice at the mercy of local gangsters who often used the fog of war and sectarian discourse to victimize local Christians, for instance, to steal homes and other real estate. Nevertheless, accounts that reduce the civil war to a communal struggle between Christians and Muslims obscure many important political dynamics that had major significance in shaping the trajectory and events of the war as well as the many actors with genuine dedication to secular ideology and governance.

Christian Militias

The other wartime coalition consisted of several militias with almost exclusively Christian fighters and extensive popular support among the Christian community, especially among Maronite Catholics. For this reason they often get labeled "the Christians," which is as reasonable a moniker as any, with the obvious caveats that not all Christians supported these militias and that a small number of Muslims did. Other scholars have called them "the Right" or "the Conservatives," on the understanding that they fought to uphold the status quo. I do not like either moniker. First, those names obscure the fact that Christian leaders among themselves had major differences on whether to maintain the existing, rigidly sectarian regime or to ultimately replace it with a different institutional design. Second, some Muslim elites within the LNM may have been quite happy to maintain some version of existing institutions in exchange for more power within this framework, making them somewhat conservative in orientation. Third, it is hard to say that Christian militias defended the status quo when in their minds the status quo in 1975 was that their country was under foreign military occupation. By their own account, the Christian militias were fighting for Lebanon to remain an independent and sovereign nation, which required an end to the armed Palestinian presence. Some observers therefore refer to them as "Lebanese nationalists," but this moniker is also somewhat confusing as most Muslim and left-wing organizations that sought radical change were nevertheless committed to the Lebanese nation defined by its contemporary borders and demographic makeup. There were, in a sense, many different "Lebanese nationalisms" among the wartime contenders.

The dominant member of the Christian coalition was the Lebanese Phalange Party (Hezb Al-Kataib Al-Lubnaniyya), colloquially known in Arabic as Katayyib and often shortened in English and French as the Phalangistes.[38] While technically secular, the party denies Lebanon's Arab heritage, claiming that the Lebanese are a distinct people with a unique history and identity and that Lebanese independence and sovereignty are therefore paramount. This ideology promotes an inclusive national identity that acknowledges and seeks to accommodate Lebanon's tremendous social diversity within a unified political system. However, this conception of Lebanese nationalism primarily resonates with Christians, especially Maronite Catholics and Greek Catholics. Katayyib has always rallied an almost exclusively Christian following.[39] The group originated as a political youth league with paramilitary characteristics, inspired by contemporary movements in Fascist Europe, but evolved into a political party and eventually gained numerous seats in Parliament after independence. From that point on, it has viewed itself primarily as a mass party.[40] Other Maronite Catholic elites also rallied to defend their vision of Lebanese nationalism, including the president, Suleiman Frangieh, and former president Chamoun. In short, most of the Christian political establishment formed a united coalition that opposed the Palestinian armed presence in Lebanon.

When the civil war broke out, Christian political and military leaders quickly realized they needed a more coordinated approach to mobilize their resources at the strategic level and to acquire and deploy heavy weapons. In response, they established a political command, named the Lebanese Front, to coordinate all allied militias.[41] The organization included senior politicians, intellectuals, and religious figures, and it had three primary purposes: to establish political control over the military effort, to develop and implement unified strategic planning, and to coordinate military activities among the disparate militias. In theory, this political body would make key strategic decisions and decide on political goals and considerations. Military operations would subsequently be planned and implemented by a unified military command consisting of commanders from all allied militias. Katayyib dominated the Lebanese Front in light of its military dominance within the group. Eventually most of these militias merged into a single political entity and military fighting force, known as the Lebanese Forces.[42] However, it took some time for all these developments to materialize, and the earliest days of the war were often marked more by chaos, confusion, and disorganized and uncoordinated behavior among Christian forces.

The Christian militias aspired, in their own eyes, to defeat all competing militias on Lebanese soil and to reestablish the Lebanese state as an independent and sovereign entity. Their conception of how independent Lebanon should be governed might differ from Muslim desires, and they intended to retain the presidency for one of their own leaders at least in the immediate postwar situation. However, both coalitions contesting the civil war sought military victory in order to enact major political change: it is important to understand that neither party to the conflict desired partition of Lebanon into new homogenous nation states based on sectarian identities. Many Christians dreamed of political solutions—none of them particularly realistic—whereby the Palestinian refugee community would relocate entirely from Lebanon to other jurisdictions. Some Christian elites, political activists, and militia operatives—particularly from the smaller and more ideologically extreme factions—spread hateful speech and slogans that incited violence against Palestinians. Individual Christian fighters engaged in performative acts of violence against Palestinians, such as tying the dead bodies of enemy fighters—and sometimes live captives—to the backs of cars and dragging them along the highway.[43] As we see in the next chapter, which delves into quantitative data, Christian militias perpetrated more extensive ethnic cleansing against Palestinians than against Lebanese Muslim communities.[44] However, the Christian war effort aimed to reestablish control over the entirety of the country and to rule it as an intermixed body politic. Its war effort was not separatist or secessionist in nature.

Historiographical Controversies

One of the most salient historiographical debates surrounding the civil war concerns how to attribute blame for the outbreak of armed hostilities. At a general level, all historians and other observers agree that a mix of domestic political conflicts, in particular tensions over the sectarian political system, and regional politics, especially the Arab–Israeli conflict, share the blame for this enormously destructive war. Yet different observers diverge sharply in how to apportion blame among these distinct factors. One reason this debate remains so salient is most likely that many historians, journalists, and other prominent observers are themselves affiliated with different parties to the conflict. These affiliations range from tacit supporters to some who served as formal officials within these parties or even fought on the front lines of various armed factions. While these affiliations present obvious sources of bias and incentives for misrepresentation, they also present unique perspectives and evidence. My purpose here is not to review the entire literature but merely to bring the enduring controversies to the reader's attention. The most important historiographical perspectives can be roughly grouped into three clusters, although far from all works fit neatly into this categorization or necessarily take a firm stand on the question.

The first perspective places blame for the civil war primarily on the Christian leadership and its hardline followers.[45] Proponents of this view note that Christian leaders stubbornly refused to compromise on the rigid power-sharing formula of the National Pact even though their share of the population was widely assumed to have slipped far below the point of constituting a majority. Ethnocentric political ideologies dominated the Christian political scene, and many Christians harbored chauvinistic views of Muslims in general and Palestinians in particular. Other sectarian communities could be no more expected to respect this existing order than contemporary Black populations facing minority rule in Rhodesia and South Africa during the same period. Furthermore, it was the decision by Christian leaders in 1973–1974 to arm their followers that produced the military arms race that spiraled into open hostilities during the spring of 1975. Having lost the ensuing military contest, they subsequently invited first Syria and then Israel to invade Lebanon in the mistaken beliefs that outside powers would implement their agenda for them.

In contrast, a second perspective argues that the presence of the Palestinian national movement constitutes the critical component that transformed a manageable political conflict into a civil war.[46] Until the armed Palestinian factions relocated to Lebanon starting in the late 1960s and started to train and arm their Lebanese allies, no domestic party possessed the kind of military capabilities necessary to initiate a civil war. Palestinian arms transformed the refugee camps into safe havens for its armed factions as well as for ordinary criminals—and sometimes it was difficult to tell the two apart. Extortion, racketeering, and other crimes plagued Lebanese civilians in the vicinity of the refugee camps, generated enormous resentment, and undermined trust in its police and military. It was the failure of the army to stop Palestinian militancy in 1973 that finally convinced many Christians that alternative solutions were required. Furthermore, this perspective notes that while the Lebanese faced intense domestic political conflicts by 1975, all its major political actors and sectarian communities had otherwise acclimatized to the realities of Lebanon as an independent state in the Middle East. Pan-Arab nationalism had lost its regional luster, and, unlike in 1958, Sunni elites and masses no longer harbored any desire to subsume Lebanon into another Arab state.[47] In tandem, Christian parties recognized that Lebanon was a de facto part of the Arab community of states, and Christian delegations increasingly visited Damascus, Cairo, and other Arab capitals to advance their interests.

A third perspective blames the regional environment.[48] The point of this account is not to absolve the warring parties of blame for their shortcomings but to suggest that any country facing the external environment that Lebanon has would likely experience strife as a result. No factor is more important in this assessment than the Arab–Israeli conflict. Aside from producing an enormous refugee flow in 1948, this conflict has also involved Israeli invasions of Lebanon in 1978, 1982, 1996, and 2006. The presence of refugees is a destabilizing factor in itself; note that the Arab–Israeli conflict also sparked a civil war in Jordan in 1970–71, even though that country does not have the same sectarian fault lines that Lebanon does.[49] Neither are negative external influences limited to the Arab–Israeli conflict, as intra-Arab rivalries at various points made Egypt, Syria, Iraq, and Saudi Arabia major players in Lebanon by backing various domestic factions. The struggle over pan-Arab unity sparked the UAR merger of Syria and Egypt in 1958, which contributed to cause a brief civil war in Lebanon that only ended with the deployment of U.S. Marines, but also rocked Jordan and Iraq. Syria invaded Lebanon in 1976 and remained as a de facto occupying force until 2005, partly driven by the regional ambitions of Syrian president Hafez al-Assad. The Cold War aggravated many conflicts in the Global South as Western powers and the Soviet Union searched for local proxies to supply with enormous quantities of arms, especially in the

Middle East and sub-Saharan Africa during the 1970s and 1980s.[50] Even a country with the most enlightened rulers would suffer consequences from such a destabilizing regional environment.

The Outbreak and Major Phases of Civil War

Tense political clashes marked the spring of 1975 as open displays of hostility gradually escalated between the two major coalitions. For instance, at a political demonstration in the city of Saida unknown gunmen opened fire killing a Sunni Muslim member of Parliament. Historians traditionally date the beginning of the civil war to a duo of violent incidents in the Ain el-Rummaneh neighborhood in Beirut on April 13, 1975.[51] On that day, members of a Palestinian group had opened fire on the baptismal proceedings of a powerful Christian political family, leaving several people dead. Later the same day a bus with armed members of a Palestinian group was stopped by Christian gunmen directing traffic while traveling through the Christian neighborhood of Ain el-Rummaneh in southeast Beirut, and a minor altercation sparked a gun battle leaving several people dead. After this day violence erupted between the two sides, and public order broke down as armed groups became the dominant political forces within the country and organized violence sidelined all other forms of politics. The civil war lasted for fifteen years and caused immense human tragedy and physical destruction.[52] However, the war can be divided into a few distinct phases of intense combat operations interspersed with periods of relative calm. The three most significant phases occurred during 1975–1976, 1982–1985, and 1986–1990.[53]

1975–1976: The Two Years' War

The first phase of the war, known in Lebanon as the Two Years' War, lasted for about eighteen months from April 1975 until the fall of 1976. Various bouts of violence afflicted all areas of the country, but the most important military battles—involving conventional military forces and clear front lines—took place in Beirut and its vicinity. The two most important sets of military operations involved militias fighting for control of the city center, particularly its hotel district, which afforded high ground in urban combat, as well as major efforts by both coalitions to secure full military control over their side of the front lines by expelling hostile populations. Both coalitions committed major atrocities—including ethnic cleansing—in connection with the second objective. The Palestinian forces and their allies eventually gained the upper hand in the military struggle and looked increasingly certain to break through Christian lines by extending their offensive beyond Beirut and attacking also in a pincer movement through its mountainous east.

The prospect of PLO control over Lebanon alarmed Syrian president Hafez al-Assad.[54] He worried that PLO-controlled Lebanon would spark a new Arab–Israeli war, dragging Syria into renewed hostilities on foreign soil with unpredictable and uncontrollable dynamics. Furthermore, all PLO factions and Lebanese left-wing groups had a multitude of Arab and Eastern Bloc sponsors, and Lebanon might thus come under de facto Egyptian, Iraqi, or Soviet control. Finally, a radical populist Sunni-dominated regime in Lebanon might threaten the stability of Assad's own regime within Syria, based partly on a heavy Alawi dominance of its military and security forces ruling over a majority-Sunni population. In late 1976 regular Syrian forces therefore entered Lebanon in full force and ended the first phase of the war through a de facto occupation of big swathes of the country. The next several years featured an array of notable local flare-ups and sparked a couple of international diplomatic crises but did not see a return of nationwide warfare.

1982–1985: The Israeli Invasion and the War of the Mountain

On June 6, 1982, Israel invaded Lebanon in an attempt to eliminate the PLO as a military force and install a friendly regime in Beirut.[55] Its forces engaged both Syrian and Palestinian units as they pushed north to reach Beirut and their Christian allies. At this point several Western powers intervened and deployed forces to Lebanon as a joint mission labeled the Multinational Force in Lebanon. Fearing a bloodbath if Israeli or Christian forces tried to defeat Palestinian forces in West Beirut and the refugee camps, the Multinational Force evacuated Yasser Arafat and all key PLO personnel from Beirut into permanent exile in Tunisia. However, subsequent Israeli plans to install a friendly, Christian-dominated government unraveled when a key ally, Maronite Catholic leader Bashir Gemayel, was assassinated. Days after the assassination, his supporters massacred an estimated eight hundred Palestinian civilians during an Israeli-organized incursion into the Sabra and Shatila refugee camps in events widely interpreted as revenge attacks. The Israeli public rapidly soured on the war, and in late summer of 1983 the Israel Defense Forces withdrew to a security buffer zone in south Lebanon. The key architect of the war, Israeli defense minister Ariel Sharon, was forced to resign in disgrace.

One result of this hasty withdrawal was to rearrange the military balance between Lebanese militias, and this process proved particularly consequential in the southern parts of Mount Lebanon. Under Israeli military cover, many Christian militia fighters had returned to parts of the Mount Lebanon region south of Beirut that was mixed mostly between Maronite Catholics and Druze and had been controlled until 1982 by Druze forces. When Israeli forces withdrew, they left behind a situation in Mount Lebanon where an intermixed area contained two rival militias, one Christian and one Druze, that both sought local military supremacy. This volatile situation precipitated a vicious war in August–September of 1983 that ended with a complete victory for the Druze. In the course of their military advance, Druze forces perpetrated numerous massacres of Christian civilians that remained in the area. Many Christians heard of these massacres and elected to flee before Druze fighters reached their villages. In 1984–1985 the violence spread south from Mount Lebanon into the two neighboring districts of Saida and Jezzine, where Sunni, Palestinian, and Druze forces displaced most of the Christian community. The result was a "quasi-complete" expulsion of the Christian population from the affected region: roughly 163,000 individuals displaced, about 2,700 disappeared, and 1,155 confirmed dead.[56] Figure 2.1 shows all 211 locations where Christians were ethnically cleansed between 1983 and 1985.[57]

In 1975–1976 Druze militias had killed and forcibly displaced some number of Christian residents in this area, an episode that forms part of the empirical evidence I examine in the next three chapters. Furthermore, in 1977 Druze forces killed a number of local Christian residents as retaliation for the assassination of Druze leader Kamal Joumblatt (even though he most likely met his fate at the hands of Syrian soldiers, rather than local Christians).[58] So why did events play out so differently in 1983? Why did Druze

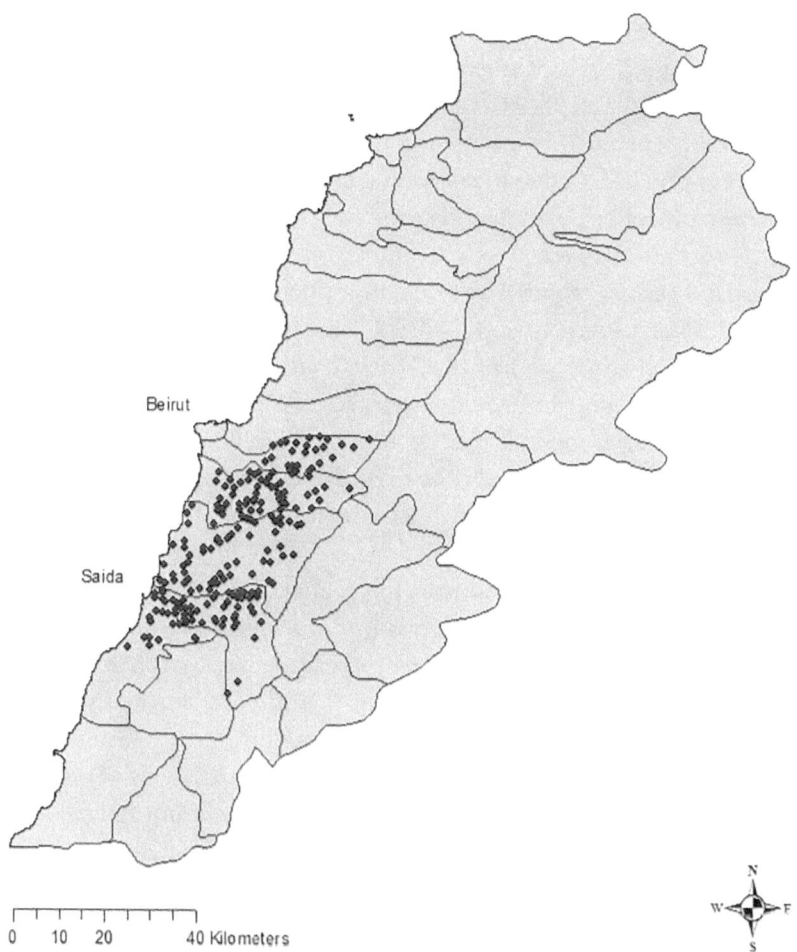

Figure 2.1 Christian villages cleansed in 1983–85

forces decide to perpetrate the ethnic cleansing of an entire community of Christians, most of whom had not previously been perceived as a compelling security threat? And how does this episode relate to my argument about intelligence?

The answer lies in the return into, and subsequent activities of Christian militias in, this region.[59] After Israel took military control of the area, many Christians who had previously been displaced from this region in 1975–1976 started to return, first spontaneously and later as a concerted strategic effort by Christian militia forces. Under Israeli protection, they reasserted themselves as the new masters of this area, including by engaging in harassment and humiliation of local Druze. More importantly, they set about installing permanent military infrastructure to ensure permanent domination of the region, including fortifications, barracks, checkpoints, and telecommunication wires. In effect, they thereby turned the Christian villages of the region into military bases. As part of this process they mobilized and trained new, previously apathetic Christian residents to participate in both military and civilian operations. These developments had several effects. First, the Christian military presence presented a mortal threat to Druze control over the one region of Lebanon where most Druze are concentrated and widely consider their ancestral home. Second, Christian actions sparked an enormous desire for revenge. Third, as Druze began to resist this presence by sniper attacks and other ambushes, local Christians rallied further to Christian militia forces for protection.

After the Israeli withdrawal from this region, Druze leaders mounted a major military effort to push Christian militia forces out of the region.[60] As part of this military campaign, senior leaders exhorted their followers to join with powerful rhetorical appeals that did not clearly distinguish between enemy fighters and the Christian community. In the ensuing combat episodes, Druze soldiers frequently perpetrated massacres of unarmed Christians. There were likely several reasons why this campaign devolved into communal warfare, including the emotional effect on Druze of what they perceived as an Israeli-installed Christian military occupation as well as the failure of senior leaders to urge moderation. However, it would also have been difficult for Druze forces to target Christians in a selective manner at this point. Their prior information about political allegiances was no longer accurate, as many previously apathetic Christians had now joined the Christian war effort. The behavior of Druze militants is thus consistent with my argument about how military mobilization of a civilian community can cause trust and moderation to break down. The ethnic cleansing of Christians from Mount Lebanon during 1983–1985 represents a heinous crime and an extensive case of human rights violations that affected many innocent people. However, the events do not represent a particularly compelling puzzle for social scientists. There is also little in the way of micro-level variation in patterns of violence and displacement to be explained. For these reasons I do not rely on the War of the Mountain for empirical evidence, even though the episode with all requisite certainty represents ethnic cleansing.

1986–1990: From Military Stalemate to the Taif Agreement

The last few years of the war were marked by mostly stable front lines between the main combatants coupled with severe infighting among technically allied militias on both sides. In what remained of the Muslim and left-wing coalition, conflicts were particularly severe between the Shia Amal Movement and the Palestinian community for control of the refugee camps, resulting in an episode of hostilities known as the War of the Camps.[61] Another conflict cleavage emerged between what had been the main Shia political actor, the Amal Movement, and the newly emergent Hezbollah—created in response to the Israeli invasion and grown powerful by a steady supply of Iranian arms and money—for control of the Shia community.[62] On the Christian side, open warfare ensued in East Beirut as Lebanese Armed Forces commander Michel Aoun tried to revive the Lebanese army and use it to impose the authority of national state institutions over both the militias and the Syrian forces.[63] However, none of these efforts had much impact on the front lines, and none of the violence had either the primary intention or consequence of causing permanent inter-ethnic displacement. While many families were temporarily displaced during this phase, particularly during the intra-Christian and Syrian–Christian battles of 1988–1990, most displaced were able to return to their original homes shortly after violence abated.

The war eventually ended with the Taif Agreement, drawn up under Saudi auspices and signed in 1990 under heavy pressure on the militias by their foreign patrons.[64] The 1991 Gulf War forced outside powers to cooperate against Saddam Hussein, and Syrian hegemony over Lebanon was a price paid by the United States for support in Operation Desert Storm. In accordance with the Taif Agreement, all militias subsequently demobilized and surrendered substantial amounts of their equipment—especially heavy arms and military vehicles—to international actors. The exception remains Hezbollah, which chose not to demobilize; at the time, they were waging a low-intensity insurgency against Israeli forces, which occupied a buffer zone in southern Lebanon. The military campaign by Hezbollah eventually forced Israel to withdraw from all Lebanese territory in 2000. Syria, on the other hand, continued its military presence—and dominated foreign and security policy—in Lebanon until forced to withdraw in 2005, following public protest in the aftermath of the assassination of Prime Minister Rafik Hariri.

Many accounts of the Lebanese civil war discuss its madness, its utter chaos, and its seemingly disorganized violence perpetrated under the fog of war; some even make these features the defining characteristics of the conflict. Conversely, in this chapter I present a different narrative that emphasizes order, structure, and rational planning. I do not deny that wars unfold in unexpected ways, that leaders often have limited abilities to implement their most preferred strategies, or that some instances of violence may appear irrational on the surface. Nevertheless, I do believe that we can explain a significant share of this variation as the outcome of rational decisions once we have a clear picture of the actors. At its outset the war was largely fought across an ethnic cleavage, and both parties to the conflict engaged in egregious acts of ethnic cleansing; Lebanon is sometimes even referred to as a canonical case of this gruesome practice.[65] Yet this chapter also shows that none of the participants in the war had separatist ambitions. Both sides fought to impose a new social contract on the country in its entirety, and all major leaders understood that the polity would remain intermixed. Neither side had the kind of political goals of homogenizing territory that motivated ethnic cleansing in Greece and Turkey, India and Pakistan, or eastern Bosnia.[66] What stands out about ethnic cleansing in Lebanon, as compared to other conflicts such as Bosnia, is not the extent of cleansing but rather the extreme in-case variation in outcomes of violence and displacement.

CHAPTER III

Demographics, Migration, and Violence

Our archives? They were destroyed by Syrian shelling in 1986.
—FORMER MILITIA PRESS SPOKESMAN, FEBRUARY 2014

It is very challenging to do quantitative work on Lebanese politics because it is hard to obtain detailed and reliable data. The country has not conducted a census since 1932, and its true demographic situation remains the subject of heated political disagreements. Those who fear they would lose out if parliamentary quotas more accurately reflected true demographics resist official updates. The historical record of the civil war remains contested as Parliament passed a blanket amnesty law after the war ended and has not tried perpetrators for war crimes. Neither has the government compiled the kind of comprehensive official documentation on truth and reconciliation that characterized transitions to postconflict governance in countries such as South Africa.[1] Many official archives, of official state institutions as well as of parties and militias, were destroyed during the war. Some of the political and military organizations that contested the war no longer exist, at least not within the country. For instance, the PLO was evacuated to Tunisia under American sponsorship in 1982, and none of its senior political or military leaders remain in Lebanon. Members of the Israeli-sponsored Christian militia operating on the Lebanese–Israeli border, the South Lebanon Army, left the country in 2000 when Hezbollah pushed the last Israeli troops from Lebanese soil.

In the face of these challenges, I devoted long stretches of time in the field to identifying and obtaining useful data sources. My first cautious interviews with academics at American University of Beirut lead to other meetings at think tanks, research institutes, nongovernmental organizations (NGOs), and private companies. Along the way I discovered not only what a fractured country Lebanon has become but also how to benefit from political divides. I only wish that I had realized sooner what different intellectual cultures and what wealth of additional material I would encounter at the francophone Université Saint-Joseph as compared to anglophone American University of Beirut, and realized the differences between what gets published in English, French, and Arabic. While I knew what I was looking for in terms of data, I had no idea where to find it. Most material surfaced somewhat randomly, often during interviews that had initially dealt with different topics. For instance, forty minutes into a meeting at a think tank, my gracious host suddenly realized I might find use for a summary of the complete national voter registration rolls sitting on his shelf and helped me obtain my own copy. Like several other important resources, it turned out that this work was readily available for purchase from the local Librairie Antoine bookstore three blocks from my apartment.

This chapter explains how I have used all of these weird and wonderful sources of fine-grained data to provide quantitative evidence for my argument. The result is a novel nationwide data set that covers demographics, migration, and violence for over 1,400 rural villages and urban neighborhoods.[2] No previous account of the Lebanese civil war contains micro-level statistical analysis using systematic data, and producing this dataset involved some challenges. Yet the data is particularly valuable for assessing my theoretical argument because it allows us to test two key observable implications. My argument implies that militias should use violence to target political and military opposition; when they use violence, the kind of violence used subsequently depends on the level of intelligence they possess in a local area. In intermixed locations with a high share of coethnics, militias are more likely to access detailed and reliable intelligence, which allows them to discriminate among neutral and hostile non-coethnic individuals and to leave the former in peace. We should thus see more selective violence in those locations. Homogenous non-coethnic enclaves, on the other hand, are more prone to experience ethnic cleansing. Systematic data allows us to test this simple proposition in a rigorous fashion.

To assess my argument I have relied on this village- and neighborhood-level, cross-sectional data set that covers the first period of the war in 1975–1976. As previous chapters explain, I focus on this period because it has both some of the most extensive campaigns of forced migration and the most puzzling variation in outcomes. The dataset has two dependent variables: selective violence and ethnic cleansing. The independent variables are, first, the demographic share of residents in a local area who were coethnics of the militia in military control and, second, results from the last prewar parliamentary election that indicate where different parties—that subsequently turned into wartime militias—had a geographic concentration of political support. The specific binary measure of where parties had support is, for each electoral district, whether they successfully elected at least one parliamentary deputy there during the 1972 election. The data I collected shows that about half of Christians in Palestinian-controlled territory were displaced while the other half remained in place; similarly, about half of Muslims in Christian-controlled territory were displaced while the others stayed in their original homes.

The chapter proceeds as follows. The first two sections describe the sources and nature of the data I compiled, their relative strengths and weaknesses, and the coding rules I used to create a systematic, nationwide, micro-level data set. I begin with how to code village-level demographics, which is the most complicated variable to measure empirically among the ones that feature in my dataset. The third section contains descriptive statistics. The fourth section tests my argument about how militias used different kinds of violence in areas where they had a high share of coethnics, compared to areas where militias had few local supporters. The following section uses prewar elections data for a subset of the country to test the other key observable implication of my argument, that violence primarily targeted political and military opposition rather than all non-coethnics.

Data and Sources: Demographics

To estimate the 1975 demographic composition of each village or neighborhood, I used data from the official Lebanese voter registration rolls. Because of the elaborate and rigid sectarian nature of electoral politics in Lebanon, its voter registration rolls contain the sectarian identity of each voter. Voter registration information comes from the civil registry, maintained by the Ministry of Interior and Municipalities, which is used to produce birth certificates, marriage licenses, and death records. Voter registration rolls contain the number of voters from each of eighteen officially recognized sectarian subgroups in each of over 1,400 so-called cadastral zones. Cadastral zones are roughly the equivalent of a municipality: almost all cadastral zones correspond precisely to one rural village or urban neighborhood and bear the exact same name.[3] The cadastral zones aggregate into twenty-eight electoral districts, which in turn form six administrative regions.[4] I have access to the complete set of nationwide voter registration rolls at the village or neighborhood level for the election in 2009 as well as data at the level of twenty-eight electoral districts from the 1953 voter registration rolls.[5] There is also a small but highly competent academic literature—mostly in French—on the prewar demographics of Lebanon, wartime migration flows, and how the country has changed as a result.[6]

I used the 2009 voter registration rolls, together with two key amendments, as a village- or neighborhood-level estimate of the number of residents from each subgroup present at the outbreak of war in 1975. At first glance, this approach seems wildly inappropriate: how can we use postwar data to estimate prewar demographics when we know that the war caused extensive demographic change? The answer is that the rigidity of the voter registration process means that the voter rolls largely preserve a demographic picture from decades past, which is no longer accurate in the present. For political reasons, it is very difficult for Lebanese citizens to switch registration location. As a result, the 1953 and 2009 registration rolls look more similar than one might imagine, even though the civil war caused extensive demographic change.[7] In many ways the 2009 voter rolls are more indicative of what demographic settlement patterns looked like before the war than at present. Ironically, this aspect of the data is very useful for assessing local demographic patterns in 1975, which serves my purposes.

In general, Lebanese citizens vote not in their current residence but in the ancestral village of their family.[8] The voter rolls are based on Lebanon's civil registry, and in theory anyone can apply to switch their residence after living in a new location for at least three years. However, such an application needs approval by the *mukhtar* (roughly equivalent to an elected mayor at the village or neighborhood level) in both the original and transfer location, by the local police or gendarmerie, and by the Ministry of Interior—all of whom exercise de facto veto power over the transfer of official residence. In practice, only exceptionally well-heeled and politically connected individuals manage to get through this byzantine process, where any number of actors have strong incentives to veto the transfer. A splendid pyramid of clientelism, vote-buying, election-rigging, and dazzling intricacies of corruption rests on the fulcrum of the civil registry, and its beneficiaries guard it accordingly.[9] As a result, many Lebanese return to "their" village—even if the family has not lived there for decades—to vote and to apply for official documents such as a driver's license or passport.

One of the best illustrations of how contemporary voter rolls reflect prewar demographic patterns comes from the areas affected by the War of the Mountain. As the previous chapter explains, during 1983–1985 Druze, Palestinian, and Sunni forces displaced virtually the entire Christian population from over two hundred villages across the five electoral districts of Baabda, Aley, Chouf, Saida/Zahrani, and Jezzine.[10] After the war ended in 1991 some Christians returned, but many stayed permanently in their new homes in Beirut or overseas. By 2007 only about 20 percent of displaced Christian families had returned to the area affected by the War of the Mountain as permanent residents, according to detailed village-level surveys.[11] Christians thus make up about 10 percent of permanent residents in this region at present. However, the 2009 voter registration rolls show the area as almost 50 percent Christian because most of those who were displaced and never moved back are still registered there.[12] This figure is very close to the 1953 voter data, which indicate that Christian residents constituted 53 percent of the population in this area in that year.[13] Since the five districts affected by the War of the Mountain are among the ones with the most extensive wartime demographic change, they most vividly illustrate my point: voter rolls have not been updated in a systematic and comprehensive fashion, and they typically reflect prewar demographics more accurately than present-day settlement patterns.

Further evidence on demographics comes from the *National Survey of Household Living Conditions 2004*, published jointly between the United Nations Development Programme and two branches of the Lebanese government, the Ministry of Social Affairs and the Central Administration for Statistics.[14] Since there has not been a census in Lebanon since 1932, there is a dearth of reliable official statistics, and the aforementioned agencies therefore cooperate on extensive surveys of Lebanese demographics in order to better provide public planning and services. Among other things, the report contains data on where actual residents in different regions are officially registered. Table 3.1 shows the percentage of actual residents in each

TABLE 3.1
Percentage of residents correctly registered in the region where they reside

Region	Correctly registered residents (%)
Beirut	60.9
Mount Lebanon	48.4
North Lebanon	98.9
Bekaa Valley	98.6
South Lebanon	89.3
Nabatieh	95.3

Source: UNDP 2006

region who are officially registered in the region where they currently reside.

This data highlights that, in four out of six regions, the vast majority of residents are officially registered in their correct location. These numbers reflect how the cities in Lebanon have changed significantly over time, especially in Greater Beirut, while the countryside remains much more mired in traditional ways, including regarding ethnic settlement patterns. In general, rural villages are significantly more likely to be homogenous than are urban neighborhoods, although there are some that are demographically intermixed. The exact sectarian balance of intermixed villages has likely changed since 1975 because of differing sectarian migration patterns and birth rates. But while the exact balance of intermixed locations may have changed, I believe that the voter rolls provide a fairly accurate measure of which locations were intermixed and which were homogenous when the civil war broke out. This aspect makes the data particularly useful for testing my hypotheses, which can easily be falsified if violence does not conform to my predictions regarding differences between intermixed and homogenous villages and neighborhoods.

The data highlights that Greater Beirut has changed enormously over time and shows that almost half of the people who currently live there are registered elsewhere. Rapid urbanization has affected both the formal administrative region known as Beirut, which encompasses only the center of the city, and the Mount Lebanon administrative region that includes all suburbs as well as some parts of Greater Beirut that are by now widely recognized as regular neighborhoods of the city.[15] The report shows that particularly large numbers of current residents are registered in the Bekaa Valley, South Lebanon, and Nabatieh. The latter two regions are heavily dominated by Shia Muslims, many of whom now inhabit the southern suburbs of Beirut known collectively as "Dahiyeh." By all demographic accounts, the in-migration of poor rural Shia began in the 1950s and 1960s and accelerated after the Israeli invasion of Lebanon in 1982.[16] This fact once again illustrates how the voter rolls preserve a demographic picture that more closely resembles what Lebanon looked like before the civil war. However, we also know that substantial in-migration of poor rural migrants, heavily Shia Muslim, occurred in the decades before the civil war broke out. For that reason, I have added data on the major shantytowns that sprung up around Beirut before 1975.

Shantytowns Surrounding Beirut

A large pool of (overwhelmingly Muslim) poor migrants failed to enter the formal housing and labor markets during the great migration waves of the 1950s and 1960s and ended up in a string of emerging, improvised, and informal shantytowns surrounding the city.[17] The shantytowns do not appear in voter registration rolls, and I have used secondary sources to include them in the dataset.[18] Academics, NGOs, and political parties of various stripes provide ample documentation of the names and locations of shantytowns as well as somewhat less reliable estimates of their demographic composition. Poor migrants generally segregated along sectarian lines, and for our purposes we can code the major shantytowns as homogenous Muslim neighborhoods.

Data on Palestinians

Finally, I have added data on the Palestinian camps from the United Nations Relief and Works Agency for Palestine Refugees in the Near East (UNRWA).[19] Palestinian refugees arrived in Lebanon in waves starting with the war of 1948; while very small numbers of Palestinians have received Lebanese citizenship, the overwhelming majority has not and therefore do not appear in the voter registration rolls. The community mostly remains in twelve decades-old refugee camps run by UNRWA.[20] While UNRWA registers contain about 450,000 Palestinian individuals in Lebanon, recent studies suggest that this number vastly overstates the true figure, which may be as small as 260,000.[21] Many Palestinians lost hope of a promising future in Lebanon and traveled abroad to work, for instance, in the Persian Gulf, or to seek asylum, especially in Germany and the Scandinavian countries. Current estimates indicate that about 62 percent of Palestinians live inside the twelve camps, and a large majority of the remaining 38 percent live in improvised gatherings directly adjacent to established camps as the original sites are becoming overcrowded.[22] Information on the camps therefore provides fairly accurate representation of where the Palestinian community resides, even if estimates of the true number of inhabitants in any one camp are unreliable. Together with the amended Lebanese voter registration rolls, this data provides a full demographic picture of the country, save for migrant workers and a small number of stateless seminomadic Bedouin.

Summary Statistics

The resulting data set contains a nationwide set of 1,453 inhabited villages or neighborhoods. A majority of locations were homogenous, but 24.7 percent were intermixed with both Muslim and Christian residents.[23] For simplicity of analysis, the category "Muslim" here includes all Lebanese Muslims and Druze as well as all Palestinian residents regardless of their confessional identity.[24] The category "Christian" includes all Lebanese Christians regardless of their confession, including Armenians. As for population size, the median location has 1,000 registered voters. The minimum population size (of voters aged twenty-one or above) is 50, while the maximum is 81,700, as there are a handful of outliers at the top of the distribution (mostly neighborhoods of Beirut) that dwarf the typical village or neighborhood in size. The first and third quartile of locations have 450 and 2,250 registered voters, respectively, while the modal number is 350. The typical location in the data set is thus fairly small and represents what we may think of as a village or a neighborhood: a social space where residents participate in community life and that typically has no more than one commercial center or school.

Data and Sources: Elections, Violence, Displacement, and Control Variables

This section describes how I obtained and coded data on military control, prewar elections, violence, forced migration, and a range of geographic and other control variables, as well as how I use this data to construct my independent and dependent variables.

Military Control

I include in the dataset a variable to capture whether each village or neighborhood was under military control of a Christian militia or controlled by the PLO factions and their Lebanese allies.[25] By my estimates, 955 locations were controlled by the Palestinian factions and their Lebanese allies (66 percent) and 498 by Christian militias (34 percent). Military front lines are available in some secondary sources, but I also asked former militia members during interviews to draw the front lines on maps for the periods in question. Since the war was fought mostly through conventional warfare, with military units facing each other across established front lines, there are relatively few controversies about where those front lines were located. Front lines did shift some during 1975–1976, although mostly in the two regions of Koura and Zahle, which mark the northernmost and easternmost reach of Christian military control. Neither area had clearly demarcated front lines, unlike those dividing Beirut. However, the number of locations affected by the shifting front lines is at most a couple of dozen rural villages. Given a dataset of over 1,400 observations, this change over time is very small.[26] Beirut was an early battleground, but the infamous "Green Line" front lines—named for the lush vegetation that sprung up among the thin strip of buildings leveled by artillery bombardment—quickly separated the capital into east and west.

For the first independent variable—coethnic presence—I have constructed a continuous measure for the share of residents in each location that is coethnics of the armed group in control. One feature of the data is that a majority of locations have 100 percent coethnics of the militia in control, and we would not expect ethnic violence in such areas. There are 638 locations containing non-coethnics of the locally preponderant militia, of which 479 were controlled by the PLO and 159 by Christians; I consider these to be areas at risk for ethnic violence, and I subset most analysis to focus on these locations only.

Prewar Elections

The second independent variable captures whether the location contained political opponents of the militia that controlled it militarily. This variable is quite difficult to operationalize, but in line with recent scholarship, I have used prewar election results as a proxy variable.[27] Several wartime militias had previously operated as political parties in prewar politics, and we can use electoral support in the last prewar parliamentary elections of May 1972 to assess where these parties-turned-militias had geographic concentrations of support.[28] In particular, I have focused on concentrations of prewar support for two parties: Katayyib and the National Liberal Party, both of which were hardline Lebanese nationalist parties, deeply opposed to the Palestinian military presence, with an almost exclusively Christian following. Both parties had a long history in Lebanese electoral politics, were well known across the country, and had returned multiple parliamentary deputies in all elections after independence. Crucially, these two parties organized the most powerful Christian militia forces and dominated the early war effort.

The electoral data has two key limitations. First, we can only study support for Christian parties. The PLO did not contest elections and most left-wing groups, such as the Lebanese Communist Party, were not organized enough to win any seats in prewar elections. It is therefore more difficult to ascertain where those parties held concentrations of public support, except in the Palestinian refugee camps. The one left-wing party with a strong parliamentary presence, the Progressive Socialist Party, won no seats in areas that subsequently became controlled by Christian militias.[29] Second, electoral returns are reported at the level of twenty-eight electoral districts, not for individual municipalities, so the variable in all likelihood codes some locations as supporting a particular party even though hardly anyone in that particular location actually voted for them. Nevertheless, we can use this data to assess empirically whether violence—of any kind—by the Palestinian, Muslim, and left-wing alliance targeted locations where those Christian parties that contested the civil war gathered strong support before the war broke out, as my argument implies that they should.

I constructed a dummy variable of whether a location was controlled by the Palestinian-led coalition but located in an electoral district that elected at least one member of Parliament in 1972 from a Christian-dominated political party that subsequently became a military actor by 1975. Out of twenty-eight districts, four elected at least one deputy from either the Katayyib or the National Liberal Party in the 1972 elections but subsequently saw villages or neighborhoods with Christian residents under military control by the Palestinian groups and their allies in 1975–1976: Metn, Baabda, Chouf, and Jezzine. Out of 955 locations controlled by the Palestinian-dominated coalition, 192 (20.1 percent) were located in the four districts where the two hardline Christian parties won seats in the 1972 election.

Selective Violence and Forced Displacement

My two dependent variables are selective violence and ethnic cleansing. Selective violence can occur without causing any displacement, and forced displacement can take place without violence; we therefore need data on both phenomena. As a key source on displacement, I have used a report by the Ministry of the Displaced (1996), a government ministry created after the war to resettle and compensate those displaced during it. The report is based on extensive surveys carried out by ministry employees in 1992, shortly after the war ended, and contains individual entries for each village- or neighborhood-level episode of displacement. Each entry provides a date, an indication of whether displacement concerned specific individuals or a whole community along sectarian lines, whether it concerned Christians or Muslims (or both), and whether it was accompanied by militia actions and bloodshed or whether it reflected general security concerns on behalf of migrants. The report does not provide numeric estimates of the number of displaced, and it does not cover some parts of southern Lebanon that remained under Israeli occupation at the time.

To code violence, I have also used a report on wartime violence against civilians published in 2013 by the Beirut office of an international NGO, the International Center for Transitional Justice (ICTJ).[30] The report compiles a rich material and organizes it as incident reports in chronological order. Among other sources, it includes the complete wartime news coverage from newspapers *Al-Nahar*, *Al-Safir*, and *L'Orient-Le Jour* as well as reports by Amnesty International and Human Rights Watch and books published in English, French, and Arabic. *Al-Nahar* and *As-Safir* represent opposite ends of the Lebanese wartime political spectrum, which should help to mitigate political bias.[31] ICTJ hired a team of about a dozen people to work on this project over four months, with the intention of collecting all publicly accessible documentation on wartime violence in a single place. Since the Lebanese government has not conducted anything even remotely approximating comprehensive truth and reconciliation programs after the war ended, the intentions behind the ICTJ report were to produce a first attempt at systematic documentation and to spur others into action.[32]

The ICTJ report contains data about quite different events, ranging from combat episodes to abuse of civilians. One downside of the ICTJ report is that most Lebanese media sources operate from Beirut, and incidents in its vicinity receive more attention than do rural locations, where there may have been events that we thus fail to capture.[33] There were in all likelihood some incidents of selective violence that this dataset does not record because they never generated news coverage. However, the number is likely to be very small, and we can control for geographic factors that should correlate with reporting standards, such as distance to Beirut.[34] Another problem is that not all phases and combatants of the war received equal media coverage. In particular, Syria and its local allies managed quite effectively to block media coverage during many episodes of human rights abuse. Nevertheless, the report represents a treasure trove for quantitative researchers as it synthesizes all publicly available information from the most widely cited primary and secondary sources on wartime violence, displacement, and human rights abuse. In general, the report is strongest for the 1975–1976 period and for human rights abuse by Palestinian and Christian militias, which is precisely the topic I focus on. The report is much weaker for the latter half of the 1980s and for atrocities committed by Syria and its allies such as Hezbollah and the Amal Movement. Those time periods do not feature in my empirical work, and this shortcoming of the report thus has little consequence for my purposes.

Coding modalities of violence involves many judgment calls. In the dataset, I have coded all locations as experiencing either ethnic cleansing, selective violence, or no violence: all locations in the data set experience one of those three outcomes, and no location experiences more than one.[35]

In general, I have coded as cases of selective violence those locations that witnessed either selective assassinations, as indicated by the ICTJ report, or forced displacement of select individuals only according to the ministry report.[36] About half of all incidents of lethal violence in the ICTJ report have an estimated body count, but the rest are only described in general terms, so I therefore constructed a dummy variable rather than a continuous measure. The incidents that I coded generally involve one specific military group perpetrating violence against a select number of individuals in some particular location. In some cases, the source material clearly notes that the victims were targeted because of their political affiliation or militant status (real or imagined). However, I acknowledge the limitation that we do not generally have any kind of statement by the responsible group that they believed the targeted persons were political activists or militants.

Ethnic cleansing proves even more difficult to code, and I have used two different coding protocols—one more conservative and one more permissive—to ensure that the results are robust to different conceptualizations of the variable. My definition of ethnic cleansing involves militants from one ethnic group perpetrating intentional forced displacement against members of a different community. At a minimum, a restrictive coding scheme should therefore code a location as experiencing ethnic cleansing if a militia from one ethnic group attacks the location, intentionally displaces all members of the other community from the location in a systematic manner by active use of force, and does not allow those who were displaced to return. This coding scheme is conservative and transparent. However, this coding scheme would fail to capture ethnic cleansing in locations that a militia intended to forcibly displace but where the civilian population preempted militia action by choosing to flee in anticipation of an attack. I have therefore also employed a second, more permissive coding scheme that codes every case where the 1996 government survey reports a "general wave of displacement along sectarian lines" as ethnic cleansing.[37] The first measure likely underreports ethnic cleansing, and the second measure likely overreports it, making them useful as complements.

In my main model specifications below, I have used the more permissive rule for what counts as ethnic cleansing. According to this coding protocol, there are fifty-two cases of ethnic cleansing and seventy of selective violence. The benefit of this measure is that it provides a clear behavioral measure of migration flows. The downside of this coding scheme is that it does not capture intentionality. As a result, it likely includes some cases where militias may not have had any intention to attack a certain location but where locals chose to leave out of fears that may or may not have been motivated by facts on the ground. In the second, more conservative protocol I have coded only those locations as ethnic cleansing where we observe an actual militia attack with the clear intention to cause forced migration of non-coethnics. By this rule, fifteen locations were ethnically cleansed in a systematic manner, of which six by the Palestinian-led alliance and nine by Christian forces, and there are ninety-eight areas that experienced selective violence, of which fifty-eight were at the hands of Palestinian and left-wing militants and forty at the hands of Christian militias. In the fifteen locations coded as experiencing ethnic cleansing, not only were civilians driven out at gunpoint—and sometimes even physically removed by being placed on buses and trucks and transported across the front lines—but these areas were also either systematically destroyed or the homes and buildings were confiscated and resettled by new residents. In none of those fifteen cases were civilians allowed to return. The areas that were ethnically cleansed by this metric tended to have large populations, with mean and median values of 9,300 and 5,000 residents, respectively.

Control Variables

From the demographic material I also constructed some control variables, including total population size of each village or urban neighborhood, and dummy variables for which sectarian subgroups were present in the location and which electoral district and administrative region it is located in. As of the 2009 election, Lebanon contained twenty-eight electoral districts that further aggregate into six administrative regions.[38] I also created an urban dummy variable that combines the three electoral districts that correspond to the city centers of the three largest cities in Lebanon: Beirut, Tripoli, and Saida.

Finally, I used distance to Beirut to simultaneously measure two relevant control variables: economic wealth of the location and its military-strategic importance. Distance is a defensible choice in both regards. Beirut increasingly became the dominant center of the national economy in the last few decades before the war, and especially for the most lucrative sectors such as international trade and finance. The war of 1975–1976 centered on control of the capital, and locations in its vicinity generally had more strategic importance than remote rural areas. It is of course far from ideal to use one measurement to capture two theoretical variables, and the measure is far from perfect for either variable. For instance, there were many slum neighborhoods in Beirut and many wealthy coastal towns further to its north and south. As for strategic value, many remote locations far from the capital held strategic importance as they mattered for control of international borders, high ground, or important roads.[39] However, despite some effort, I have not managed to obtain better measurements.[40] I determined the distance of each location to central Beirut in kilometers using the individual global positioning coordinates of each village or neighborhood and a single reference point.[41] The mean distance of a location to central Beirut is fifty-one kilometers.

Descriptive Statistics

This section combines all of the above data sources to produce descriptive statistics that help convey several key quantitative results. Figure 3.1 contains an estimate of prewar Lebanese sectarian demographics. The map reveals several things: Beirut is generally quite intermixed, both in the sense that it contains intermixed neighborhoods and that it has many neighborhoods that are ethnically homogenous but located in very close proximity to non-coethnics. The Christian heartlands start in East Beirut and run east and north, between the coast to the west and the peaks of a mountain range to its east (this mountain range is noticeable in the map as a blank spot of very limited settlement, which runs north–south and almost divides the country into two halves). Immediately south of Beirut is Aley and the Chouf district, a rural and mountainous region intermixed between Christians and Druze. Shia Muslims dominate in the Bekaa Valley that makes up the eastern part of the country (between the central mountain range to the west and the Syrian border to the east) and in the south. Sunni Muslims traditionally concentrate most heavily in the northern region of Akkar and in the cities of Beirut, Tripoli, and Saida. However, as the map shows, in 1975 all regions contained a fair number of Christian towns and villages as well.

The next two figures explore the spatial incidence of violence. For visual clarity I have used the alternative, more restrictive coding of ethnic cleansing.[42] Figure 3.2 exposes the data through a scatterplot. On the x axis, the

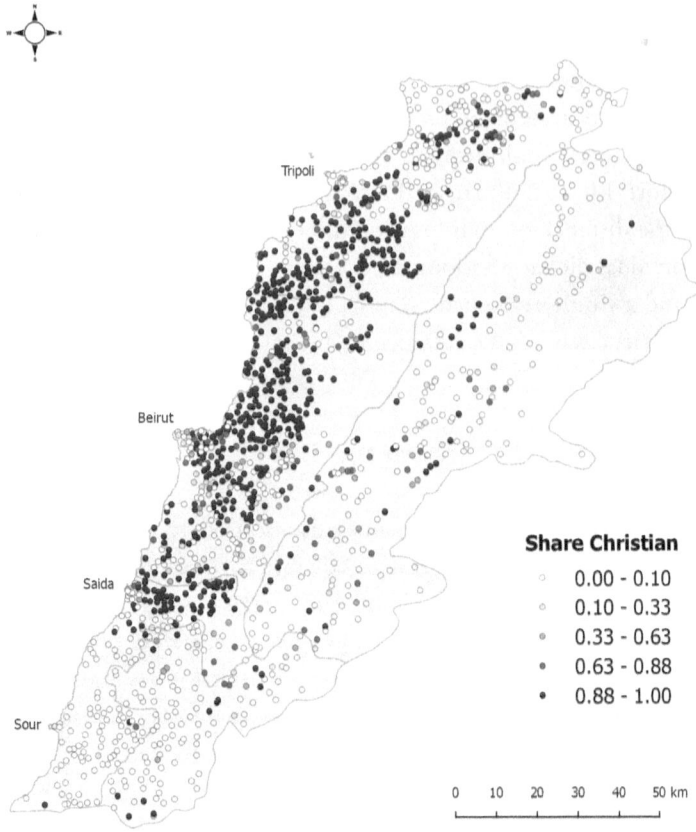

Figure 3.1 Map of prewar demographics

data is organized by "share of coethnics," meaning that locations further to the left are either Christian-controlled areas with a mostly Muslim population, or vice versa. The y axis shows locations by their distance to Beirut. We can notice here that locations experiencing ethnic cleansing—the diamonds in the plot—cluster strongly in the bottom left of the graph. These are areas where the militia in control had a smaller share of coethnics; in particular, most of the affected locations fall on the y axis, where zero percent of the population were coethnics of the militia in control. Note that some of the diamonds overlap in the bottom left corner of the

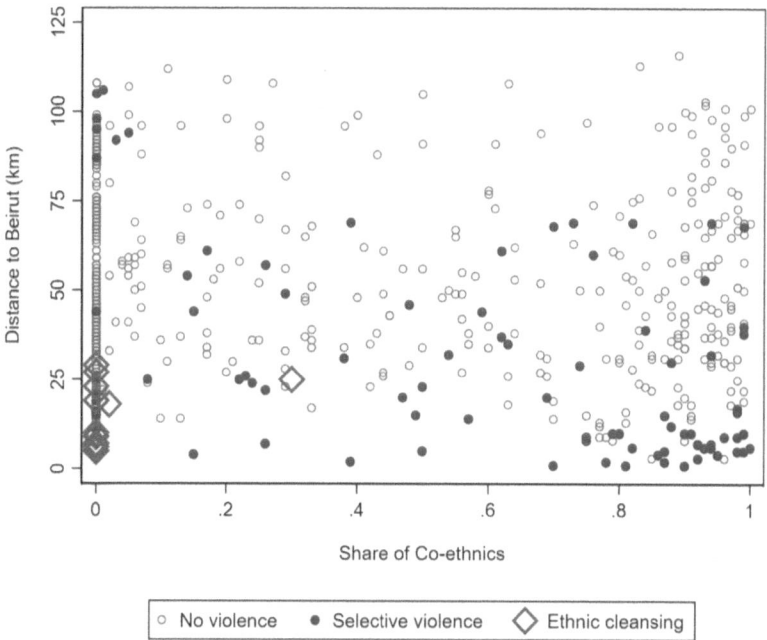

Figure 3.2 Distribution of violence across locations

graph, which somewhat obscures the visual effect. Locations that experienced selective violence are indicated by solid dots. These incidents show more geographic dispersion but with a distinct cluster further to the right in the scatterplot, indicating locations where the militia in charge had a higher share of coethnics. It is also noticeable in the scatterplot that violence is significantly more common as we move toward the floor of the graph, meaning in locations that are geographically closer to Beirut. The most intense and closely contested battles of 1975–1976 centered on control for the capital. The data is subset to include only "at-risk areas," meaning those where the militia in control had non-coethnics.[43]

The figure raises one concern: if selective violence frequently occurred in locations where non-coethnics were a relatively small share of the population, how do we know that this violence did not de facto cleanse these locations even if the total number of targeted people was relatively limited simply because the non-coethnic population was very small? The data in table 3.2 addresses this concern by providing information on numbers killed

TABLE 3.2
The ten largest body counts among instances of selective violence

Location	Body count	Size of non-coethnic population	Share of non-coethnic population killed (%)
Chekka	100	4,200	2
Hamat	100	2,200	5
Mtein	53	2,500	2
Bashoura	50	1,800	3
Rahba	50	5,800	1
Taalabaya	35	2,100	2
Minet el Hosn	30	2,700	1
Salima	29	850	3
Tal Abbas	24	2,000	1
Kab Elias	16	3,600	0

Sources: Eid 2010, ICTJ 2013.

and total population of the targeted ethnic group for the ten instances of selective violence with the largest body count. We do not have body counts for all instances of selective targeting, which is why I have coded this outcome as a binary dummy variable, but we do have this information for about half of all incidents. As table 3.2 confirms, the total number of non-coethnics killed by militias in each of these attacks is only a fraction of the total non-coethnic population in that location.

Geographic Information System mapping also reveals a few important points about the geographic distribution of violence. The most fiercely contested battles of the military campaign in 1975–1976 centered on Beirut, and figure 3.3 shows the incidence of violence in the area surrounding the capital. The thin line bisecting the central city indicates the military front lines, the "Green Line." This line separated Christian militias, in the northeast part of the map, from the PLO and its allies to the south and west. On the Christian side we notice that militants emptied all homogenously Muslim neighborhoods in East Beirut but refrained from ethnic cleansing in any of the intermixed neighborhoods. Many intermixed neighborhoods witnessed selective violence, but some escaped violence altogether. On the PLO-controlled side we notice that not a single neighborhood in

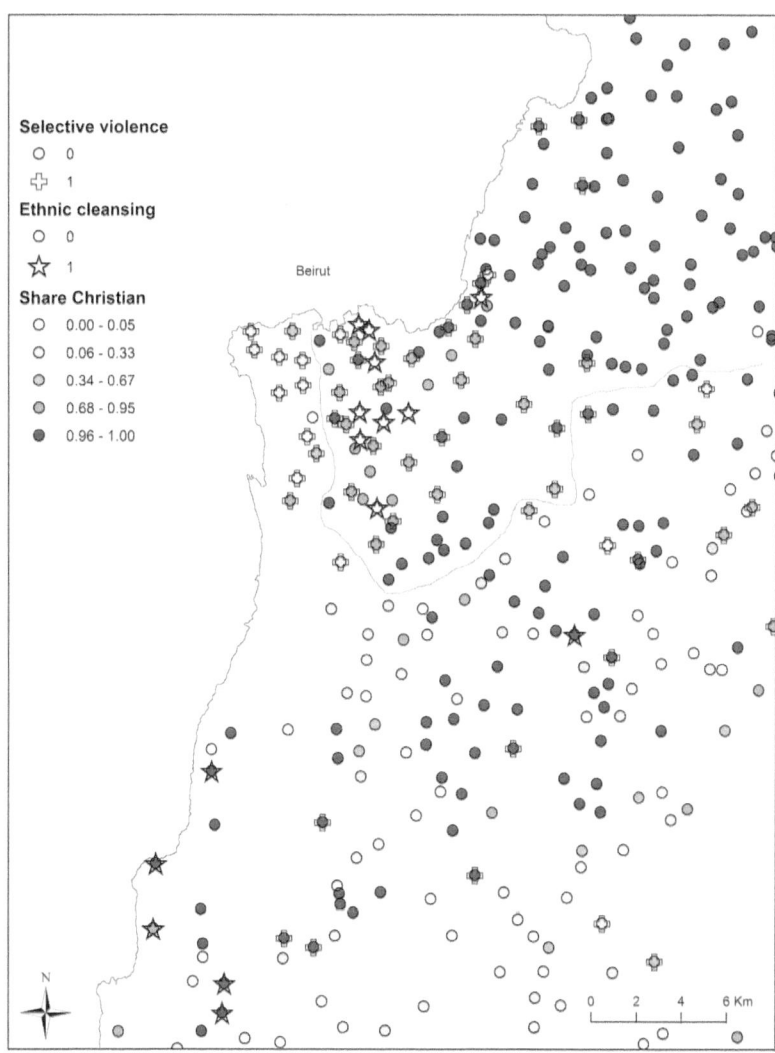

Figure 3.3 Map of Beirut attacks

thoroughly intermixed West Beirut was ethnically cleansed, although most of them witnessed some form of selective violence. On the other hand, PLO-affiliated militants ethnically cleansed several villages south of the capital. Most of those villages were homogenously Christian, although at least one was somewhat intermixed.

The map shows that violence and displacement did not cluster neatly around military front lines, in proximity to combat zones, or in conjunction with territorial contestation.[44] Neither did violence cluster around areas of nationalist or religious importance; in fact, the country contains few religious sites of any significance.[45] Other established theories of forced displacement fare similarly poorly in explaining patterns of violence in Lebanon. The early phase of the war was fought mostly through conventional warfare with clear front lines, and variation in levels of military control across contested space therefore cannot explain variation in violence.[46] There is no evidence that variation in violence stemmed from limited military capabilities that stopped militias from implementing more extensive strategies of violence and displacement.[47] Acts of violence or displacement were often followed by looting, and perpetrators were frequently intoxicated by drugs and alcohol. However, there is little evidence that the large instances of mass displacement that occurred were primarily motivated by economic gain.[48] In fact, there is every reason to believe the opposite: some of the targeted areas were slums and shantytowns and thus among the poorest neighborhoods in the country, while many nearby wealthier areas escaped predation. In sum, the patterns of violence are quite difficult to explain by established theories.

Model Choice, Specifications, and Results

I have estimated conditional logit regressions on whether violence occurred for each location in the sample and, conditional on violence occurring, whether it took the form of selective violence or ethnic cleansing. Since my theoretical argument implies a two-step decision-making process, the conditional logit model is the most appropriate statistical model since I code the two outcome variables as binary dummy variables. I argue that militias first gather intelligence from loyal coethnics on where there is militant activity on behalf of the enemy and thus a need to respond by violence; they then choose between selective violence and ethnic cleansing, depending on the information they possess about this local area (which is in turn a function of demographics, according to my argument). The conditional logit model mirrors this logic, as it first estimates the correlates of violence and then, conditional on violence occurring, the kind of violence employed. The main specification of the conditional logit model uses

TABLE 3.3
Conditional logit regressions on violence and ethnic cleansing

VARIABLES	(1) Violence	(2) Ethnic cleansing
Share coethnics	-0.418	-1.381***
	(0.274)[a]	(0.461)
Distance (km, log)	-0.836***	0.0551
	(0.197)	(0.144)
Population (log)	1.028***	0.313
	(0.244)	(0.210)
Christian control	0.290	0.762*
	(0.197)	(0.403)
Constant	4.484*	-1.443
	(2.514)	(1.662)
Observations	623	122

[a] Robust standard errors in parentheses.
* $p < 0.1$
** $p < 0.05$
*** $p < 0.01$

standard errors clustered at the electoral district level to ensure that the results are not a statistical mirage of spatial autocorrelation.[49] Table 3.3 displays the results.

The first column of the results table establishes the correlates of violence. The model shows that violence (either selective violence or ethnic cleansing) is more likely to occur in rural villages or urban neighborhoods that are closer to Beirut and that have a larger population; however, there is no correlation between the share of militia coethnics in a location and whether the militia uses violence there. The model also fails to detect a statistically significant difference in the likelihood of violence occurring in areas controlled by the PLO-led alliance or by Christian militias. Note that the sample size falls from 638 to 623 observations once we add controls because a few areas do not have global positioning coordinates and thus have missing values for distance.[50]

The second step of the conditional logit model, displayed in the second column of the table, shows the correlates of ethnic cleansing occurring, conditional on violence taking place. The sample in this second step consists of only those 122 locations that experienced some form of violence, meaning either ethnic cleansing or selective violence. The result in this column is clear: ethnic cleansing was more likely to occur in locations where a militia had fewer coethnics, which also means—by necessity—that the inverse is true, and that selective violence was more likely to occur in locations where a militia had a high share of coethnics. Including control variables in the model does not change the result in meaningful ways. Christian control is weakly correlated with an increased probability of ethnic cleansing occurring instead of selective violence, but the relationship is only marginally significant at conventional levels. In short, the quantitative results conform precisely to the empirical predictions of my theoretical argument.

Substantive Effects

The probability of a location witnessing ethnic cleansing depends on what values it registers for the explanatory variables.[51] The probability of a location witnessing ethnic cleansing—conditional on violence taking place in that location—differs across Christian-controlled and PLO-controlled locations. The following values all pertain to locations that did witness violence. A location with zero percent Christians in Christian-controlled territory has about an 81 percent chance of witnessing ethnic cleansing if it suffers violence, which falls to 61 percent for a location with an even mix of both Christians and Muslims, and further down to about 40 percent in a location with 90 percent Christian residents. The corresponding probabilities of ethnic cleansing are systematically and considerably lower on the other side of the front lines. A location with zero percent Muslims in PLO-controlled territory has about a 53 percent chance of violence taking the shape of ethnic cleansing, which falls to a 32 percent risk in locations with an even demographic balance, and reduces further to 17 percent in a location with 90 percent Muslims. These differences may reflect that the Palestinian factions had more support among Lebanese Christians than Christian militias did among Muslims, and that Christian militias were more prone to use ethnic cleansing against Palestinians than any militia was against any other sectarian subgroup.

Robustness Checks

I conducted a series of robustness checks to assess how sensitive the findings are to coding decisions and model choice and specifications. The robustness checks address six specific concerns. First, as discussed above, I have employed both a very conservative and a more permissive rule of what events count as ethnic cleansing, which in turn affects how many locations are coded as experiencing selective violence. I therefore reran the models above, which use the permissive rule, using the more conservative measure. The only difference between the two is that one of the control variables (Christian control) slips from weak significance to insignificance when using the conservative coding scheme.

Second, I reran the main specification using a linear probability model instead of the probit model. I retained the conditional setup and ran both a model for correlates of violence (of any kind) and then a subsequent model on correlates of ethnic cleansing (for those 122 data points that experience violence of any kind). One difference obtains: Christian control now exhibits a statistically significant correlation with ethnic cleansing taking place, conditional on violence occurring. Christian control remains uncorrelated with more violence taking place overall, in the first step of the model.

Third, variation in ethnic cleansing could also result from differential effects of different demographic subgroups. For instance, perhaps the Palestinian factions primarily displaced Maronite Catholics rather than Greek Orthodox, while Christian militias displaced Palestinians but not Lebanese Muslims. To control for such effects, I reran the models using interaction effects to control for the effects of Maronites present in PLO-controlled territory, and for Palestinians present in Christian-controlled territory.[52] I used a dummy variable for whether Maronites and Palestinians were present in a location, respectively, and interacted both measures with non-coethnic military control. Finally I ran both sets of models using both the conservative and permissive coding rules for ethnic cleansing. The interaction of Palestinian presence with Christian control is positive and significant at the 5 percent level with both coding rules, but the interaction of Maronite presence with PLO control is not statistically significant in either. Across all four models the independent variable, "share of coethnics," remains significant at the 5 percent level. While sectarian subgroups clearly matter, and Christian militias used particularly heavy-handed displacement strategies versus Palestinians, sectarian subgroup effects do not offer a full explanation for variation in strategies of violence.[53]

Fourth, I reran the main specifications while including region-fixed effects to control for unobservable region-specific factors.[54] With this specification the share of non-coethnics now has a statistically significant negative effect not only on whether violence takes the shape of ethnic cleansing in the second column but also on whether violence occurs at all in the first column. Christian control is also weakly significant for predicting violence. However, these are small changes, and they do not alter the main result: a higher share of coethnics is significantly correlated with a higher probability of selective violence, rather than ethnic cleansing.

Fifth, as a robustness check I ran two separate regressions for selective violence and ethnic cleansing instead of using a conditional model with two separate steps. For each of the two outcome variables I thus ran one regression, with full controls, to see how the share of coethnics correlates with the incidence of each outcome across all 623 observations. On the one hand, this setup is conceptually unsatisfying because it estimates the correlates of one outcome occurring as opposed to any other outcome. So, for instance, models of selective violence now estimate the likelihood that a location experiences selective violence as opposed to either no violence at all or ethnic cleansing. Nevertheless, these are about the simplest models used in social science, and they involve an absolute minimum of underlying assumptions. For this reason, I ran each model with both probit and linear probability models and with both the conservative and permissive coding of ethnic cleansing, for a total of four models for each dependent variable or eight models in total. The coefficient on "share of coethnics" shows the correct sign and is statistically significant across all eight models.

Sixth, I reran all of the above results using robust standard errors instead of block bootstrapped clustered standard errors. On the one hand, the block bootstrap technique produces more conservative estimates, which is why the technique is widely used as an antidote to various common threats to inference. On the other hand, the technique is likely somewhat obscure to many readers, and because it involves simulations, it produces marginally different results every time we estimate the model. The latter aspect is unfortunate as we generally desire replicability of results as a methodological principle. For these reasons I reran all of the models reported above using robust standard errors instead of block bootstrapped clustered standard errors. The main result on the independent variable still holds across all specifications and, as we would expect, a few more control variables now show statistical significance as well.

In general, when using robust standard errors (instead of block bootstrap techniques) the coefficient for Christian control often shows statistical significance at the 5 percent level. In some models, areas with Christian control are more prone to violence overall; in other models, Christian control is associated only with a higher probability that violence takes the shape of ethnic cleansing. Finally, in some models there is no change at all. Consequently, this variation across models is somewhat difficult to interpret. Perhaps this pattern merely is a statistical mirage, which more conservative estimation techniques successfully dispel. However, these results could also suggest that Christian militias were indeed more prone to use violence overall and more likely to use particularly brutal strategies of violence against civilians, such as ethnic cleansing, compared to Palestinian forces and their Lebanese allies.

Omitted Variable Bias

The data does not allow us to identify causal relationships, so we need to consider endogeneity effects. Reverse causality seems implausible—it is hard to imagine that wartime violence caused prewar demographic settlement patterns—but the estimated models could suffer from omitted variable bias or simultaneous causality. Examples of the former could be that individuals with an affinity for non-coethnics sort into intermixed locations or that cohabitation changes preferences for instance by causing tolerance. There likely is something to these concerns, but it is unclear how strong the effect is: as the data shows, there is no correlation between share of coethnics and whether violence occurs, only between share of coethnics and the *kind* of violence that militants engage in. Second, some characteristic of a location could make it more likely both to become ethnically intermixed and to suffer wartime violence. For instance, intermixed locations in Lebanon are more likely to be urban than rural and, partly as a result, tend to be wealthier. Clustered standard errors help us assess concerns about the effect of urbanization as I use standard errors clustered by electoral district, and the three largest cities—Beirut, Saida, and Tripoli—each constitutes its own district. If urbanization caused both intermixing and violence then the correlation between the two should disappear when we employ clustered standard errors, which is not the case. As a final robustness check, I tried estimating the main models while including an urban dummy variable instead of using clustered standard errors. The urban dummy variable does not show statistical significance at conventional levels, while the correlation between ethnic intermixing and modalities of violence still does across both coding rules for what constitutes ethnic cleansing.

Prewar Electoral Support for Christian Parties

A limitation of the previous set of models is that they lack one critical variable. My argument is that armed groups first determine where to use violence, as they want to pacify enemy militants and political opponents, and then in a second step decide what kind of violence to use. However, the first step of my model in the preceding table does not contain any variable to test whether violence in general correlates with some kind of observable indication of political or military opposition in the targeted location. This section rectifies that shortcoming by using data on prewar elections as a proxy variable for political loyalties. As I describe above, electoral data is only relevant as a test for whether violence correlates with political loyalties among Christians in the PLO-dominated zone, where we can identify locations that had elected deputies in 1972 from one of the Christian-dominated parties that subsequently turned into a major militia force. For that reason, the following analysis subsets the data set to those 479 locations that were controlled militarily by Palestinian factions and their Lebanese allies but had a presence of Christians. Table 3.4 displays the results using a conditional logit model with robust standard errors.

The results in the first step of the model, displayed in column 1, conform to my predictions. The regression shows clearly that the PLO and its allies were more likely to use violence in villages or neighborhoods located in electoral districts that elected Christian members of Parliament in the 1972 election that represented the two dominant hardline Lebanese nationalist parties in the Christian community at the time. Assuming that those electoral results indicate where said parties had their strongest geographic concentrations of support, this result suggests that wartime militias primarily targeted political opponents among their non-coethnics. Furthermore,

TABLE 3.4
Prewar electoral returns and wartime violence against Christians

VARIABLES	(1) Violence	(2) Ethnic cleansing	(3) Ethnic cleansing
Christian hardline MP, 1972	0.465**	0.519	0.388
	(0.186)[a]	(0.506)	(0.556)
Share coethnics	−1.076***	−3.219**	−3.069*
	(0.264)	(1.525)	(1.745)
Distance (km, log)	−0.474***		−0.204*
	(0.119)		(0.123)
Population (log)	1.370***		−0.346
	(0.231)		(0.583)
Constant	−0.405	−1.039**	2.178
	(1.590)	(0.415)	(2.613)
Observations	467	64	64

[a] Robust standard errors in parentheses.
* $p < 0.1$
** $p < 0.05$
*** $p < 0.01$

the second step of the model—displayed in column 2 and then again in column 3, with the full battery of controls—shows that the presence of political opponents determined only *whether* militias used violence but not what *kind* of violence they employed. The decision of what kind of violence to use, in turn, is correlated with the share of militia coethnics, just as we found in the previous model for the full dataset including both Palestinian- and Christian-controlled territory.[55] These findings conform to the empirical implications of my argument. The results are robust to different coding rules for ethnic cleansing and to substituting linear probability models for probit models.[56] The result for Christian hardline member of Parliament also survives the inclusion of region-fixed effects across all models.

The quantitative data reveals two important pieces of evidence. First, there is a strong and robust correlation between demographic configuration and the type of violence a location experienced: the greater the share of militia coethnics in a location, the more likely it is that violence takes the shape of selective violence rather than ethnic cleansing. Second, electoral data shows that Palestinian and left-wing groups more frequently used violence—of any kind—against Christians in those parts of the country where nationalist Christian political parties commanded significant support in prewar elections. Since the wartime Christian militias largely originated as prewar nationalist political parties and movements, electoral data is a good proxy for where they had geographic concentrations of support when the war broke out. However, these quantitative results leave one major question unanswered in assessing my argument: how do we know that the correlation between demographics and repertoires of violence takes place through an information transmission mechanism? Even if we had access to more data, it would be hard to answer such questions using any kind of quantitative techniques. The next two chapters therefore turn to qualitative material—drawn from secondary sources and about seventy interviews—to address this question.

CHAPTER IV

Lebanon's Christian Militias

What a beautiful house!
Thank you. It was our wedding gift from [Christian warlord] Bashir [Gemayel].
—INTERVIEW IN BROUMMANA, APRIL 2014

On March 12, 1976, a senior political official from the largest Christian political party in Lebanon stepped off his yacht in the middle of the night and boarded an Israeli gunboat anchored off the Lebanese coast.[1] The sturdy craft raced through the night and brought its guest to the Israeli port of Haifa for a face-to-face meeting with foreign minister Yigal Allon, who listened patiently as his counterpart pleaded for an overt Christian–Israeli alliance to crush the Palestinian national movement once and for all. Israel had aided the Christian war effort for some time, by modest shipments of small arms smuggled into the port of Jounieh on the northeastern outskirts of Beirut, but contacts were confined to mid-level Mossad officials and their Christian counterparts to provide senior leaders on both sides with plausible deniability. Yet as the war intensified, so did the Christian–Israeli relationship, and by August 1976 the mess of an Israeli missile ship hosted former Lebanese president Camille Chamoun and Israeli prime minister Yitzhak Rabin for what was in effect a diplomatic summit at the highest level.

Rabin was as hesitant about formal Israeli involvement in Lebanon as he was enthusiastic about Lebanese militias fighting against the PLO, and he turned down a request by his own foreign minister, who wanted to visit Christian leaders in Lebanon. Nonetheless, to assess the situation and determine how best to aid the enemy's enemy in what was by then an intensifying civil war, he commissioned a team of senior Israeli intelligence agents and army officers to enter the country as guests of former president Chamoun. On a cloudy night, they made the transfer from an Israeli gunboat to a luxury yacht commandeered by Lebanese militiamen, which took them to a waiting motorcade north of Beirut and ultimately a lavish dinner in a swank mountain villa. Over the next few days the team followed a tight schedule. Their days consisted of frontline visits to inspect the troops and their evenings of fashionable cocktail parties to mingle with all factions and commanders worth knowing within the Christian war effort.

Upon their return to Israel, the professional spies compiled a comprehensive report for Prime Minister Rabin that included a litany of complaints about their informal allies. They found the Christian forces poorly trained and equipped, deemed them mostly unable to stage military operations outside of Christian areas where they commanded popular support, and held severe misgivings about the character and competence of some of their leaders. The militias lacked adequate communications equipment and could not coordinate maneuvers. Their fighters were mostly volunteers, with little or no military training, and some fought with outdated weapons such as antiquated hunting rifles. They had insufficient artillery, and fighters were inept at using even what precious little they possessed. Troops were divided across too many different organizations under too many different commanders, and jealous rivalries characterized relations between units and commanders.

However, the experienced Israeli soldiers noticed that the Christian forces were thoroughly committed to the fight against the PLO and that they commanded a remarkable degree of popular support in the Christian community, particularly among Maronite Catholics. The fight to maintain Lebanese independence and sovereignty had a powerful ideological appeal with enormous resonance in the Christian community. Most fighters were volunteers, and a lot of militia resources were donations or volunteer efforts by community members. Even those Israeli spies who were otherwise deeply skeptical of the Christian war effort could not avoid being impressed by this level of popular support. As consummate military professionals, they fully understood the value of this resource. In fact, they noted, this deep support across broad layers of the community was probably the militia's greatest asset.

This chapter uses primary interview evidence and secondary literature to fully convey this point: Lebanon's Christian militias were deeply embedded within their sectarian community. Prewar political parties, community organizations, and social networks based on education and worship were mobilized into wartime service and became the cogs and wheels that kept the war machine turning. The Christian political parties had developed a detailed understanding of political opposition in areas they controlled, especially within East Beirut, for several years before the war. Palestinian factions and left-wing parties had maintained a loud and bold presence in the area for some time, and many groups took pride in challenging law and order as part of their revolutionary appeal. Local Christian residents resented the militants, who defied and challenged ordinary life, and some residents fell victim to extortion and other crimes that law enforcement agencies could not stop or prosecute. Locals nevertheless reported these activities to the police, military, media sources, political leaders, and anyone else who might listen. This continuous stream of detailed intelligence proved invaluable once the civil war broke out.

The chapter begins by describing the prewar political scene in Lebanon and its most powerful actors in the Christian community. The following section shows how these actors rallied their supporters to mobilize powerful militia forces that were deeply embedded within their sectarian communities. The third section outlines how Christian leaders organized a unified body for political leadership and how these militias eventually grew to become a state-within-the-state that collected taxes, provided public services, and governed its enclave through a sophisticated web of institutions. The fourth section explains how this level of community organization influenced the ability of armed organizations to collect and process military intelligence, and how this process differed across homogenous and intermixed locations, using a structured comparison of two neighborhoods in East Beirut.

Political Elites and Movements in Prewar Lebanon

Three sets of actors dominated Lebanese politics between its independence in the waning days of World War II and the civil war that broke out in 1975: traditional sectarian elites, a handful of political parties, and the Palestinian national movement. This section describes some of the most important prewar political actors in the Christian community and the nature of their ties to local communities across the country. The key points are that those elites and organizations that organized the early wartime effort on the Christian side had deep and extensive roots in the Christian community and that political leaders relied heavily upon this support to mobilize their militia forces. This is especially true of former President Camille Chamoun's National Liberal Party and of the Katayyib party, the two dominant Christian military actors in 1975. As we will see, their deep ties across the Christian—and especially Maronite Catholic—community also gave them access to networks of supporters across the country that acted as a powerful source of information once the war broke out.

Traditional sectarian leaders made up about two-thirds of members of Parliament in Lebanon before the civil war.[2] Many journalists and academics, particularly those with left-wing sympathies, have been quick to point out the fundamentally illiberal character of how Lebanese democracy worked in practice. One account portrays these traditional sectarian elites, "whom the Lebanese would describe as 'honoured families' but whom the average Westerner would quickly identify as mafiosi," and recounts that their "conspicuous wealth, bodyguards, cruelty, education and private armies proved more efficacious than any electoral appeal."[3] Another account similarly highlights the mafiosi aesthetics of older men with an affinity for cigars, Cadillacs, and Italian suits who conducted business over three-hour lunches.[4] Vote-rigging and patronage politics have always been a defining feature of Lebanese elections.[5] This corruption, while allowing parliamentarians to dole out favors to their clients, prevented the country from developing a truly representative electoral system or a rational and efficient bureaucracy. Left-wing opponents of the sectarian regime derided it as an elite cartel more interested in serving their own class interests than the welfare of the people.[6]

One effect of the clientelist nature of Lebanese elections was that traditional elites generally had deep personal ties to voter-clients in areas they controlled through the long histories of exchanges, bargains, and mutual favors that constitute patronage politics. Traditional elites also were called upon for arbitration, dispute resolution, and advice on major decisions by residents; their roles typically extended far beyond the traditional demands of a parliamentarian politician, to a position of wider community leadership. Once the war broke out, some elites relied on their clientelist networks to mobilize rudimentary militia organizations among their loyal supporters. One striking example of this process is the president of Lebanon in 1975, Suleiman Frangieh, whose family had for generations served as the premier Maronite Catholic political leaders of the mountainous Zghorta district in northern Lebanon.[7] Drawing on these deep personal ties to local residents, the president organized a militia called the Marada Brigade controlled by his son Tony Frangieh. As a result, his militia came to dominate this area but had little presence elsewhere. Furthermore, the elements of a military organization may not have been an entirely novel creation, as Frangieh had always maintained a number of loyal gunmen to guarantee his electoral grip on Zghorta.[8]

Another member of the traditional Maronite sectarian elite, former president Camille Chamoun, mounted a significantly more extensive military organization than Frangieh by drawing on a much more extensive popular base of support. Chamoun relied on the same clientelist electoral tactics as other elites and his formal political party, the National Liberal Party, was more of a vehicle for elite-level electoral bargains across districts than a genuine mass party.[9] However, Chamoun had gained prominence first during the struggle for independence from France in the 1940s, and again in 1958 when Lebanon experienced a brief civil war.[10] He therefore commanded a certain personal status and political following in the Christian community, where he was widely seen as a strong leader who could be counted on to stand up for Lebanese nationalism, an ideology with genuine grassroots appeal in the Christian—and especially Maronite Catholic—community. As a former president, he held significant gravitas as an éminence grise among Christian elites. His party maintained local branches across large swathes of the country and published a newspaper, the Voice of the Free (*Sawt Al-Ahrar*), that commanded a respectable circulation among Lebanese Christians. Finally, Chamoun's extensive history of patronage politics not only allowed him to distribute arms to trusted supporters but had also involved securing employment in the army and other branches of law enforcement and the security services for a particularly large number of his Christian constituents, who remained loyal to him personally as much as to any other institution of government. He eventually organized an official militia organization, the Tigers, headed by his son Dany Chamoun.

Finally, prewar Lebanese politics did include a few political parties that differed in character from the hollow entities operated by most traditional elites. The most important one, and the one with the most extensive organization across the country, was the Christian-dominated Lebanese Phalanges Party (Hezb Al-Kataib Al-Lubnaniyya), often known simply as Katayyib.[11] Katayyib was the closest thing to a traditional Western-style mass party in Lebanon by 1975, at least within the Christian community. However, the party also differs in character from a traditional Western mass party in several key respects. Katayyib was founded in 1936 as a youth organization by a small group of Maronite Catholics dedicated to Lebanese nationalism and determined to work for Lebanon to gain independence from France. At this point Lebanon was still ruled by the French mandate, and the French had banned all political parties and organized activities such as political demonstrations. Pierre Gemayel, the founding president of the organization, had visited Berlin during the 1936 Olympics as a delegate for the Lebanese Football Association and was impressed by contemporary European youth movements in Fascist Italy, Nazi Germany, and Phalangist Spain. Upon his return to Lebanon, Gemayel was convinced that a strong youth movement based on order and discipline was the best way to advance his nationalist agenda for Lebanese independence. In addition, given the French ban on political parties, a youth movement based around sports and social events was a convenient outlet for underground political activities.

Katayyib was thus founded as a formally apolitical youth organization with a strictly hierarchical and paramilitary mode of organization, similar to the Boy Scouts, which organized its thousands of mostly young members into local chapters based on geographic location. With a hierarchical organization emphasizing order and discipline at their disposal, its leaders could organize extensive events such as sports tournaments, festivals, lectures, and social events, all of which were infused with a political content and character. Despite the formal ban on political activities, Katayyib constantly pushed the strict boundaries set by the French and was at times outlawed.[12] For instance, when French administrators outlawed political marches, Katayyib skirted the measure by organizing two meetings the same evening at two different locations. Its members would then walk in formation from one location to the second, wearing the same distinct clothing, thus producing a political march in all but name. Larger meetings featured various forms of chants and salutations that turned the congregation into a de facto political rally, regardless of what the formal occasion for the meeting might have been. Finally, the party was not above a more rough-and-tumble kind of street politics that was on display, for instance, when its members burned down the local office of a rival party after a brawl in 1949.

The movement reorganized formally as a political party in 1952 and has had several members in every Parliament since independence. However, it retained its paramilitary structure as well as its emphasis on sports and youth activities. By the late 1960s, records show that the party had over 54,000 members: 91 percent were under forty-five years of age, and 77 percent had been members for less than five years.[13] These numbers highlight that the party remained a youth-oriented organization with a broad presence across its community and had a relatively high turnover of members. Its membership was heavily Maronite Catholic and Greek Catholic. The base of the party was among the working- and middle-class Christians who had relocated to urban areas relatively recently and thus had been dislocated from their old political networks in rural locations. Nevertheless, the party had local chapters in most Christian villages and neighborhoods across the country.[14] It published its own newspaper, *Al-Amal*, and periodically disseminated pamphlets and posters. The movement had several wings: a parliamentary wing, a youth wing focused on sports and social events, a public services wing focused on social relief, and others, including ones focused on health and education.[15] The organization is more multifaceted and has broader and deeper community ties than a typical Western mass party.

Communal Support for Lebanon's Christian Militias

When the civil war broke out, established Lebanese political elites and parties used their positions in their respective communities to mobilize volunteer efforts into wartime service and create militia forces. On the Christian side, Katayyib had a central leadership role. Since it already had a hierarchical nationwide organization with paramilitary characteristics and a loyal youth following, it was relatively easy to turn this infrastructure into a militia by arming its members. Former president Camille Chamoun also distributed significant amounts of light arms to loyal supporters of his party and created a sizable militia organization. Both parties served as central nodes that attracted new volunteers who rallied to the struggle, although certain smaller organizations also mounted their own efforts. The Christian coalition included a number of smaller and marginal groups, such as the ultranationalist Guardians of the Cedars and the Tanzim, a small military outfit clandestinely set up by renegade Christian personnel from the Lebanese Army as an underground movement in the early 1970s. These groups lacked extensive ties to civilian bases of support developed through mass politics and eventually merged with the larger military outfits. Yet they brought smaller networks of ideologically and personally committed cadres into the struggle, many of whom had military training. Finally, many Christian villages and neighborhoods also witnessed the rise of impromptu "youth committees" consisting of local volunteers.[16]

Recruitment

When the war broke out, "[Lebanese] militias were little more than neighborhood groups," says a Christian fighter.[17] "We were volunteers, not employees. We were not an invading army. People fought in their own neighborhoods." A striking feature of militia warfare is the extent to which it relied on temporarily mobilizing community members who otherwise maintained normal civilian lives. "When there was a cease-fire, everyone would go home. Most weapons were individual, in the closet," according to the same fighter. "As were uniforms. [Many] people fought locally so there was no need for transportation. The militia could disappear and reappear in a day." Most frontline fighters served in or near the areas where they lived, and many were high school or university students living with their parents. Many militia fighters with regular jobs would only join the fight if it affected their own neighborhood, but more dedicated militia fighters would travel from other parts of the country to join a local fight, if only for a few days at a time. Those who participated in wartime militias unfailingly refer to their efforts as "self-defense" in interviews and describe how they wanted to defend their sectarian community, their neighborhood, their homes, and their families.

The defining feature of recruitment in the early days of the war is that most Lebanese fighters were young volunteers who fought in their own neighborhood, and they counted on others in the community to contribute to the struggle as well. "I would not separate the two," says a Christian fighter when I ask what relations were like between the militia and the Christian community; in his mind, the community and the militia were to a large extent the very same thing.[18] Some fighters received a salary, especially if they played key leadership roles and would not otherwise be able to fight.[19] Many others, however, received little compensation and fought as volunteers because the fighting involved their local area, because of ideological commitment, or because they hoped to benefit in future from either promotions or other opportunities for financial gain. Some fighters had other interesting financial arrangements that highlight the extent to which militias relied on community support. "We could not afford to pay everyone," says one fighter. "So I maintained my regular engineering job at the factory. When I needed to, my boss would let me go to do my duties. I did not ask for this arrangement, he offered. My salary was part of the aid society was giving to what we were doing."[20] The fact that an employer would allow an employee to dedicate substantial amounts of time—at stochastic intervals—to militia activities shows the extent to which they were willing to make a privately costly sacrifice to aid the militia efforts.

The militias recruited heavily among the urban working class, but their social composition included members from all walks of life such as university students and young professionals like lawyers and engineers.[21] Both fighters and commanders were generally young. One former Christian mid-level commander claims that militia fighters were generally youth about sixteen to twenty-seven years of age, and that his group "refused kids at fourteen, fifteen who tried to join."[22] Another Christian fighter with a leadership position, however, gives an age range of "thirteen to fifty, all tasks included."[23] The youngest would serve as lookouts or perform other simple tasks, like bringing food to the front lines, while older volunteers often contributed in logistical operations rather than frontline combat. Many fighters maintained normal civilian lives and attended school or university or held regular jobs, in parallel to their volunteer militia activities. All militias recruited heavily among high school and university students. "We would have regular lectures on [Lebanese nationalist] ideology," explains a Christian fighter who was recruited by her high school headmaster.[24] "It was like an extracurricular activity." Estimates of the share of female fighters among the Christian militias range from about 2–7.5 percent, while in many noncombat roles (especially cooking and health care) at least as many women as men participated.[25]

Most of the volunteers who fought in the early days of the civil war had little or no military training. Army defectors and others with prior military training or experience were therefore particularly valuable recruits, and they often trained others in turn. The Christian militias retained a number of sympathizers within the officer corps of the Lebanese Armed Forces, which was more heavily Christian than its rank and file, and many provided various levels of advice or support for the fledgling militia forces.

Some of those relationships predated the war, and a small core of committed adherents had secretly provided clandestine military training to members of Katayyib university student chapters starting as early as 1969.[26] Sympathetic small businesses or landowners provided suitable training grounds in remote parts of Mount Lebanon, and senior party leadership had encouraged, although rarely outright sponsored, these activities.

Logistical Support

Community support was an integral component of all aspects of militia operations, from the most mundane to the more complex. Among simple services, the role of cooking recurs in interviews as local volunteers often sustained combat operations by providing fighters with meals. Fighting would often unexpectedly erupt on some particular section of the front lines, and locals would rally to defend their neighborhood while more committed activists trickled in from other parts of the country; sympathetic local residents would often volunteer to cook food for the fighters on these occasions. Community volunteers also contributed relatively simple public relations services such as designing, printing, and distributing flags and posters to display in public, as a show of support for militia forces and to mark territory, as well as pamphlets for dissemination. Sympathetic community members organized feasts, parades, and other ceremonies to honor and decorate their fighters. Among slightly more costly services, community activists and sympathetic health care professionals also volunteered to provide for wounded fighters, including by setting up and operating improvised health clinics in private homes.[27] One important source of coordination was militia-operated radio stations. The main militia-affiliated station in the Christian community was the Voice of Lebanon (Sawt Lubnan) radio station that mixed pop music with political news. "Everyone listened to it. When it reported about incidents, people did not wait for orders, they just showed up," says a Christian fighter.[28] Later on during the war the major militias also started their own television stations, most of which still broadcast in Lebanon at present, including the LBC channel affiliated with the Lebanese Forces.[29]

A more expensive service was to stock militia arsenals, and the issue of guns also highlights the complex relationships between the militia organizations and their supporters. The first phase of the war was fought predominantly with small arms, rifles, machine guns, and mortars. In the last few years before the war, political elites in the Christian community purchased and stockpiled arms that they subsequently provided to trusted and loyal supporters. Some volunteers also purchased their own guns, partly as a contribution to the cause. "Most fighters got guns from the militia, but some also bought their own. The party made a profit by connecting its supporters to arms dealers. Everyone knew this. It was a double contribution," explains a Christian fighter.[30] A double contribution, that is, as the fighter would both pay for their own gun, so the militia would not have to, and allow the militia to earn a commission on the transaction. The militia armed the community, and the community armed the militia.

The Christian militias got substantial support from the Maronite religious establishment, especially from monastic orders who ran a range of religious, social, and educational institutions.[31] Because of its history of sectarian divisions and a weak central state, the confessional establishment in Lebanon retains substantial powers, including in such legal matters as family law. Historically, many religious orders have also played a substantial role in providing welfare services, including health and education.[32] Maronite monks ran not only a large number of Catholic schools in Lebanon but also one of its largest institutions of higher education, Kaslik University. The Maronite Church is a major landholder and has significant financial resources at its disposal. The details are murky, but a multitude of sources claim that the Church used considerable amounts of money to purchase arms for the Christian militias immediately before the civil war broke out. For instance, Kaslik University reportedly financed large purchases of light arms from dealers in Eastern Europe in the early 1970s; these guns were easily recognizable because the organizers outfitted the rifle stocks with Virgin Mary decals before distributing them among students.[33]

Business owners provided other modes of costly support. For instance, many vehicles used by the Christian militias came from sympathetic small businesses. Heavy weapons like mortars and machine guns were often mounted on otherwise civilian trucks when needed. "The trucks could be painted and repainted to play alternatively civilian and military roles," says a Christian fighter.[34] The vehicles usually belonged to small businesses whose owners sympathized with the political cause, and once fighting ended along some particular stretch of the front lines, the trucks were returned to their civilian purpose. Sometimes the same crew could operate the same vehicle as frontline soldiers one day and as carpenters or plumbers the next. Business owners also shared storage space, while large corporations or very successful businesses contributed cash assistance. Sympathetic Lebanese in the diaspora not only contributed funding but often acted as intermediaries in foreign relations and represented militias to foreign publics and governments.

All major militias eventually received considerable arms shipments from foreign donors. "The enemy's enemy is a friend," says a former member of the executive council of the Lebanese Forces, the group that unified most Christian militias after 1980.[35] "You'd sit down with them and they'd ask, so, what do you need? And then things started arriving. Heavy weapons came in fits and pieces, over time, from many places. Foreign security services aided us versus the PLO. Arab governments aided us. First it was Syria, when we were against the PLO, and then later on Iraq and Libya gave aid when we were against Syria. And there was Israel, of course."[36] Israel eventually became the largest foreign donor to the Christian war effort by quite some margin. However, in the early days some Christian leaders also received arms from the United States, Jordan, and Iran based on their status as pro-Western proxies against Eastern Bloc–aligned groups like the PLO.[37] Until 1975, shipments mostly included rifles and small quantities of machine guns and mortars, but from 1976, foreign donors gradually started to provide increasingly sophisticated weapons systems.

Political Leadership and Governance

One further illustration of how broad the community support was for Christian militias, and how difficult it can be to even separate the community from the militia movement in some cases, comes from their political leadership. In 1976 Christian political and military leaders created a formal political command, the Lebanese Front, intended to unify their war effort.[38] In theory, the Lebanese Front was to define broad political goals and subsequently delegate military planning to a joint command council with representatives for all militia factions. Aside from traditional political leaders such as Camille Chamoun and Pierre Gemayel, who by that point controlled the major Christian armed factions, other members of the Lebanese Front included Abbott Boulos Naa'man, head of the Permanent Congress of the Lebanese Monastic Orders; Dr. Charles Malek, former minister of foreign affairs and former president of the UN General Assembly; and

Dr. Fouad Boustany, former president of Lebanese University.[39] This composition highlights how the Christian militias sought—and, to a large extent, succeeded—to rally broad swathes of their community behind the war effort.

Christian wartime leaders firmly maintain that their strategic goal was to defeat the PLO and its left-wing allies but not to indiscriminately attack Lebanese Muslims who remained neutral or apolitical. Senior leadership claims their view was that the country would remain demographically mixed and that their fates were inextricably linked to that of their Muslim compatriots. A former chairman of the Katayyib party describes the ultimate war aim with the following words: "Ultimately it was about reestablishing the Lebanese state. The state had to take back its place. We were with the government, with the army, with the state. . . . Whatever happens, we will always have to deal with the Muslims in a political solution."[40] A former member of the executive War Council of the Lebanese Forces echoes similar sentiments. While he calls them "a foreign factor," he charitably describes how the "PLO gets diversity" and how "it wasn't a Muslim threat to Christians. . . . Not [a sectarian conflict] like Iraq."[41] He specifically denies that the war arose from sectarian animosity. As a result of these wartime goals, according to a senior political aide to wartime leadership, the Katayyib implemented a specific policy of general restraint: "The party had a clear policy: no to displacement of Muslims, no to destruction of mosques. It was by consensus, there was no real opposition within the party. Those [Muslims] who were original inhabitants, those who were peaceful: they could stay. But those who fought had to go. It was political cleansing, not ethnic cleansing."[42] It is hard to overstate how often I heard variations on the final sentence of this quote. This line represents the consensus view among senior decision-makers: they believe they were cleansing their political opponents, meaning active supporters of the Palestinian factions and various Muslim and left-wing military organizations, but they argue they had no intention of displacing or otherwise harming the Lebanese Muslim community in general. The problem, in their eyes, was the presence of armed Palestinian groups violating Lebanese independence and sovereignty. While most Muslims and left-wing faithful saw the PLO as an ally to be leveraged for political change, many Christians thus took a diametrically opposed view. "It was a military occupation," says one Christian fighter.[43] Christian leaders generally claim that they were willing to negotiate the political future of the country—and they actually differed among themselves to a surprising extent in their preferences in that regard—but they were not willing to do so until the immediate threat to national sovereignty had been conclusively resolved.

Christian parties and political leaders continuously debated political goals and strategy during the first few years of the civil war, including in formal conferences such as the 1977 conclave of Sayyidat Al-Bir.[44] Some leaders believed that the existing framework of sectarian quotas according to the National Pact could be amended, while others considered it a failed experiment that should be abolished. Some believed that federalism offered a promising way to rearrange political affairs, but federalism was highly contentious even though it rarely took the shape of concrete or workable plans or designs. By late 1977 few Christian leaders advocated federalism, and none advocated outright separatism. Their ambitions were eventually summed up in a 1980s wartime slogan, "10,452," the number of square kilometers within the country: the civil war was a fight to the death for control of every square inch of Lebanon and the power to rule every single one of its inhabitants.[45]

As the war ground on over time, several Lebanese militias began to take over operations of public management and social services from the government in areas they controlled.[46] This process played out with particular strength among the Christian forces, which came to run the areas under their control essentially as a sovereign state. Militia encroachment of state activities began in a rather innocent manner as student groups "volunteered to clean the streets and drive the idle municipal garbage trucks."[47] Gradually, the Lebanese Front took over and centralized governance operations. By the end of 1977, it had organized 1,400 activists across 142 local committees to maintain public services previously provided by the government as well as new tasks such as housing displaced persons. Later, these activities were organized as a set of "Popular Committees" with clearly defined geographic jurisdictions and operational responsibilities. Most of the official institutions of the Lebanese government remained in existence, and they miraculously managed to perform some activities and operations throughout the war years. However, militias gradually took over most of their ordinary operations.

Governance became more systematic and organized after most of the Christian militias finally merged under the moniker Lebanese Forces in 1980. The Lebanese Forces raised revenues in a range of different manners.

In areas they controlled, they eventually implemented a systematic tax policy with a graduated surcharge on households and ad valorem taxes on consumption goods, such as restaurant meals and gasoline.[48] Aside from taxation, all major militias also made money from operating ports and imposing excise duties. Port facilities allowed militias to smuggle not only arms and other commodities into Lebanon but also lucrative hashish out of the country to reach customers in Europe and elsewhere.[49] The Lebanese Forces used their war chest—bulging with revenues from taxation, donations, and smuggling—to build up enormous armies with infantry divisions, heavy artillery, and mechanized units. Yet they also spent a sizable share of the proceeds on social relief and public services.[50] Social relief wings operated health clinics and educational institutions and helped displaced families find new housing. Public management wings took responsibility for traffic control, public transit, street cleaning, garbage collection, provision of water and electricity, and maintenance of the telephone system. Media wings published newspapers and operated radio stations. Youth wings organized sports and recreational activities. The Lebanese Forces operated parking lots staffed by disabled ex-fighters, who needed civilian employment opportunities, and even opened a public beach. Its foreign affairs wing conducted public and private diplomacy in foreign countries, particularly the United States, and tried to reactivate dormant Lebanese embassies under its management.

The development of state-within-a-state sectarian organizations was neither immediate nor inevitable. However, it was possible precisely because the organizations that led those efforts had deep roots in prewar politics. The Christian militias possessed the institutional skeletal frames that allowed them to accomplish these tasks because they commanded support from a set of political parties and other institutions dating back decades before the war. Some of these organizations already had wings dedicated to social relief, public services, youth activities, media production, and public relations in addition to parliamentary wings. This institutional heritage allowed them to rapidly harness volunteer and community contributions when the civil war broke out and to expand, formalize, and scale up their operations. Preexisting institutions, in turn, allowed these organizations to mobilize and channel popular desires to contribute to the wartime effort. The seeds of wartime sectarian quasi-states were sown a long time before the first shots were fired.

Intelligence Capabilities Among the Christian Militias

The largest Christian-dominated party, the Katayyib, had a formal intelligence section by the time the war broke out. One interviewee who worked in military intelligence, eventually rising to be deputy head of military intelligence and acting head for a brief stint in the 1980s, claims that at first the intelligence section consisted of "six or seven people."[51] Later the intelligence section grew and split into separate branches focused on local security, military intelligence, and external relations. The militia also benefited from close collaboration on intelligence matters with sympathetic Christian personnel in the military and law enforcement agencies, including especially in the officer corps of the army. The intelligence section remained somewhat fragmented throughout the war because of the impact of local leaders, branches, dynamics, and opposition forces; at various times the Christian forces had up to twenty-seven separate incarceration centers. However, the real roots of wartime military intelligence capabilities stretched back several years before the war broke out.

The military front lines divided Beirut into predominantly Muslim West Beirut and mostly Christian East Beirut. East Beirut had witnessed tremendous social and economic change in the last few decades before the civil war. Poor rural migrants arrived in Beirut starting in the 1950s, searching for urban employment opportunities.[52] Some managed to enter the formal labor and housing markets and joined the growing ranks of the middle class. Several new working-class Christian neighborhoods emerged through this process of urbanization, such as the suburb of Ain el-Rummaneh southeast of the city center. Less fortunate migrants ended up in a string of emerging poor neighborhoods that sprung up in a semicircle engulfing the outskirts of Beirut, and the very poorest neighborhoods tended to be almost exclusively Muslim with a concentration of Shia.[53] Some areas, such as Nabaa, were low-income neighborhoods of very cheap rental housing. Other areas, such as Karantina and Haret el-Ghawarneh, were outright shantytowns with shacks built out of corrugated iron and plastic tarp. The Lebanese process of urbanization mirrors similar developments in other Third World countries during this period, including in Latin America, South Asia, and sub-Saharan Africa.

As a result, Beirut in 1975 was encircled by a string of predominantly Muslim slum areas and Palestinian refugee camps known collectively as the "Misery Belt" (Hazaam Al-Bou'as).[54] Since slum dwellers were generally unable to register to vote in their new urban homes—and since Palestinians lacked citizenship—they faced little but neglect from formal government institutions and the patronage machines of established politicians. These areas became fertile grounds for progressive, Communist, and sectarian Shia movements, including the Lebanese Communist Party and the Organization for Communist Action. Yet no other organizations could rival the political and military clout of the Palestinian factions, which began to attract Lebanese recruits as well. All of these organizations, except some sectarian Shia groups, had some Lebanese Christian members. However, since left-wing and Palestinian movements had limited appeal among Christians, these organizations in practice focused mostly on mobilizing Muslim communities at the mass level. While these organizations had an extensive presence throughout the area, they were a dominant force in the slums, shantytowns, and refugee camps. Some of the organizations also provided services in underserved neighborhoods, sometimes alongside apolitical and nonsectarian charitable organizations such as the Mouvement Social, founded and operated by the Greek Catholic bishop of Beirut, Father Gregoire Haddad.[55]

Left-wing and pro-Palestinian militants grew increasingly bold and acted with brazen disrespect for law and order. Militants frequently brandished their weapons, fired in the air, and generally marked their presence. Street politics became increasingly radicalized at a time when the Palestinian community was resolved to the necessity of armed struggle to liberate Palestine, and many left-wing Lebanese organizations questioned whether parliamentary politics was the correct vehicle for social change. "In 1969–70 kidnappings became a big issue," says the director of a Lebanese think tank.[56] The East Beirut suburbs are the center for industry in Lebanon, and militants would enter these areas to erect checkpoints and arbitrarily impose fees on commercial traffic. Many local businesses paid protection money to various groups. "Palestinian rackets and extortion was a huge cost," says a Christian fighter.[57] "Criminal elements, murderers, rapists, would escape into [Muslim slums and Palestinian camps] and disappear. The police couldn't go in there," says another Christian fighter who grew up in a nearby neighborhood.[58] Extortion, racketeering, and kidnappings generated enormous resentment within the Christian community: how was such activity, deep inside Lebanon and targeted at Lebanese civilians, supposed to advance the ostensible goal of liberating Palestine?

Lebanese Army intelligence chronicled all incidents whereby Palestinian factions ostensibly violated the terms of the 1969 Cairo Agreement, which was supposed to regulate the Palestinian presence in Lebanon. A 1973 report recounts a litany of incidents during 1971–1972 classified into specific categories.[59] Some categories of incidents highlight the bold way militants behaved: publicly displaying weapons, carrying unlicensed weapons and explosives, aimlessly firing guns, establishing checkpoints and searching cars, and arresting and kidnapping civilians. Other categories of incidents underscore their defiance of law enforcement agencies by actions such as entering restricted military areas, refusing to stop at army checkpoints, shooting at Lebanese military targets, and killing with premeditation civilians and military personnel. Some incidents highlight the general military buildup among Palestinian forces and their allies, as shown by the events categorized under "training and arming Lebanese citizens." Finally, some categories of incidents indicate that militants also exploited their status and position to engage in ordinary crime, such as conducting armed robberies, occupying houses, and collecting contributions by force. These activities were not necessarily planned or sanctioned by senior leadership. PLO leaders would often negotiate understandings with Lebanese security services only to see smaller and more radical factions violate the terms to gain attention and recognition. Palestinian militants occasionally clashed with Christian vigilantes. Sometimes Palestinian factions also clashed among themselves.

Local residents in all affected areas reported detailed information to their political leaders and demanded action to restore law and order. In the early days, victims of specific crimes would report those events to the police. Community members might also report such incidents as firing of unauthorized weapons or other instances of illegal and antisocial behavior. When it became clear that the police were powerless to curb the behavior of armed Palestinian factions, detailed information and deep frustration trickled up from victims, community members, and police to the Lebanese Army. After 1973, when the Lebanese Army failed to subdue Palestinian militant groups despite its most vigorous attempts to date, the status of Palestinian forces became the defining political issue for many Christians. At this point, Christian political leaders had been receiving a steady stream of information about their adversaries and their activities for the better part of a decade. Furthermore, most radical left-wing or pro-Palestinian groups were not trying to hide their activities; on the contrary, they often publicized their actions as they jockeyed with one another for status and recruits, and many maintained formal party branches and physical offices, especially in the slums and shantytowns.

When the war broke out, the Christian political parties-cum-militias had already developed a sophisticated understanding of the political ecology of East Beirut as well as channels for receiving a steady stream of continuous information. Their most valuable source was ordinary Christian residents in affected areas. "Civilians who lived nearby would let the militia know about activities and movements," says a Christian former intelligence operative.[60] Most of these residents wholeheartedly supported militia action to end the oppressive presence of Palestinian and other militants, and many eventually came to participate in militia activities—or assist with simple logistics—as the civil war broke out. The militias could act on this information by implementing violence to break down political and militant opposition on their side of the main front lines that bisected Beirut. However, the nature of the intelligence that the groups possessed differed systematically among neighborhoods. These differences in intelligence had important effects for how and where the militias implemented violence. In particular, there was a major difference between the type of information they possessed in intermixed neighborhoods, where they had local supporters, versus what they knew about homogenous Muslim neighborhoods.

Structured Comparison

The next two subsections contrast intelligence collection in two nearby areas: Jdeideh and Karantina. Both areas were located in predominantly Christian East Beirut and were no more than a couple of kilometers apart. Both areas had a sizable population of poor and working-class Muslims who had migrated to the area in the preceding few decades looking for work. Karantina had both Sunni and Shia residents, while Jdeideh Muslims were mostly Shia, but both areas contained Muslim individuals who participated as activists in left-wing and pro-Palestinian parties and movements such as the Lebanese Communist Party, the Syrian Social Nationalist Party, and the Organization for Communist Action. However, Jdeideh was an intermixed working-class neighborhood with a majority Christian population, while Karantina was a homogenous Muslim enclave. As a result, Christian militias gained access to very detailed information in Jdeideh and selectively targeted only those Muslims who were active in a hostile party. Most Shia remained in Jdeideh throughout 1975–1976. In Karantina, on the other hand, Christian forces viewed all locals as potential enemies and did not trust anyone to remain in the area; this neighborhood was ethnically cleansed in January 1976. Since both cases occurred within Lebanon within a relatively short span of time, variation in outcomes cannot be explained by national-level or temporal variation in any variable.

Intermixed Neighborhood: The Jdeideh Municipality

Prewar Beirut exhibited a fairly high level of communal segregation into residential neighborhoods dominated by different sectarian communities, and the very poorest neighborhoods in East Beirut were almost exclusively Muslim.[61] Yet there were also plenty of intermixed neighborhoods where Christians and Muslims lived side by side, even though one community was usually a decisive majority. One example of a majority Christian working-class neighborhood with a sizable Muslim population is the Jdeideh municipality. While technically located in the Mount Lebanon administrative region, the municipality is part of the Beirut conurbation and generally regarded as an eastern suburb. The Shia community constituted about 20 percent of the population when the war broke out in 1975. The municipality had five schools at the time, and all five were intermixed with both Muslim and Christian students.[62] Shia families often worked for the municipality doing menial labor, which put them in direct contact with Christian coworkers and managers. There was an element of residential clustering, with Shia concentrated in certain streets or buildings, but the community was sufficiently intermixed that all residents used the same shops and other local amenities.

Some Shia in Jdeideh were attracted to various left-wing groups, particularly the Lebanese Communist Party because of its emphasis on secular politics and radical economic redistribution. Some joined the party and partook in its political activities. Once the war broke out, local Christians who sympathized with the war effort supplied information to their local militias about suspected Communists and other allies of the PLO. "We got information from locals about who was a known Communist, who had been in demonstrations, who used Communist language, who received Communist newspapers in the mail. We would interrogate them and, if the suspicion was strong, search their house to see if they had Communist literature, if they had weapons," says a Christian former deputy head of military intelligence. In some instances, Christian militias also obtained formal rosters or other lists of the membership of particular political parties or extra-parliamentary left-wing groups. Local Communist activists included both Christian and Shia individuals.[63]

Intermixed schools played an important role in this process as most political movements had youth sections.[64] During the 1960s it was common for high school students aged fourteen and older, as well as for students at universities and other institutions of higher learning, to join political clubs. Political parties often had youth, high school, and university chapters loosely sponsored and affiliated with the main party organization. As the war broke out, all militias recruited heavily among sympathetic high school and university student organizations. In communities where Christians and Muslims had mixed in any kind of educational setting before the war, militias faced particularly good opportunities to collect reliable intelligence. Youths typically knew who in their school was or had been affiliated with political clubs or other activities, and adult community members could often recall political sympathies of their former classmates. All political conflicts that sparked the Lebanese civil war predated the war by many years, and in some cases decades, and there had not necessarily been any reason for people to hide their views before the war.

Media consumption was another important proxy for political views as most media sources—both newspapers and radio broadcasts—were openly sympathetic to a particular political party or ideology. All large political parties, including the Lebanese Communist Party, published their own newspaper and other kinds of print periodicals, and many of those reached a sizable circulation. There were rather few, if any, major media sources that did not have any political connotations, and local residents tended to note what media sources their friends and neighbors consumed. In urban areas in particular, people would typically notice what newspapers and periodicals their neighbors received in the mail. Densely intermixed social space therefore offered a multitude of informational cues whereby individuals assessed others' political views.

Once the war broke out, most Lebanese therefore had access to a wealth of intelligence about specific individuals and families within their local community. "Communists were very loud. Everyone knew who we were. It was easy to identify," says a former Communist party member who participated in East Beirut activism.[65] The Lebanese Communist Party and other hard-left outfits had members from all communities, including Christians. Christian militias were particularly adept at identifying Christian Communists. Since Christian Communists were embedded within the same networks of family and community that Christian militias mobilized into wartime service, the militias had abundant information about this group of individuals. Because these left-wing activists were Christian, and some even had family members who served in Christian militia forces, the militias often eschewed lethal violence when targeting this group. For instance, one historian notes of a nearby town:

> In 1975–76, when combat was raging, the formerly communist families of Bikfaya were made an offer to stay in this small town, fiefdom of the Gemayels; their security was guaranteed on condition that they revoked their membership of the Communist Party. . . . In the leftist parties, this ultimatum provoked such a copious haemorrhaging of the Christian militants that the Communist Party of Lebanon, for example, whose leadership remained, however, primarily Christian, appeared as the ally of the Muslims, and was sometimes denounced as the defender of Shi'i communitarian interests.[66]

Wartime processes thereby reinforced the sectarian character of the armed groups involved.

Senior Christian political officials describe the process of selective violence in very general terms in some of our interviews. "There was nothing written. It was an understanding," says a former chairman of the Katayyib of relations with those Muslims who remained in East Beirut after the war broke out.[67] "You can remain in this part of the country and you will be protected. But you cannot take up arms. . . . It was self-defense. . . . We closed our sector." A former senior aide to wartime leadership uses the particular terminology of "original inhabitants" to distinguish between local Muslim residents.[68] "Those [Muslims] who were original inhabitants, those who were peaceful: they could stay. Those who fought had to go. [It was] self-defense [and] also affected Christians who fought against us." The term "original inhabitants" partly reflects the specific difference between those Muslims who were registered voters in East Beirut and the recently arrived, unregistered inhabitants of slums and shantytowns.[69] More generally, "original inhabitants" also seems to refer to families that had been present in the area for a long time, often for several generations, and that were well-integrated into the social fabric of the neighborhood. While intermarriage rates were anemic, Christian and Muslim residents in mixed locations would attend weddings, funerals, and even religious feasts across sectarian lines in addition to mixing in schools and workplaces.[70] In this particular context, the term "original inhabitants" therefore also signifies Muslims who were well-known to their Christian neighbors. Needless to say, the interviewee did not consider Palestinians to be "original inhabitants" of Lebanon.

The exact operational response, once someone was identified as a Communist or other pro-Palestinian activist, seems to have varied depending on local and personal circumstances. Christian militia operatives claim that they often interrogated suspects, or searched their house looking for weapons or documents, and that those found to be "active"—a somewhat nebulous term that recurred in interviews—might receive a warning to cease and desist or might be exiled from the area. A Christian former intelligence official claims that Communists were exiled or attacked if they "had weapons, documents, were active in any way."[71] One former Communist activist confirms this behavior. "[Christian militia leader] Bashir Gemayel came to my house and had tea with my mother. He said I had to leave the area, that I wouldn't be safe anymore, because of my activism. But they wouldn't target me without warning since I was from a political family," says the contemporary Communist activist whose mother briefly served as a member of Parliament, and who sought refuge in France during the war.[72] Other members of contemporary pro-Palestinian organizations claim in interviews that many of their comrades were simply assassinated without warning.[73] There were also cases where entire families were exiled over alleged Communist or other pro-Palestinian sympathies, a mode of operations often tied to expropriation of housing.

Homogenous Enclave: The Karantina Shantytown

The formidable intelligence capabilities that Christian militias commanded in intermixed areas form a stark contrast to the relative poverty of information they possessed when attacking homogenous Muslim neighborhoods. Of course, in one sense they retained quite a sophisticated understanding of these environments as they knew what neighborhoods were likely to pose a military threat. The militias knew what hostile parties and movements had local branches in what neighborhoods, what groups were flying flags and putting up posters, and what factions commanded men with guns. Some neighborhoods were very clearly bastions of support for the Palestinian war machine. Conversely, other homogenous Muslim villages or neighborhoods had no presence of Palestinian or radical left-wing organizations, no history of hostile political activism, and no other indications that the location posed a threat.

One example of homogenous locations that did not appear threatening is Shia villages in the Jbeil district north of Beirut, mixed predominantly between Maronite Catholic and Shia Muslim residents. When the civil war broke out in 1975, the district had a Maronite Catholic majority but a significant Shia Muslim minority of about 20–25 percent of residents.[74] Yet these Shia villages were not threatening to Christian leaders because they were firmly entrenched in the local Christian-dominated political patronage machine and had no history of political activism or militancy. Parliamentary elections followed a familiar pattern: the dominant local party, the National Bloc, always designated a unified slate of two Maronite and one Shia candidate, and this list always won the election in a landslide.[75] "Everyone trades favors, in social life, in politics. The Shia were poor. They needed help getting government jobs, services, if they wanted an army job, licenses, permissions. They would go to a Christian notable," says a Christian former Member of Parliament for Jbeil.[76] As the war broke out, local leaders—Christian and Muslim—worked together to stop wartime violence from spreading to Jbeil.[77] "People would come to my house every Sunday. We would listen to complaints. Plus I'd spend time traveling the district by car to meet with villagers and maintain relationships," says a former secretary-general of the National Bloc party that dominated local politics.[78] Their work appears to have been successful, as systematic work on wartime violence and displacement fails to record any bloodshed or forced displacement in any of the Shia villages of the district.[79]

An extreme example of the opposite—a homogenous area that clearly posed a military threat—is the Palestinian refugee camp of Tel al-Zaatar.[80] The camp was first established in 1948 to house Palestinian refugees following the creation of the state of Israel and was "liberated" by Palestinian militants in 1969, meaning that it became inaccessible to Lebanese police and military forces after that point. By the time the civil war broke out in 1975, Palestinian forces had purposefully turned Tel al-Zaatar into one of its main military bases in Lebanon. "It was a fortress," says a Christian mid-level commander.[81] "They had East bloc weapons, West bloc weapons, Swiss weapons, Swedish weapons. . . . They had heavy machine guns on hydraulic lifts." The whole camp was surrounded by fortified walls and barbed wire, plastered with posters and flags of particular factions and parties, and had formal checkpoints manned by uniformed soldiers at all entrances. "Things were not hidden. They were there openly," says another Christian fighter of Tel al-Zaatar.[82] Tel al-Zaatar was located on a hill overlooking the rest of East Beirut, and once the war broke out, it proved an excellent staging ground for mortars and other artillery pieces that could shell vast tracts of nearby Christian residential and commercial areas. There was no doubt in the minds of Christian political and military leaders that Tel al-Zaatar posed a major military threat that they would have to solve if their canton of the country was ever going to be militarily defensible.

The Christian militias thus had a relatively firm ability to judge whether a homogenous Muslim village or neighborhood posed a threat but had little ability to discriminate between neutral and hostile residents on an individual basis. One prominent example of this dynamic is the case of Karantina, a shantytown located near the harbor and populated by poor Muslim residents—Lebanese Sunni and Shia, stateless Kurds, Syrian guest workers, and a few Palestinians—who mostly worked as day laborers in the port facilities.[83] The residents were largely "poor families," according to the assessment of a former resident of Karantina and current staff member at the Ministry for the Displaced.[84] Most residents had arrived from the countryside in the preceding decades looking for work. Starting around 1971 some Palestinian families who moved into the area brought their own light weapons, which they kept hidden in their homes, but this activity was not organized in any way or by any particular faction. Factions arrived in Karantina later, and by 1975 there were some formal representatives of groups like Fatah and the Popular Front for the Liberation of Palestine. Fatah relied on local operatives in Karantina for intelligence, and some Palestinian factions maintained caches of rifles and other light weapons in the area as well.[85] Some local militants also used Karantina as a base of operations to engage in the kind of harassment and crime characteristic for the period, mentioned above.

Christian militias perceived Karantina as a threat since it hosted hostile militants. "They fired on us," is the terse explanation of a former senior aide to wartime leadership.[86] Palestinian militants also used the position of

Karantina next to a highway to periodically disrupt or close down traffic by erecting temporary roadblocks or checkpoints. This highway represents a crucial traffic artery connecting central Beirut to Christian conurbations along the coast to its north, and the Christian militias needed full control over this route to make their enclave militarily defendable. This strategic location influenced Christian views of the enclave. Finally, the shantytown had been erected on land that technically belonged to private landowners, local businesses, and Maronite monastic orders.[87] These landowners vigorously encouraged the militias to sack the shantytown so they would thereby regain access to potentially valuable commercial real estate in close proximity to the port of Beirut. However, Karantina was a residential area, demarcated partly by the aforementioned highway, and was not fortified or enclosed by walls or checkpoints.

Christian forces surrounded the neighborhood on January 15, 1976.[88] Several different militia forces participated in the attack, which was relatively uncoordinated and not particularly well planned or executed from a military perspective.[89] However, as the location was primarily a residential shantytown defended by some armed local residents and a small number of Palestinian commandos, the attackers quickly overran the defenses when they entered the area on January 18.[90] The day before the attack Christian leaders had telephoned Yasser Arafat and suggested a temporary cease-fire on the main front line the next day at noon. After that they contacted the army, the Red Cross, and local businesses and requested to borrow all available buses and trucks. On the day of the attack, after they overran the defenses, Christian forces rounded up all survivors and put them on the hastily assembled vehicles. Shortly before the temporary cease-fire took hold at noon, they left in a convoy down to the main front lines, where they allowed civilians to enter into permanent exile in the PLO-controlled western side of the city. As arranged over the phone the day before, PLO leadership had begun contingency planning to provide for the displaced and eventually settled most of them into a handful of southern villages that they conquered around the same time and where they in turn had expelled all Christian residents, as well as in empty hotels and apartments in West Beirut.[91] Similar fates struck several other neighborhoods that were similar in profile to Karantina, such as Nabaa, Haret el-Ghawarneh, and Sebnay, which were all on the Christian side of the front lines.

Why did Christian forces displace all civilians who survived the attacks in areas like Karantina while they used selective violence in areas like

Jdeideh? Even some Christian fighters talk about "civilians" when describing survivors of the Karantina attack, and they are well aware that most of those who were displaced were not militants. The answer shines through in the following interview with a former deputy head of military intelligence who at the time fought for the Katayyib.

"Why were [Muslims in Karantina] displaced?"
"If they stayed, we didn't know that they wouldn't start up again in 24 hours. There could still be cells active."
"Why could you not use surveillance or guards?"
"It was not guaranteed. We were not organized enough. It would have required hundreds of troops, thousands of troops. We did not have it. Frontline battles were very intense. Displacement was lower risk. . . . We didn't have the manpower for anything else."[92]

Note how the exchange highlights two motivations: militias wanted to minimize risk and to conserve manpower for frontline battles. Traditional forms of counterinsurgency, such as surveillance, guards, and patrols, require significant numbers and discipline of manpower. Furthermore, counterinsurgency operations sometimes fail despite the best of efforts: the strategy therefore entails accepting a significant degree of risk. Note also the word choice in the sentence about how there could "be cells active," using terminology normally describing terrorist organizations; the implication is that, in the eyes of the interviewee, all residents remained potential militants and could not be trusted. The twin motivations of scarce resources and risk aversion prodded Christian forces to engage in ethnic cleansing for military-strategic reasons in situations when they could not identify their enemies by any characteristic other than their sectarian identity. Karantina had military-strategic importance because it sits adjacent to a main highway. However, many nearby locations of similar strategic importance—including Jdeideh—experienced selective violence against certain Muslim individuals only. Strategic importance influenced *what* locations Christian militias would attack but not *how* they would attack them.

In April 2019 the Katayyib party opened an "Independence Museum" in the Haret Sakher neighborhood of Jounieh northeast of Beirut, less than a mile away from the Maronite Patriarchate in Bkerké, to commemorate its wartime militia organization. The festive inauguration featured appearances by an array of party notables but also from the Maronite Patriarch, Bechara Al-Rahi, who blessed the new museum and gave a speech. "Hadn't it been for those martyrs, we wouldn't have been here today. They died so that we would live. . . . Unfortunately, the truth has been forgotten because we are suffering from allegiances and affiliations to other countries. This is why the Kataeb did not hesitate to speak up even if this would be to its own detriment," said the patriarch in a formal speech at the event.[93] The fact that the highest religious official in the Maronite Church would make such a statement in support of an effort by a political party to change public perceptions of their militant past underscores the enduring support for these efforts in large segments of the Maronite Catholic community. Most models of civil war violence theorize interactions between militias and local residents as a bargaining process between actors with divergent interests, but in Lebanon local Christian residents were the backbone of militia operations. Many Christian volunteers fought the civil war in their own villages, their own neighborhoods, and sometimes even in their own homes. This simple fact explains why the militias developed remarkably powerful military intelligence capabilities in most areas where they operated, but also why they lacked meaningful local intelligence once they ventured outside the areas where they could count on locals to volunteer for their war machine.

CHAPTER V

Palestinian, Muslim, and Left-Wing Armed Groups

> So you kept arms in the house?
> I still keep arms. I have a gun under my shirt right now.
> —INTERVIEW AT CAFÉ PAUL, APRIL 2014

Because of the general amnesty law, most Lebanese militia fighters returned to civilian life after 1991, and as I proceeded to interview former fighters and commanders I found myself talking to an assortment of individuals that included high school teachers, lawyers, engineers, and more than one political science professor. The civil war was mostly fought and directed by men and women in their twenties; since it broke out in 1975, many participants were nearing retirement during my fieldwork. One interviewee was watching his grandkids when I stopped by his house to talk about militia policy on ethnic cleansing; his grandchildren were perhaps a little too young to grasp how their grandfather spent his prime working years. In Lebanon the civil war still lurks just beneath the surface, like the clown-faced antagonist of a Stephen King novel. As a researcher, one faces many conflicting emotions when interacting with this motley crew of characters, but the conversations offer an unparalleled treasure trove of information for understanding and elucidating wartime processes. Besides, the interviews are quite fun.

I anticipate two objections to the empirical evidence I present from my interviews. First, some critics will argue that I put too much emphasis on the rationality and organization of violence. As I discuss elsewhere in the book, there were egregious acts of ethnic hatred, including major massacres, perpetrated by members on both sides. Both coalitions also had their cracks and fissures between different parties and militias, and neither side ever resolved all internal rivalries and acts of insubordination among their disparate members. Turf warfare broke out on both sides, especially over control of tax collection and other sources of revenue. Decision making under the fog of war is chaotic at best, and combatants always struggle to make sense of the intentions of those on the other side of the front lines. Minor incidents force the hand of major players, and sometimes it is not clear either during or after the fact what the exact sequence of events may have been or what actions triggered what response. We cannot assume that all acts of war follow directly from premeditated decisions made at the top of wartime military organizations or that senior leadership can effortlessly direct complex organizations to do their bidding. I concede that there is some merit in this critique.

Second, I imagine that some readers will accuse me of "ethnographic seduction" and of whitewashing the crimes of some quite chauvinistic organizations that killed and maimed many innocent victims on the flimsiest suspicions.[1] This risk only magnifies when the researcher relies heavily on interviews, as I do, where pleasant interactions with the interviewee humanize former perpetrators. There is a fine line between understanding an organization and its actions, on the one hand, and normalizing or misrepresenting distasteful ideologies and practices, on the other. I describe Palestinian factions as acting with "moderation" even though they severed Christian limbs with welding irons on the faintest suspicion of the wrong political sympathies, and describe Christian militants as "restrained" even as followers engaged in performative acts of violence, such as tying their victims behind cars and dragging them along the highway. Do I describe these perpetrators in a flattering way because I sat in their living room, ate their cookies, and drank their wine? Did the kind old man who offered me a blanket as we spoke on his balcony on a sunny day in early spring trick me into believing that he never harbored ill will against his fellow man?

In light of these critiques perhaps the best way to explain what I mean by moderation and restraint among Lebanese and Palestinian militias, without overstating their magnanimity or whitewashing their crimes, is to compare them to combatants in a few other conflicts that featured extensive ethnic cleansing. Serbian militias in east Bosnia used ethnic cleansing precisely because they wanted to displace as many Muslim Bosniaks from as large of a territory as possible in order to join these areas with the new independent Serbian state. The Sudanese government in Khartoum wanted its Janjaweed militia clients to displace entire tribes in South Sudan as a form of counterinsurgency. Partition between Greece and Turkey in the 1920s or India and Pakistan in the 1940s involved extensive population transfers with millions of families uprooted from their homes and reintegrated into novel ethnonational entities. My argument is not that Lebanese or Palestinian militants were tolerant liberals or enlightened humanitarians; but in its simplest form, my argument is that neither side fought for ethnonational designs involving the creation of homogenous sectarian polities. Lebanese war planners had many different political goals but, unlike military enterprises in many other conflicts, ethnic separation was not among them.

This chapter mirrors the previous one in structure but focuses on the Palestinian factions and their Lebanese allies on the political left and in the Sunni, Shia, and Druze communities. The first section explains the prewar origins of the various Lebanese armed groups that played major roles during the civil war. The second section describes how all of these groups developed and relied upon strong ties to local communities in areas where they operated, and the third section outlines the origins and operations of the Palestinian national movement and its armed factions. The fourth section outlines how this military coalition developed structures for political decision making and governance. The fifth section delves into how this coalition collected intelligence and contains a brief paired comparison to show how intelligence capabilities differed in different types of geographic locations. In intermixed areas, local residents with various ties to the armed groups would report suspicious activities among their Christian neighbors but, crucially, also vouched for friends, neighbors, and acquaintances. Many Christians used personal connections to relay their neutral, left-wing, or pro-Palestinian views. As a result, many Lebanese Christians remained in areas controlled by Palestinian and allied groups.

Prewar Political Parties and Movements

The Sunni, Shia, and Druze communities had traditionally been governed mostly by a set of sectarian elite families, but during the 1960s and early 1970s traditional Muslim elites found themselves increasingly challenged by other actors. These rising movements included some secular left-wing parties, but particularly the Palestinian factions. As political conflict and polarization deepened across the country, many traditional elites struggled as they could not compete with more radical alternatives, either for ideological fervor or for access to guns and military training. This process was particularly pronounced within the Sunni community, where the urban base of support for traditional elites became increasingly radicalized and began to look to the Palestinian factions and other groups for political leadership. Once the war broke out, armed groups became the dominant players at the expense of traditional elites who lacked the requisite means to participate in the politics of armed conflict.

At independence in 1943 a small set of established elite families dominated Lebanese society, politics, and business. These powerful leaders were often referred to as *"zaim"* personalities, using the Arabic word for leader, and discussions of post-independence politics often references a specific *"zuama"* culture (using the plural form of the word).[2] Power often passed from father to son in this family business: some electoral districts had returned members of the same family in every single election since independence, such as the Joumblatt family (Druze) in the Chouf district and the Frangieh family (Maronite Catholic) in Zghorta. Sunni strongmen included the Karame family in Tripoli, the Salam family in Beirut, and the Solh family, originally from Saida. All three families had long histories of political leadership stretching back into Ottoman times, including service in the Ottoman Parliament in Istanbul.[3] The electoral system mandated a certain sectarian power sharing, and the *zuama* controlled the electoral districts; partly by design, these elite families therefore served not only as parliamentary deputies but also as formal communal leaders for their sectarian groups.

Clientelism and patronage politics constituted the base of *zuama* rule as leaders who often owed their positions to feudal practices in the Ottoman era adapted to modern times by recasting themselves as business tycoons and parliamentary politicians. The *zuama* were often major landholders, and in some rural areas they dominated ownership of agricultural lands such that many voters were also their tenants. The clients supported their local leaders in national elections and in return expected that their patrons would use government positions to deliver goods and services such as schools, running water and sewage, paved roads, and electricity. Urban leaders were more frequently asked to supply government jobs, licenses and permits, and other derivatives of a notably corrupt and inefficient national bureaucracy. Furthermore, the traditional leaders typically dominated their electoral district by running a full slate of candidates on a unified ticket to win all seats in the constituency. To fill the seats, they usually brought on board representatives of major economic interests, such as bankers and industrialists, who in turn helped finance these political campaigns.[4] Finally, most *zuama* also retained the services of a handful of musclemen in case they needed to resort to various tactics of street politics during election times. Elections were rarely competitive.

Some of the traditional elites formed political parties to maintain a façade of electoral legitimacy. However, most political parties in Lebanon before the civil war were just that: electoral vehicles for certain families or for groups of elites that had agreed to contest elections on a shared platform. This behavior was particularly true of the traditional sectarian elites in the Sunni community. Their political parties generally had no paying members, local offices, internal mechanisms for deliberations, transparency, and certainly no internal elections. One brazen illustration is the bylaws of the National Appeal, a party created by the Solh family that dominated Sunni politics in the city of Saida, that simply specified that all powers rest with its president.[5] Most political parties functioned primarily as campaign organizations and had few operations outside of election times, although many published their own regular newspapers to disseminate their point of view. Elections usually involved a hefty dose of patronage politics and buying, monitoring, and rigging the actual voting process; political parties were often key institutional vehicles for such practices. That said, traditional Sunni leaders did have some genuine popular appeal as champions of the pan-Arab nationalist cause in general and the issue of Palestine in particular; as a group, these elites were known for their rhetorical abilities and elaborate speeches.

Outside of the Sunni community, there were a few political parties with committed followers and deep roots in prewar politics that came to play an important role once the civil war broke out. Perhaps the most important was the Progressive Socialist Party (PSP), founded in 1949.[6] The party was founded by Kamal Joumblatt, the scion of a powerful family of feudal origins that had held a leadership position in the Druze community for several hundred years. Its ideological platform is based on reformist social democracy, which originally attracted a mix of middle-class professionals, intellectuals, and workers from all sectarian communities. The party has had members elected to Parliament consistently since 1943, representing various districts. However, because of Joumblatt's status within the Druze community, which he rallied to support the party, it was founded with a Druze plurality of members leading one observer to describe it as "a nucleus of intellectuals dedicated to socialism surrounded by a sea of Druze peasants who joined the party to express their loyalty to their leader."[7] The party originally had healthy contingents of support within all sectarian communities, with over 20 percent of its members being Christians in its early years.

The main distinguishing feature of the PSP in the prewar years is how it gradually evolved from a political party ideologically committed to social democracy into a political movement with a Druze sectarian character. Most Christian members left the party after the crisis of 1958.[8] By the late 1960s the party had about ten thousand members, who were largely Druze peasants and craftsmen in the traditional Druze stronghold of Aley and Chouf districts.[9] The Druze represent no more than a few percent of the Lebanese population, and communal solidarity has always proved a powerful political appeal. Furthermore, the central role of the party in the Druze community also reflects the position that Kamal Joumblatt held in this community, where he combined the roles of tribal, spiritual, parliamentary, and business leader.[10] To sympathetic eyes he was simultaneously "a military leader, a skilful parliamentarian, a maker and breaker of governments, a feudal chieftain, a religious authority and a progressive Third World militant."[11] Once the war broke out, the PSP quickly lost most of its remaining non-Druze members, while many previously apolitical Druze rallied to the party out of communal solidarity and looked to Kamal Joumblatt as the undisputed leader of their sectarian community. The share of Druze in the PSP membership had hovered around 40–50 percent ever since 1949 but rapidly shot up to about 85 percent by the end of 1976.[12]

Another influential political party was the Lebanese Communist Party, originally founded in the 1920s by intellectuals protesting against the famine and poverty that followed in the wake of World War I.[13] It is a secular political party with genuine cross-sectarian appeal and a membership that included sizable shares of Christians, Shia Muslims, and minority groups such as Armenians and Kurds. The party is fairly small: by the late 1960s it most likely had no more than several thousand members across the entire country, with a particular concentration in Beirut.[14] It often ran candidates for Parliament but never won seats in prewar politics. However, its influence lay neither in its numbers nor in parliamentary machinations but in its dedicated membership of energetic activists and intellectuals. Lebanese

Communist Party members held a number of high-profile leadership positions in trade unions, civil society organizations, and universities. These members thus gained prominent platforms from which to spread their message and influence the wider political landscape. Furthermore, its activists were generally genuine devotees with a high degree of ideological commitment to their political cause.

The most important political actor in the Shia community was the Amal Movement, which was technically the armed wing of the political organization Movement of the Dispossessed.[15] This organization was founded by Imam Moussa Sadr upon his return to Lebanon from Iran in 1959. Sadr realized that he could use social service provision as a political tool to draw poor Shia supporters to his movement and away from their previous landowning political patrons.[16] To this effect, he deployed significant funds that he gathered from traditional centers of Shia power in Iran and Iraq to fund schools and orphanages. Service provision created strong ties between the Amal Movement and poor Shia beneficiaries; later on during the civil war Amal would use these ties—and generous financial and military support from Syria—to develop a formidable military machine. However, when the war broke out Amal was still a fledgling and incoherent movement with little political experience, limited resources, and few guns and that exerted no meaningful territorial control. It grew in capabilities and importance during the 1980s primarily because of Syrian patronage.

One final party merits attention and requires explanation: the Syrian Social Nationalist Party.[17] Its founder, Anton Saadeh, was a Greek Orthodox Lebanese national who grew up in South America around the time of World War I.[18] Returning to Lebanon as an adult, Saadeh immediately became frustrated with the underdevelopment of his native country and blamed this outcome on its sectarian divisions. At that time, Levantine emigrants in the Americas generally described themselves as "Syrian" regardless of what present-day country they hailed from; to Saadeh, the Syrian nation was the natural unit of governance, and he dedicated many years to fanciful writings about the ancient, pre-Islamic origins of this mythical nation. His proposed remedy for all contemporary problems was to unite the Syrian people under the rule of an iron-fisted leader. The party thus originated in the 1930s as a national socialist, right-wing, fiercely secular, explicitly antidemocratic ideological outfit emphasizing order, discipline, and elite rule. With Maronites and Sunnis dedicated to Lebanese and Arab nationalism, the Syrian Social Nationalist Party drew its supporters from minorities present throughout the Levant including some Druze and Shia Muslims but especially Greek Orthodox Christians. Anton Saadeh was executed in 1949 after a sham trial, and the party was subsequently banned for a time, during which it existed only as underground cells. By 1975 it was a minor player in national politics, but it retained a dedicated cadre of activists (numbering in the thousands) and a regional presence in some areas that became important during the war, such as West Beirut and the Metn district. Having opposed pan-Arab nationalism and the United Arab Republic in 1958, the party eventually grew closer to its left-wing counterparts because of its support for the Palestinian armed struggle.

Community Ties Among Muslim and Left-Wing Militias

The armed Palestinian factions took center stage in the war effort once armed hostilities erupted. They already possessed a standing fighting force akin to a small national army and drew on their dominant position and well-oiled institutions of governance in the Palestinian community to sustain this military organization. As a result, they largely sidelined the traditional Sunni elites who lacked military capabilities. However, Lebanese elites in the Shia and Druze communities fared better than their Sunni counterparts precisely because they catered to the political moment. For instance, the PSP rallied the Druze community in a fashion that mirrors what the Katayyib and National Liberal Party accomplished among Maronite Catholics and eventually developed a rather powerful armed wing. As the rest of this section shows, all Lebanese militias relied heavily on volunteer efforts to create, organize, sustain, and direct their militia efforts. Furthermore, even the Palestinian factions developed strong ties to local communities in many places where they operated because they recruited many Lebanese fighters, developed ties to Lebanese political parties and organizations, and sponsored Lebanese ancillary militias.

In terms of recruitment, the Lebanese militias relied heavily on local volunteers to control the front lines. "The militia wasn't separate from the local population. That's who we were, we were a part of the neighborhood, guys who knew each other from school. The militia didn't fall down from the sky," says the former military commander of the armed wing of the Lebanese Communist Party who fought in the predominantly Shia neighborhood of Nabaa.[19] The role of schools recurs in interviews. One member of the Syrian Social Nationalist Party argues that most of their recruitment took place in high schools and universities.[20] One Palestinian source argues that the factions recruited heavily in high schools and that there were strong network effects in recruitment whereby individuals joined factions that had attracted their friends or family members.[21] Many fighters in Lebanese militias did not receive a salary but fought out of ideological commitment or from a sense that they were defending their neighborhood or their community. Most fighters I talked to, from both sides of the frontline divide, stated that they believed at the time that their efforts represented a form of self-defense. While some have since reevaluated their past actions, others remain unrepentant.

The issue of logistics also highlights the deep ties of militias to local communities. The Palestinian factions drew heavily on their deep well of support in the refugee camps, and while the war forced these organizations to adapt and improvise, they had a head start on the Lebanese militias that scrambled to organize an effective military fighting force.[22] The latter groups found themselves heavily reliant on volunteer efforts for even the simplest forms of logistics. "The locals cooked for us," says a former Communist fighter.[23] "They would make a hot lunch and then bring it to the front lines, in the middle of battles, at great personal risk. Then they would come back, bring us tea, bring us coffee." Sometimes activists would also organize communal cooking sessions remotely and then deliver the food to frontline fighters, especially in situations where it was possible to plan ahead somewhat. Another logistical issue that highlights community ties is health care.[24] The major parties and militias organized their own health wings and rallied volunteers to provide improvised clinics, health care staff, and dispensaries. The PSP showed particular prowess at this activity in the Druze-dominated areas they controlled in Mount Lebanon.

The main source of military training for the Lebanese Muslim and left-wing militias was the Palestinian armed forces.[25] Many of the most dedicated activists had sought out opportunities to train before the war either in Palestinian camps in Greater Beirut or in South Lebanon close to the border with Israel where Palestinian military units exercised de facto sovereignty. Army defectors also played a key role in creating the Druze military organization, including by running military training and command functions. As the war progressed, some army units and commanders defected outright and fought alongside sectarian militias.[26] Defectors included a predominantly Sunni Muslim splinter faction, the Lebanese Arab

Army, commanded by Lieutenant Ahmed Al-Khatib. Aside from providing a competent fighting force, training, and command functions, army defectors were also an important source of new weapons. Palestinian factions had some heavy artillery before the war broke out, while most Lebanese militias only got access to heavy artillery of their own about a year after the war started once army defectors joined their ranks.

Many Lebanese left-wing groups received arms from the Soviet Union and other Warsaw Pact nations. "It is no secret that [Druze leader] Joumblatt was close to the Soviet Union," says one of the vice presidents of the PSP party. He further recounts that arms were presented as gifts since "we could not afford to pay for them. . . . Joumblatt sent men to train in the Soviet Union, including on very advanced weapons systems."[27] The Soviet Union sponsored innumerable formally socialist militant-revolutionary Third World organizations during the Cold War, and the PSP may have seemed a suitable client in a strategically important region. The Lebanese Communist Party also sent commanders to train in Moscow and received some shipments of arms, but, unlike the PSP, it did not have a strong and vital communitywide base of support. This factor made the PSP a more suitable ally to arm. From 1977, the Soviet Union poured tanks and artillery into the Druze war machine and even offered to supply a fleet of helicopters.[28] Among the Druze, who predominantly live in rural and mountainous areas, gun ownership was already quite common. The vice president of the party, who joined the party before the civil war, said of the very early days of the war, "It was individual weapons only, not organized, no central decision. Rifles, Kalashnikovs, light arms."[29]

The gender composition of fighters varied widely among Muslim and left-wing armed groups.[30] In some left-wing groups the share of female fighters was as high as 15 percent, which likely reflected not only party ideology but also the related fact that these organizations had sizable cadres of female activists before the war broke out. On the other end of the spectrum, the Shia communal guardian Amal Movement had barely any female fighters at all. The Shia community traditionally had the lowest levels of socioeconomic development in the country and consequently tended to be particularly traditional on issues such as gender; furthermore, the movement did have some Islamist undertones and was founded by a Shia cleric. Many Shia Lebanese activists with progressive views therefore preferred the left-wing parties, such as the Lebanese Communist Party, which had a healthy Shia membership. The tension between formal ideology and community preferences is perhaps best illustrated by the PSP. In theory, this was a social democratic party committed to gender equality. In practice, it came to serve as communal guardians of the Druze, a rather conservative community with highly traditional views on family matters; as a result, the party had very few female fighters. Yet all militias drew heavily on the volunteer work of women to organize logistics.

The Palestinian Movement

The Arab defeat of 1967 sparked the Palestinian movement for national liberation through armed struggle, and groups such as Fatah and the Popular Front for the Liberation of Palestine surged to power as leaders of this effort in the West Bank, Jordan, and Lebanon.[31] At first these various factions possessed very limited military capabilities, and they fought their very first skirmishes with small arms and grenades that they received as token gifts from friendly Arab regimes or acquired by scavenging for supplies left behind in the battlefields of the West Bank and Golan Heights. However, the largest factions—especially Fatah—rapidly improved their military capabilities and built quite sophisticated military organizations outfitted by Egypt and Syria, who saw them as proxy units in the struggle against Israel, and by Eastern Bloc countries like China and Vietnam, who saw them as a fellow national liberation movement struggling against Western imperialism. The groups rapidly gained popularity in the Palestinian community, and by the late 1960s they attracted more volunteers in Jordan, Syria, Lebanon, and the West Bank than they could feasibly train and incorporate into their armed wings. The Palestinian national movement rapidly grew into an organized nationalist mass movement.

Palestinian leadership preferred Jordan as a base of operations because of its long border with Israel and its large Palestinian civilian population. From this base they conceived of their struggle against Israel as a guerrilla war inspired by Ho Chi Minh and Che Guevara, who had both managed to defeat the United States through insurgency tactics. Yet what the Palestinian national movement built up in Jordan was something much broader than merely a military fighting force and increasingly resembled a state with "its own military police, security apparatus, revolutionary courts, information offices, media, trade union movement, and, of course, full-time armed forces and 'liberated zones' in the refugee camps."[32] The movement had much deeper and stronger ties to the civilian Palestinian population than a typical insurgency. It is best understood—and was largely understood by its own members and supporters—as a national liberation movement aspiring to create and rule an independent and sovereign country called Palestine.[33]

After the PLO departed Jordan in 1971, virtually all of its political and military operations were located on Lebanese soil. Because of their origins as secretive underground organizations, both the PLO and most of its constituent factions developed fragmented and divided institutional designs. It appears that no one besides Yasser Arafat and his closest associates ever fully understood its financial or operational status at any point in time. Nevertheless, we know that what the PLO possessed in Lebanon during the early 1970s amounts to a veritable state within the state. Until 1969 the Lebanese government had maintained police stations in the refugee camps with formal checkpoints at all entrances. The camps were under strict curfews, and many Palestinians needed travel passes to enter and leave their residential locations. This strict regime generated huge resentment within the community. Starting in the late 1960s, the PLO established a more prominent political and military presence that shifted the balance of power in this regard. In 1969 the PLO and Lebanese Army leadership reached an understanding, the Cairo Agreement, to regulate the Palestinian presence in Lebanon. Lebanese police and army units left the camps altogether, which fell under the de facto sovereign control of the PLO and its factions.[34]

A promising new era seemed to dawn for the refugee community. "The early 1970s was a golden era for Palestinians in Lebanon," says the Palestinian director of a nongovernmental organization with ties to the PLO.

> The [Red Cross], UNRWA, and PLO provided services. There were jobs, health care, and university scholarships. The PLO had health clinics. They had a hospital in Sabra, four stories high, with modern technology. There were opportunities to travel and to work in the Gulf. Gulf money flowed directly to the PLO, from governments, but also as remittances both directly to families and to the PLO. [Beirut slums and refugee camps] were ignored by the government so the PLO moved in and took control. They provided benefits to all who lived there without discriminating.[35]

In part, the PLO benefited from the windfall revenues associated with rising oil prices after 1973 that poured enormous amounts of money into Sunni Arab kingdoms intent to increase their regional influence.[36] Aside from Gulf Arab governments and the Palestinian diaspora, the PLO also operated the Palestinian National Fund that collected taxes in the community and paid for military expenditures. In short, to many Palestinian refugees in Lebanon, the PLO essentially functioned as a regular government: it taxed its citizens, provided services, and maintained a national army.

The Palestinian forces differed from their Lebanese counterparts in that they already brought an impressive set of armed forces when they first arrived in Lebanon, and the dominant factions already had a competent fighting force when the war first broke out. "[Fatah] had maintained a standing military organization since 1969," explains a Palestinian academic and occasional consultant to PLO leadership during the 1990s Arab–Israeli peace process.

> It had a full command structure with a unified military command and a political command in control of the military. It was more organized [than the Lebanese militias]. It understood combined arms, in particular with infantry and artillery. It was well-informed and skilled in professional military intelligence. It was well-trained and had maintained full-time soldiers since the 1960s. Many had battle experience from the West Bank and Jordan. It could operate outside of its own neighborhoods by moving reserves and reinforcements long distances with professional logistics.[37]

If the Lebanese militias originated as neighborhood volunteers, the Palestinian forces were already close to a national army when the war broke out. The Palestinian factions generally paid their fighters, whereas the situation was more mixed among Lebanese organizations. Various Palestinian factions received major shipments of arms from Syria, Iraq, Libya, Algeria, and the Soviet Union; Arab countries often jockeyed for influence by sponsoring competing factions.

The Palestinian strategy in Lebanon contained a central contradiction.[38] On the one hand, the PLO officially pursued a policy of nonintervention in Lebanese affairs. Arafat feared that civil war in Lebanon would be the second time in only a few years that his forces were depleted by fighting within an

Arab country instead of focusing on his real enemy, Israel. He therefore wanted to prevent his Lebanese allies from escalating the political conflict to the point where they would pull the Palestinian movement into an armed confrontation through chain-gang dynamics. However, on the other hand, the Palestinians had learned from their experience in Jordan that they needed a popular base of support within their host country to avoid a repeat of how the Hashemite monarchy had violently evicted them. Palestinian intellectual and political leaders therefore cultivated close ties with traditional elites, the "Sunni street," left-wing groups, labor unions, student groups, and civil society movements. The goal was to "Lebanize" the PLO by firmly rooting it to its local host community as well as to rally the Muslim and left-wing political community around support for the Palestinian cause.

As a result, the Palestinian factions developed and maintained strong ties to local communities inside Lebanon in at least three important ways. First, Palestinian factions attracted many Lebanese recruits. Lebanese Muslims and left-wing activists saw their own struggle as intertwined with the issue of Palestine and connected through ideological themes such as anti-imperialism, antisectarianism, anticapitalism, and pan-Arab nationalism. The Palestinian factions were the main agents of change for Lebanese seeking radical transformation of their country. Fatah, in particular, stood out as a broad, secular organization united around the cause of liberating Palestine, a political goal with almost universal appeal among Lebanese Sunni Muslims as well. "Fatah was non-Marxist, non-sectarian. It was easy for a Lebanese to join," says a Palestinian intellectual.[39] In addition, Fatah offered its recruits arms and a monthly salary. Through these recruits, Palestinian factions thus gained strong ties to local Lebanese communities, especially among Sunni Muslims. Furthermore, the Palestinian base of operations and support was in the refugee camps and slum areas where most Palestinians lived, and some of those slums also had poor Lebanese residents who benefited from PLO service provision. When the war broke out, many Lebanese Sunnis looked to the Palestinian factions as their de facto political representatives.

Second, all major Palestinian factions had established close working ties with Lebanese groups well before the civil war broke out.[40] Fatah made strategic alliances with the most powerful Lebanese actors while other relationships arose out of ideological compatibility. For instance, the Popular Front for the Liberation of Palestine and the Lebanese Communist Party were both devoted to similar left-wing doctrines with an emphasis on the twin problems of Western imperialism and capitalist exploitation. Likewise, the Democratic Front for the Liberation of Palestine and the Organization for Communist Action—both of which found the former two insufficiently committed to Marxist principles—united in their critique of the "reformist tendencies" of their other allies. In general, the Palestinian movement had sought for almost a decade to develop close ties with student activists, civil society movements, and labor unions to widen their base of popular support in Lebanon. Many Lebanese individuals, groups, and parties had received arms and military training from the Palestinian factions. From the Palestinian perspective, the purpose of donating arms and training to its allies was not generally to build up military capabilities but to establish strong and cordial relations with Lebanese political elites.

Finally, Fatah also sponsored or effectively created new Lebanese militias, such as Al-Mourabitoun in West Beirut and the Popular Nasserist Organization in Saida. These groups were ostensibly Arab nationalist, Sunni-dominated Lebanese political movements but in practice were entirely dependent on the Palestinian factions from whom they received all their arms and money. These groups often recruited and operated only in a particular neighborhood, consisted of locals, and had little ability to independently stage offensive operations.[41] Fatah had several reasons to sponsor Lebanese proxy militias. One was to gain political cover and portray the conflict to the largest extent possible as an intra-Lebanese affair. A second, related reason was that Arafat was reluctant to send large numbers of uniformed Palestinian soldiers into Beirut and other high-profile areas for fear of attracting outside intervention into the war. Other reasons include to increase total manpower, to reduce casualties among Palestinian soldiers, and to allow Fatah to preserve combat troops in the south where they bordered Israel. Yet, whatever the motivation behind sponsoring Sunni-dominated ancillary militias, these local groups gave the Palestinian movement genuine ties to local communities in many locations where they engaged in military contestation. They are an important piece of evidence in how even Palestinian militias—technically foreigners in Lebanon—came to possess strong and deep ties to local residents in many areas where they operated.

Political Leadership and Governance

Once the war broke out, the Lebanese National Movement set up a unified political command, the Central Political Council, to coordinate political and military activities.⁴² The problem was that its constituent members had very little in common except their fierce resistance to the status quo, and their meetings, recounted in interviews, often descended into scenes reminiscent of Orwell's Catalonia. The alliance had about thirteen constituent political parties, not counting factions of the Palestinian movement, and countless smaller organizations demanded a seat at the table as well. Individual militias and factions quickly seized control over various parts of the country—sometimes as small as a single urban neighborhood—where they jealously guarded their position from rivals who were technically their allies. Smaller groups with cadres marked by ideological devotion to various pan-Arab or left-wing causes were particularly prone to hold up proceedings over doctrinal disputes. Iraq, Syria, Libya, and the Soviet Union exercised various degrees of influence over client groups within the alliance, and larger factions sometimes approached foreign patrons directly to get minor parties to fall in line. "Decision making was not easy. The aspiration was for consensus," says a contemporary Palestinian politician.⁴³

Despite this chaos at the political level, in practice the alliance operated under a unified military command at the strategic level and deployed its forces in a largely coherent manner. The reason is that, from a military perspective, the Palestinian factions, and especially Yasser Arafat's Fatah, completely dominated the alliance. Once the war broke out, other parties shared territory with Palestinian forces but could not conduct meaningful military operations to contest or capture territory on their own. The military dominance of the Palestinian factions stems, of course, from the fact that they already possessed a formidable military fighting force built up over many years in the West Bank, Jordan, and Lebanon. While they struggled to operate a unified political command because of their doctrinal differences, none of the Lebanese left-wing and Muslim forces had the military capabilities to act as an independent fighting force, and in practice all of them relied on Arafat to command their joint war effort. The Palestinian leadership planned the war effort and took most significant strategic decisions, while other parties supplied fighters and other resources in various local areas where they already had a very strong prewar presence. Arafat acted strategically so as to keep the coalition intact by incorporating the views of other groups as well.

As the war progressed beyond the first two years, several of the most powerful militias developed states-within-the-state characteristics as they gradually took over operation of most social services and public management within their respective cantons. The formal institutions of the Lebanese government continued to exist and to operate some functions during the war but became increasingly marginalized as armed organizations muscled in on government activities. Some armed organizations simply took over control of services that were already present and reemployed former government employees to return to their old jobs under new management. The culprits typically claim that they were forced to do this because the government was no longer able to operate and to provide for citizens. There is no doubt that one reason for service provision was to convince the civilian population to stay in their homes rather than to leave the area or the country. Another, less charitable interpretation is that militias wanted more extensive and comprehensive territorial control and access to revenues. It is likely that both motives played into the gradual process of militia takeover that began shortly after the war broke out and accelerated after 1976.[44]

The most competent governance initiatives belonged to the sectarian militias that dominated the Shia and Druze communities. The Druze community was heavily concentrated geographically in its traditional heartland of Mount Lebanon, an area under full military control by the Druze-dominated PSP.[45] Its control of the area was so extensive, and its overlap with prewar patterns of governance so comprehensive, that in most cases the party simply asked civil servants and other government employees to return to their regular day jobs and perform their ordinary duties. The party collected a modest household tax but otherwise relied heavily on toll booths at military checkpoints for revenue as their territorial domains included one of the main highways running north to south along the Lebanese coast.[46] The party also operated the Voice of the Mountain (Sawt Al-Jabal) radio station that broadcast news, interviews, and music; it provided an important focal point for the dissemination of information within the community and for rallying community efforts at short notice.[47] After the War of the Mountain in 1983 left the region with substantial material devastation, the party reorganized its reconstruction and governance initiatives as the "Civil Administration of the Mountain," intended to function as a civilian governance institution.

Similar developments occurred in the Shia community a few years later, after 1978 as Shia migrants flocked to South Beirut escaping Israeli incursions against Palestinian militants in South Lebanon. During the 1980s

Shia movements Amal and Hezbollah rose to prominence and eventually established quasi-states in several Shia-dominated areas of Lebanon.[48] However, both movements relied more heavily on outside funding, and neither created as comprehensive service provision as the Christian or Druze communities during the war. One reason for this discrepancy is that the Shia community was much less economically advanced, and its political parties thus faced a steeper task. Amal and Hezbollah received considerable supplies of arms from Syria and Iran and have continued to do so ever since.[49] As these relationships continue to define Lebanese politics up until the present, they are much more sensitive topics than other modes of wartime governance, and party leaders are a lot less willing to discuss them. "There is no denying that Amal Movement has been in numerous wars. But they were all for self-defense," says the chairman of the executive committee of the group.[50] He offers a lengthy discussion of the circumstances and background that prompted Amal to organize military activities and to eventually enter West Beirut as its dominant faction in 1984, after the Israeli withdrawal and the collapse of the national army. Yet he offers little detail on operational and logistical issues.

Not all actors were equally adept at the art of wartime governance, and the Sunni community in particular suffered from weak wartime leadership on social and economic governance.[51] The Palestinian factions did not generally establish effective governance, except in the refugee camps where they were long established. Another problem was that some areas contained multiple militant groups that, while technically allied, did not manage to cooperate effectively in establishing governance. Perhaps nowhere was this problem as salient as in West Beirut. One historian notes of this area that "the armed forces of the many political factions not only manned the front lines against the Lebanese Front but jealously guarded urban strongholds, sometimes no larger than a single block, against incursions by 'fraternal' parties. . . . Shootouts in the Emergency Room of the American University Hospital in Beirut were common, as rival militiamen struggled to have their wounded treated first."[52] Citizen initiatives to provide and maintain services, such as municipal garbage collection, mostly failed. While statistics from active warzones are notoriously unreliable, the best available figures on crime suggest that Sunni-dominated West Beirut was an order of magnitude worse than Christian-controlled East Beirut.[53]

Intelligence Capabilities Among the Palestinian Factions and Their Allies

The PLO began its operations in Lebanon in the late 1960s, and largest faction Fatah maintained an intelligence organization dating back to at least 1968.[54] At that point PLO activity inside the camps was mostly limited to political operations and some service provisions, with military operations relegated to the southern countryside bordering Israel. Gathering and processing intelligence was largely secretive work conducted by underground cells. Later, Fatah developed a formal intelligence branch in Lebanon that operated centers for detention and interrogation, for instance, in the Bourj el-Barajneh, Sabra, and Shatila camps. As for the Lebanese militias, there is little evidence that they possessed formal intelligence organizations, wings, or branches before the war broke out. However, much like their Christian counterparts, these militias heavily rallied volunteers both as military recruits and to conduct their logistical functions. Most of their volunteers contributed locally in their own village or neighborhood, where they typically had deep local knowledge about conditions in their immediate social and physical vicinity.

In terms of intelligence collection, the Palestinian factions benefited enormously from the modest share of Lebanese who served in their ranks as well as from their deep operational ties to the armed wings of Lebanese organizations such as the Lebanese Communist Party.[55] "The extent to which the [Palestinian factions] relied on Lebanese [parties] for decision making, I do not know, but for intelligence, certainly. . . . The goal was to cleanse the area of threats," says a contemporary Palestinian political activist who served as student body president at American University of Beirut.[56] Activists from the Syrian Social Nationalist Party were particularly active in joint intelligence operations because the party had a strong presence in certain Katayyib strongholds such as the Metn region.[57] Along similar lines, a former deputy head of military intelligence for the largest Christian militia claims that his organization generally viewed the intelligence capabilities of the Lebanese Communist Party as a greater threat than its military prowess.[58]

Palestinian, Muslim, and left-wing groups were acutely aware of the need to pacify political and military opposition in the areas they controlled. "If you have question marks about the loyalties of a village in your back, militarily, you are vulnerable," says a contemporary Palestinian political activist.[59] During interviews in English, interviewees most often refer to their enemies as "Phalangists" or "Katayyib," using both terms interchangeably and often switching between the terms within the span of a single interview.[60] Occasionally they call their opponents "the Right," or "right-wing forces." Some civil war participants, particularly those who fought with left-wing organizations, also refer to their enemies as "the Fascists." However, it is quite rare to hear former fighters and commanders refer to their enemies as "the Christians." This is because, in their mindset, the members of the PLO-led alliance believed that they were fighting certain political groups, which happened to be heavily Christian, rather than the Christian community per se. Their enemy was not Christians as a group but rather adherents of certain ideologies and members of particular political movements or parties that espoused those ideas; in fact, some number of Christians had left-wing or pro-Palestinian sympathies. As a result it made no strategic sense to target the Christian community in an indiscriminate fashion. "The PLO did not take [general] decisions to kill Christians," says a Palestinian academic.[61]

Their challenge, then, was to separate hostile individuals from neutral or left-wing Christians in areas that the militias controlled. The rest of this section addresses the question of intelligence collection through a structured comparison between two cases, aiming to isolate the effects of demographic intermixing on outcomes of violence to the greatest extent possible. One case concerns the intermixed West Beirut neighborhood of Mosaitbe. The other case concerns a set of homogenous non-coethnic enclaves: the town and two villages of Damour, Jiyeh, and Saadiyat. This design allows us to compare how intelligence-collection efforts differed across areas with different demographic configuration (variation in the independent variable), causing militias to perpetrate either ethnic cleansing or selective violence (variation in the dependent variable). As all cases occurred within Lebanon during a relatively short span of time, national-level or temporal variables cannot explain variation in outcomes. The cases are in close geographic proximity to each other, less than twenty kilometers apart, and were targeted by the same coalition of militia groups. Both locations had Christian residents who were middle class or well off, rather than poor. Both locations witnessed violence; but as the structured comparison shows, militias had differential abilities to collect intelligence in the locations, which in turn influenced variation in the kind of violence they employed.

Intermixed Area: West Beirut Neighborhood of Mosaitbe

While predominantly Christian East Beirut occupies a vast geographic area extending east into Mount Lebanon, including large suburbs, Sunni-dominated West Beirut is relatively contained as it borders the sea to the north and west and a set of predominantly Shia suburbs to the south. Official administrative records split West Beirut into only seven neighborhoods, all of which are intermixed between a Sunni majority and meaningful minorities of Maronite Catholics, Greek Orthodox, and Shia Muslims as well as a small presence of many other groups also. When the war broke out several armed groups shared military control of West Beirut and rapidly proceeded to clear the area of Katayyib loyalists and other hostile Christian residents. However, because of the densely intermixed nature of the neighborhoods militants generally discriminated among individual Christians. The comprehensive report by the Ministry of the Displaced (1996, 9) documents forced displacement of civilians in three West Beirut administrative jurisdictions: Mosaitbe, Mazraa, and Minet el Hosn. All three cases involve selective targeting of specific Christian individuals rather than general waves of displacement along sectarian lines, and many Christians stayed in the area, especially during the 1975–1976 period of the war. Several interviews concerning the Mosaitbe neighborhood of West Beirut illustrate these dynamics.

Much like their Christian opponents, several interviewees from PLO-aligned groups mention the role of schools and universities—where many Lebanese youngsters first became politically active and joined clubs affiliated with national political parties—as a key factor in intelligence collection. "From fourteen, fifteen students would typically start to identify with one party or another. . . . From the 1960s on it was usually known who was with whom, known among locals, neighbors," says a former activist from the Syrian Social Nationalist Party who lives, and runs a bookshop, in West Beirut.[62] He mentions the growth after 1967 of the Palestinian issue as a true watershed in Lebanese politics. Some Christians with left-wing sympathies were openly pro-Palestinian in their political orientation. Yet most Lebanese Christians, and especially Maronite Catholics and Greek Catholics, opposed the armed presence of Palestinian organizations in Lebanon. Some Christians were known to be party members of the Katayyib or the National Liberal Party, open sympathizers, former members of high school or university chapters of its youth or student wings, or subscribed to newspapers published by those organizations. Those individuals were relatively easy to identify for other members of their local neighborhoods.

One Syriac Orthodox Christian interviewee from the Mosaitbe district of West Beirut describes his experience of relocating permanently in 1975 to Christian-controlled East Beirut. His father was a well-known and prominent Katayyib member, and the young man was an active student politician at American University of Beirut with outspoken views about the "Christian struggle for survival."[63] He says cryptically that his family left in 1975 after unspecified "small incidents" and "negative signs" during a time period when political assassinations were becoming a frequent occurrence in the country. In contrast, he describes those Christians who stayed behind in West Beirut as "prominent families" who were "apolitical" and says that "those [Christians] who stayed often had contacts, relationships with PLO, with [the Syrian Social Nationalist Party], with Islamists even." However, he says that he himself chose to relocate not only because of threats against his person but also because of a general sentiment that "if we stay here, we have to be *dhimmi*, be with PLO."

Let us dwell on a word from the last sentence, "*dhimmi*," which recurs in interviews with many Lebanese Christians. The word is a historical legal term for non-Muslims living under Islamic law and was used, for instance, in the Ottoman Empire. Today some Christians use it to imply a kind of general submission and deference to Muslims. One young political secretary from the Katayyib party uses the term in our interviews to describe someone who is the opposite of a "strong Christian," a "proud Christian" or a "muscular Christian." One Christian priest uses the term to describe the situation for Christians in the northern city of Tripoli during the 1980s, when it was controlled briefly by an Islamist movement, Tawheed. Tawheed had no ill will against Christians and permitted Christian residents to remain; however, they had to abide by Tawheed's version of Islamic law, including on how to dress in public, a complete ban on alcohol, and a ban on eating in public during Ramadan. "There were horseback religious police patrols," says the priest.[64] For many Christians who lived in PLO-controlled territory, the choice was between either relocating elsewhere or accepting *dhimma* status in their original place of residence. *Dhimma* status generally seems to imply to refrain from all forms of political activity or expressions and to generally maintain a low profile in community life.

Identifying the full set of Katayyib sympathizers was not always an easy task even where locals had a lot of information about their Christian neighbors. The problem was partly that allegiances within the Christian community were shifting. Katayyib had been a very strong, although not dominant, player in Christian politics, but it rapidly gained sympathies as it took a leadership position in confronting the Palestinian movement through armed struggle.[65] It was also well known that the group had many covert sympathizers among Christian army personnel and some other representatives of official government institutions. The Palestinian factions and their allies had quite a difficult time in practice deciding who was a Katayyib sympathizer and who was neutral or loyal to their cause. Targeting was thus slightly more complicated than merely working through a list of long-time activists. Sometimes other individual traits, particularly employment in certain professions linked to the military or law enforcement, could render the affected individual a suspected Katayyib sympathizer.

A Katayyib activist provides more detail on how targeting worked from the perspective of the targeted community, with references to cases from his own family. "There was pressure on [certain] Christians to leave," he says.[66] At first the targets were usually what he deems "key persons." Starting with all known affiliates of Katayyib or its allies such as the National Liberal Party, it subsequently broadened to include army personnel; police, judges, and other agents of law enforcement; and sometimes other public servants or members of what he deems "the deep state." A lecturer in history at the University of Balamand describes what this process looked like in practice based on her primary research. "It started with incidents that had no casualties," she explains.[67] Neighbors might confiscate newspapers affiliated with political parties they disapproved of, especially the Katayyib publication *Al-Amal*. In other cases militants would blow up cars or even houses belonging to persons with suspected ties to hostile groups. Many Christians at this point either left the area into exile in Christian-controlled territories, ceased various activities that were deemed suspect, or otherwise tried to convey their neutrality in credible ways. "Then they started killing people. Mostly political people, but targeting was not perfect," continues the academic. Some were killed because they did not heed warnings, and others never received a warning in the first place.

In theory it may have been easy to distinguish between "Christians" and "Katayyib sympathizers," but in practice it often proved difficult. "The distinction between Maronite and Phalangist started to disappear. . . . If you were Maronite, the assumption was you're most probably a Phalangist. . . . Unless proven otherwise. They needed contacts. Someone to vouch for you," says a contemporary Palestinian political activist.[68] "Many [Christian] socialists [were] killed by mistake," says a vice president of the Druze-dominated PSP who laments that political allegiance was not always investigated very thoroughly and that many innocent people were killed on flimsy and speculative evidence.[69] In short, those Christians who remained in Palestinian-controlled territory generally had strong political connections and relationships dating back to prewar life. They relied on their personal connections to left-wing and Muslim residents and leaders who could vouch for them.

As an illustration of this process, a Greek Orthodox former member of Parliament who spent the war years in West Beirut describes his experience of securing peaceful coexistence for himself and many of his constituents in one interview. His father was a member of Parliament before him, and they were well known in political circles with extensive contacts among Sunni Lebanese, Palestinian, and left-wing elites. While the man denies left-wing sympathies, both he and his father were known for their pro-Palestinian views. "That's how it works in Lebanon. Prominent families always talk to each other," as the man explained to me over lunch.[70] He claims that much of the violence against Christians in West Beirut after 1975 resembled "gangsterism," as midlevel commanders would use their position to try to steal Christian homes and other possessions. The former member of Parliament explains how he would often get calls from constituents in distress who had received threats to leave their homes. On such occasions, he would in turn telephone senior commanders of various local militias; jointly, they would then locate the culprit of the crime who would receive a reprimand in front of senior brass. In short, to stay behind in Palestinian-controlled territory as a Christian, it generally took strong and reliable connections, either to senior leadership in relevant militias or to community leaders who had such ties.

Homogenous Enclaves: Damour, Jiyeh, and Saadiyat

One contrasting example to the dynamics described above comes from a string of homogenously Christian settlements along the coastal highway running south from Beirut: the town of Damour and the two nearby villages of Jiyeh and Saadiyat.[71] Damour was a town with perhaps twenty thousand predominantly Maronite Catholic inhabitants, although it also had a small presence of Shia in the town or its immediate surroundings. Jiyeh and Saadiyat were very small and homogenous Maronite Catholic villages. While Jiyeh and Saadiyat thus feature as homogenous locations in my quantitative dataset, Damour was technically intermixed as it contained both Christian and Muslim residents. Damour thus constitutes an exception to my general theory. However, local Shia appear to have formed part of former president Camille Chamoun's clientelist machine, and there is little evidence of any presence of left-wing parties in these locations when the civil war broke out. Shia were much more likely than Sunni or Druze to remain neutral in the early days of the war, before the rise of Amal and Hezbollah in the 1980s. As a result, it appears that the Palestinian and left-wing groups had no local sympathizers in these locations despite the presence of a small Muslim population.

Collectively, these locations constituted a political stronghold of former president Camille Chamoun at the center of the electoral district he personally represented as a member of Parliament. His swank mansion was situated on the coast in the village of Saadiyat, and many locals had strong links to his National Liberal Party through ties of patronage politics and clientelism. For instance, the area had a particularly high share of military families as Chamoun had exerted great efforts to get his clients—the local villagers and townspeople—jobs in the Lebanese Armed Forces. The Chamoun family had a long history in this region, and the towns were adorned with statues, posters, and even street names honoring the family, which added further symbolic value to the area. When the civil war broke out Chamoun distributed weapons among trusted villagers, and many local army personnel also defected to join this nascent militia effort.

Palestinian and allied forces attacked Damour in January of 1976. There were three reasons for the attack. First, Chamoun loyalists had blocked the major national highway running by all three villages and erected checkpoints. Palestinian factions wanted to reopen this strategic coastal highway that connected their West Beirut headquarters to their military strongholds in Saida and in South Lebanon, near the border with Israel. The checkpoints effectively cut off the bulk of Palestinian forces in the south of the country from the center of military contestation in central Beirut. Second, the Palestinians wanted to hurt the personal fief, honor, and status of Chamoun who was rapidly gaining a position as one of the main Christian warlords. The attack intended to hobble his fledgling efforts to create an effective military fighting force. Third, the attack was tit-for-tat retaliation for the Christian attack on Karantina, which took place in East Beirut only days earlier. To the Christian forces, the attack on Karantina was part of a logical and necessary campaign to take full control over all parts of Beirut on their side of the front lines and to expel hostile forces that threatened to surround their enclave. To the Palestinians and their allies, however, this attack had represented an unprecedented escalation in terms of its level of violence and displacement against civilians and merited a countervailing response.

Palestinian and left-wing militants, with large contingents from Palestinian factions Fatah and Saiqa, entered and easily conquered Jiyeh while most Christian civilians fled the area as the attackers approached. As Palestinian and left-wing forces stormed the town of Jiyeh, former president Camille Chamoun personally orchestrated its defenses. He continuously and forcefully appealed to the central government to send in the army to stop the attacking Palestinian forces; in his mind, the Palestinian assault on a Lebanese town crossed a clear red line whereby the institutions of the sovereign state—first and foremost its armed forces—had to come to the defense of its citizens. For many Muslim leaders, on the other hand, Christian forces had already crossed that very red line themselves when they attacked the shantytown of Karantina only a few days prior. In the end, government ministers reached a compromise and the Lebanese Armed Forces dispatched two fighter jets to strafe the advancing Palestinian forces from the air. Yet this maneuver was more symbolic than substantive and barely slowed down the advancing ground forces. At the very last minute, when defeat appeared certain, Chamoun escaped the town in a helicopter.[72]

The attacking forces subsequently advanced on Damour and took up positions just outside the town. Palestinian forces and Chamoun loyalists fought a battle for control of Damour that raged for nearly two weeks. During this period most Christian civilians started to leave the area, and many were evacuated by boat to Christian-controlled territory in East Beirut.

Palestinian leaders would parley with their Christian counterparts and at one point offered to evacuate all remaining persons—both civilians and military personnel—from the affected villages.[73] Local Christian commanders appeared split on whether to accept this offer, but Palestinian commanders lost patience as they prevaricated and launched a final assault on the town. Secondary sources explain how the remaining Christians were "lined up against the walls of their homes and sprayed with machine-gun fire" by Palestinian forces who did not discriminate between civilians and militants.[74] The invaders proceeded to blow up the Chamoun family mansion with dynamite, perhaps an apt illustration of what they ultimately hoped to accomplish.[75] The fighters subsequently exerted the same treatment upon the local church and desecrated its cemetery. Christian evacuees were not allowed to return, and several months later the PLO installed the Palestinian survivors from the Christian attack on the Tel al-Zaatar refugee camp in Damour.[76] The ruins of the village church, along with the nearby former priest's home, was turned into a school to teach about three hundred Palestinian children resettled in the village.

Why did Palestinian forces want Damour, Jiyeh, and Saadiyat ethnically cleansed, as evidenced by the fact that they first offered to evacuate all residents and then either killed or exiled all of its inhabitants? The answer is complicated and likely reflects multiple motivations. There is no question that the attackers—many of whom were intoxicated by drugs and alcohol—wanted to inflict pain and suffering on civilians linked to the Christian militias, personified by Camille Chamoun, in retaliation for the massacre at Karantina. In addition, the very boundaries between civilians and militants were becoming somewhat blurred in these particular locations as Chamoun gradually mobilized local residents into his militia. Furthermore, the attackers used the opportunity to engage in a spectacular level of looting. One account describes how, "in subsequent days, swarms of looters stripped Damour of everything of value, down to the tiles on the roofs and the metal wiring and pipes."[77] Another Western journalist who visited Damour shortly after the attack claims to have seen Palestinian men carting away refrigerators and other household durables on motorbikes.[78] When the attackers were finished, little remained but bare concrete foundations. One reason for this ferocious level of looting was the need to scavenge supplies for the exiled population of Karantina, which was being resettled elsewhere, including partly in rapidly appropriated West Beirut beach clubs.

Yet another factor for militia behavior appears to be the inability to distinguish between local civilian residents, renegade army personnel, and Christian militia fighters. One Palestinian source acknowledges that the attackers ethnically cleansed the location but downplays the significance of this event by arguing—in a circular fashion—that those who remained must have been militants since the civilians had already left. "Most [civilians] had left already. Probably only hundreds of civilians left," says a Palestinian intellectual with knowledge of the episode, who argues that it has become "mythologized."[79] In contrast, a former midlevel military commander and press spokesperson for Chamoun claims that Damour actually contained relatively few armed militia operatives and was not the military stronghold that Palestinian sources describe it as.[80] The point here is not to verify which account is correct but to establish how they differ. Damour and its surrounding villages formed the center of Chamoun's electoral stronghold; the Palestinian factions that attacked it had no local sympathizers or informants and treated all Christian inhabitants as Chamoun loyalists in an indiscriminate fashion.

This chapter highlights my argument that the role of ethnicity as information can vary within the same one conflict. In Lebanon, as in most conflicts in plural countries, ethnic identity generally correlated with political loyalties, but it was not a perfect indicator because sectarianism intersected with other loyalties based on secular ideology or material interests. In areas where militias could access detailed information about select individuals, ethnicity was not a very useful piece of intelligence whenever militants could access better intelligence—such as political party membership—that was generally a more accurate indicator of political allegiance. Militias could then target those select individuals in a range of modalities, not all of which were lethal in nature; many individuals received some form of warning, and many chose to relocate to an area controlled by friendly forces. However, in areas where armed groups had very limited access to intelligence, they often had no alternative but to rely on ethnicity as a proxy for political loyalties. As a result, the role of ethnicity as information varied widely within this complex conflict.

Conclusion

A common narrative holds that Lebanon was a diverse and intermixed country until its civil war reinforced the role of narrow sectarian identities, poisoned interethnic relations, empowered chauvinistic militias, and tore the country apart into Muslim and Christian enclaves. I challenge this narrative by introducing nationwide data that shows how displacement was less comprehensive than sometimes appreciated: only about half of Muslims in Christian-controlled territory were displaced throughout fifteen years of civil war, and about half of Christians remained in the Muslim-dominated enclave as well. My explanation for these puzzling outcomes centers on political loyalties and military intelligence. When the civil war broke out, both military coalitions tried to systematically break down the social and military base of support that the other side enjoyed in particular segments of the population. The Christian forces fought a war against the armed Palestinian factions and their Lebanese allies. They methodically razed a string of Palestinian-controlled slums, shantytowns, and refugee camps across East Beirut and displaced their populations. However, senior Christian political leaders understood that, even if they won an outright military victory, they would need—at the very least—grudging acceptance from the Muslim communities for whatever political project they hoped to implement in victory. They had political incentives to avoid general and indiscriminate displacement of the entire Muslim community.

Palestinian forces and their Lebanese allies retaliated on their side of the front lines by ethnically cleansing towns and villages, such as the prosperous seaside towns of Damour, Jiyeh, and Saadiyat. These municipalities formed the electoral base of the Chamoun dynasty, a Maronite political family that was in the process of turning its vast electoral and clientelist machine into a powerful militia. Defeating the Christian militias would allow the Palestinian allies to form a new Lebanese government, which would provide political and military sanctuary for the PLO on Lebanese soil for its armed struggle against Israel. Nevertheless, the PLO had no political incentives to attack Lebanese Christians with indiscriminate violence and displacement. On the contrary, the Lebanese allies of the Palestinian national movement knew that they needed—and believed that they would be able—to win approval from the Christian community to rebuild the Lebanese political regime according to their ideological visions. A non-trivial number of Christians participated in the civil war as allies of the Palestinian national movement, including by fighting for left-wing outfits like the Lebanese Communist Party.

Ethnic cleansing in Lebanon—compared to many other civil wars, such as Bosnia or Darfur—is remarkable not for its prevalence but for the degree of restraint shown by militias and the quality of military intelligence that informed their decisions. Serbian militias displaced all Muslim Bosniaks from vast tracts of land in eastern Bosnia because they wanted to homogenize the territory and merge it with the independent Serbian state; their political goal incentivized them to perpetrate extensive ethnic cleansing across a wide region. In Lebanon, on the other hand, sectarian militias would often ethnically cleanse certain villages or neighborhoods while leaving nearby locations intact. I do not want to overstate the rationality of the process, the moderation of perpetrators, or the quality of their intelligence. But compared to violence in disintegrating polities like British India, Yugoslavia, or the Soviet Union, the Lebanese militias operated with remarkable precision. Ethnic cleansing in Lebanon simply does not conform to the Bosnian model, which informs so much of our research and commentary on this topic in both academic and popular discourse.

The Lebanese experience of ethnic cleansing teaches us three major lessons about ethnic conflict, civil wars, and forced migration. First, too much of our research on ethnic cleansing applies primarily to separatist conflicts, but a large minority of civil wars fought across an ethnic cleavage is non-separatist in nature. Non-separatist ethnic wars have predominantly occurred in the Arab world and sub-Saharan Africa, and regional factors—such as shared Arab culture and identity and the African norm against revising international borders—may explain why the two regions have such a prevalence of this type of conflict. In Lebanon specifically, the role of geography may have been decisive: Christian militias in particular might have pushed to partition the country if it was not already so territorially small, demographically intermixed, and economically interdependent. More generally, a lot of multiethnic countries that experience civil wars are former colonies. Perhaps we have too readily assumed that ethnic conflict in such countries will normally evolve into struggles for national self-determination, which may be true in South and Southeast Asia but much less so in other postcolonial regions. Interestingly, the dominant post-independence political responses to colonial state systems in Latin America and the Arab world were the pan-American and pan-Arab unification movements of Simón Bolívar and Gamal Abdel Nasser, respectively, rather than ethnic separatism.

Second, the way that militias in Lebanon behaved highlights the central role of intelligence, and the techniques that militants used to distinguish between neutral and hostile non-coethnics in this conflict. The key insights in this regard are how militias developed extremely close ties to residents in many local communities where they operated and how these ties provided innumerable channels to receive detailed and continuous information. These dynamics were most pronounced among Maronite Catholic and Druze militias, where the corresponding communities mobilized to a particularly impressive extent in support of certain militias. The Lebanese Sunni community did not mobilize militarily in quite the same way because they counted on the Palestinian movement to supply a formidable war machine in service of their political goals. However, all major factions of the PLO had Lebanese recruits as well, mostly Sunni Muslims. The largest factions also developed close operational ties to local Lebanese affiliates, such as the Lebanese Communist Party and the Organization for Communist Action, and some sponsored Lebanese surrogate groups like Al-Mourabitoun and the Nasserist 24 October Movement. Through these political alliances, the Palestinian movement retained deep and strong ties to broad segments of the Lebanese population. As a result, prewar patterns of interethnic trust and cooperation sometimes survived as local islands of peace, even as the country descended into a black sea of sectarian mistrust and armed conflict.

Third, militia behavior highlights how the role of ethnicity differed over time and space within this complex conflict. Debates over the role of ethnicity in civil war violence have generally lacked this kind of nuance. Existing work tends either to elevate ethnicity to the primary explanatory variable of conflict and violence, endowing it with unique abilities to shape preferences and behavior, or to write it off as a macro-level cleavage largely inconsequential to micro-level outcomes shaped by opportunism and rapid shifts in loyalties. While many conflicts may conform to either one of these two explanatory models, my argument and empirical results reveal a vast landscape of middle ground in between these two opposite extremes. Ethnicity is one kind of information: Sometimes militias can access more detailed intelligence and have no need to use this crude indicator of individual allegiances. In other situations, it may be the only information they possess. In Lebanon, both coalitions were guilty of sometimes using ethnicity as a heuristic device when assessing individual loyalties. The quantitative evidence also confirms that Christian groups were more likely to use violence against Palestinians than either coalition was to attack any other ethnic, national, or sectarian community. This finding conforms to the insight that Christian militias' tolerance of, and moderation against, Lebanese Muslims did not quite extend to the Palestinian community. Christian militias may also have been more prone to engage in ethnic cleansing in general, which could reflect the fact that the Palestinian factions had more Lebanese Christian sympathizers than the Christian militias had Muslim ones, although the quantitative evidence is mixed on this point.

The end of the Cold War and the rise of several prominent ethnic wars, which merited international intervention, forced scholars of international security to shift focus away from Great Power politics to the dynamics of substate conflict and violence. Over the past two decades a new wave of scholarship has produced an impressive body of research using state-of-the-art social science methods to elucidate the processes of political violence that bedevil large swathes of the contemporary world. We have learned many key lessons about civil war onset, dynamics of violence, rebel governance, international peacekeeping missions, and the prospects of partition for ending ethnic conflicts. While these topics are interrelated, this book deals primarily with the politics of violence in civil wars. Scholars increasingly agree on a few general principles that help explain this phenomenon. We know beyond reasonable doubt that many armed groups perpetrate savage and heinous acts of violence against civilians because it advances their military prospects, that many seemingly irrational acts nevertheless follow a strategic calculus, and that access to information usually influences what kinds of violence militants employ. My argument in these pages contributes to this body of scholarship by exploring the role that ethnicity plays in processes of selective and indiscriminate violence, the ways militias collect intelligence, and how ethnic identity compares to other sources of information.

Armed conflicts generate forced displacement of civilians because of rational strategic behavior by combatants and other processes inherent in the nature of civil war. As a result, it is not difficult to explain why the number of forcibly displaced persons across the world has shown a monotonic increase over the past several decades and currently stands at its highest level since at least 1945. According to the United Nations High Commissioner for Refugees (UNHCR), there are over 65 million displaced persons in the world at present: in other words, more than one percent of the global population is currently displaced from their original homes because of armed conflict.[1] The Middle East and North Africa region is particularly affected by this global crisis, in two ways: about 40 percent of those people forcibly displaced hail from a Middle Eastern country, and about the same share are currently hosted in this region as well, even though the region only holds about 6 percent of the global population.[2] Countries in the region shoulder the burden both of losing productive members of their population and of hosting people in need. Civil wars generate displacement, and the Middle East has experienced a number of remarkably destructive civil wars over the past two decades.

Implications for Future Research

What avenues should future research take to improve our understanding of political violence and help us develop policies that further political stability and alleviate suffering across the world? Several topics follow directly from my theoretical argument, case study, and empirical findings. First, ethnic cleansing is a complex phenomenon that serves different purposes for different perpetrators. Much previous research has simply assumed that ethnic cleansing involves an armed group trying to maximize displacement of non-coethnic civilians, subject to constraints on military capabilities.

Yet in Lebanon we find that militias typically used ethnic cleansing as a last resort and that they usually sought to moderate violence against civilians. We know that the practice of ethnic cleansing can serve either military or political goals, that its prevalence may differ across wars fought in symmetric and nonsymmetric fashion, and that its incidence may reflect constraints on manpower. But the fact that ethnic cleansing in Lebanon differs from its practice elsewhere in multiple dimensions suggests that we are still learning new things about the strategic calculus behind ethnic violence and that other conflicts may hold additional lessons. In particular, the general category of non-separatist ethnic wars remains understudied and merits more attention, especially by scholars who study the Middle East and sub-Saharan Africa, where most cases have occurred.

Second, my argument provides a novel mechanism for understanding how militias gather intelligence. While scholars increasingly use the conceptual framework of selective versus indiscriminate violence to explain violence against civilians, we are still learning about how militias collect intelligence in their theaters of operation. We have seen how militias rely on soliciting collaboration from self-interested local residents, collude with local elites, study prewar election results, and even use the process of displacement itself to generate information and increase the legibility of populations under their control.[3] The vast range of techniques used in collecting and processing intelligence suggests that we have only begun to fully understand this topic and that we still do not have a unified general theory—or perhaps even a complete set of conceptual tools—for describing this phenomenon. Furthermore, the prominence of recent U.S. counterinsurgency operations in both popular and scholarly discourse may have biased the field toward studying other combatants with very poor local intelligence about their surroundings, such as Soviet counterinsurgency in Ukraine and Russia's wars in Chechnya. My work details why and how indigenous military forces have far superior capabilities to foreign occupiers. Exploring new case studies should add new insights to our understanding of intelligence collection in civil wars, and further research should strive to move this field toward greater conceptual unity.

Third, a related issue concerns the role of urban warfare. Lebanon is a small, dense, and highly urbanized country, and I show how this social density was a key factor in how militias collected intelligence. This factor may limit the generalizability of my argument to countries like Chad, which had a non-separatist ethnic war but ranks among the poorest and least developed countries in the world. Its primarily rural population remains scattered across vast territories and is largely segregated by religion, language, and tribe. On the other hand, many scholars predict that urban warfare may become more frequent as the global population increasingly settles in urban locations.[4] If so, the Lebanese experience may be a harbinger of what warfare will look like as other dense and highly urbanized multiethnic societies descend into armed conflict. Perhaps urban intermixing will provide other militias with the requisite information to more frequently use selective violence instead of ethnic cleansing, potentially reducing the global incidence of the latter phenomenon. In multiethnic societies, urbanization generally produces greater ethnic intermixing; while intermixing may lead to competition over material goods and political power, it could also foster tolerance and diffusion of information across ethnic boundaries.

Fourth, the empirical evidence from Lebanon confirms the value of mixed-methods research designs, in general, and of combining micro-level quantitative evidence and primary interviews, in particular. Lebanon presents a particularly difficult context to gather data because various important stakeholders have an interest in keeping many data sources out of date (such as the voter registration rolls) or unavailable (such as documentation of wartime crimes). Nevertheless, with long stretches of time in the field and with ingenuity, it proves possible to piece together a range of sources into a coherent dataset. Micro-level data, in turn, provides very powerful, transparent, and falsifiable tests of a range of empirical implications. Furthermore, in contrast to its deleterious effects on the environment for quantitative data collection, the general amnesty law that followed the Lebanese civil war provides remarkably propitious opportunities for doing primary interviews. Most militia operatives survived the war, remain in the country, are still of prime age, and can express themselves openly without fear of legal consequences. Several scholars have availed themselves of these opportunities in recent years to study either wartime dynamics or postwar reconstruction using Lebanon as their primary case.[5] However, no previous work has combined the opportunities to conduct interviews with rigorous micro-level data to study wartime processes.

These empirical results permit a few observations about future methodological directions in conflict studies. While scholars have made enormous contributions to the study of political violence using an amazing array of methods and approaches, mixed-methods research designs based on extensive fieldwork remains perhaps the single most prominent way to study substate conflict. Each new case seems to teach us new insights, and there is plenty of promise in researchers exploring new and understudied cases. One downside of this approach is that the requisite level of country specialization places great demands on time and effort; one researcher cannot reproduce the level of empirical evidence this book brings to bear on Lebanon across several conflict zones. Some scholars have solved this problem by combining in-depth case studies using micro-level data with additional cross-country data, and future researchers may want to emulate this approach to the greatest extent possible.

On a related note, in recent years the wider community of political science researchers has placed a premium on research designs that include experimental techniques for causal identification. Causal identification has proved a valuable tool in social science, including in conflict studies. However, no institutional review board will —or should—permit researchers to manipulate outcomes involving violence, while survey experiments primarily capture public opinion and the set of interesting questions about public opinion and political violence remains rather narrow. We cannot limit our studies of armed conflicts to specific topics where researchers happen to discover clever natural experiments. Consequently, we should expect conflict studies to remain a field that primarily uses other techniques—such as observational data and interviews—to study topics that we cannot ignore because of their grave consequences for foreign, security, and humanitarian policy.

As for future research topics we have an increasingly sophisticated understanding of the conflict processes that generate displacement but a more limited understanding of how forcibly displaced persons behave. This deficiency is alarming because the scale of the global refugee problem is immense in magnitude, growing at a rapid clip, and has frustrated all attempts by international policymakers to address its roots and effects. The nexus of issues surrounding displaced persons, refugees, and conflict-related migration therefore stands out as the next frontier in conflict research. We know that civilians in conflict zones have agency, that they choose whether to cooperate with armed groups according to a strategic logic of their own, and that they frequently choose to depart their homes as a rational response to the risk of facing violence. Traditionally, humanitarian and aid agencies assumed that displacement was an indirect consequence of armed combat; that during spells of displacement, refugees primarily need temporary assistance with food and shelter for basic survival; and that once warfare subsided, displaced persons would mostly return to their original homes as if through magnetic attraction.[6] Contemporary policymakers reject these assumptions as flawed and unrealistic, but we do not have much work on how forcibly displaced persons behave either during their spell of displacement or when making decisions about whether to return after civil wars end.

This intellectual shortcoming frustrates our ability to design adequate policy responses. Future research should address a range of topics, starting with questions about how forcibly displaced behave during their spell of displacement. Recent research emphasizes that we need to study forcibly displaced persons as individual agents making rational decisions rather than passive actors merely waiting for the tides of war to turn. If displaced persons are strategic agents with better knowledge of how to deploy their resources to increase their own welfare than any bureaucrat could ever hope to attain, then we need to better include their behavior and decision making as key drivers and inputs of humanitarian relief efforts and other related policy areas. This insight pertains to decisions that individuals make during their spell of forced displacement for instance about labor market participation, family decisions such as marriage and child rearing, and whether to enroll their children in schools. In addition, we want to know more about under what conditions forcibly displaced persons choose to return to their original homes after wars end.[7] If we better understand the decision to return, we can better determine whether to respond to spells of displacement by focusing policy on return migration, reintegration in the host society, or resettlement into a third location.

Another important topic, which pertains immediately to the study of political violence, is the politics of refugee communities during their spell of displacement. For instance, in the late 1960s the Palestinian refugee camps in Jordan and Lebanon became hotbeds of radical politics and armed struggle; this armed movement produced civil wars in Jordan and Lebanon without improving their odds of returning to their original homes in present-day Israel. What will happen if Syrian refugees remain in Jordan, Lebanon, and Turkey indefinitely? At a more general level, we need to better understand the conditions that make refugees and their communities likely to radicalize and to engage in violence. What factors contribute to making refugee communities support and participate in armed organizations, and when does political mobilization take nonviolent shapes?

Policy Implications

What lessons do my theoretical argument and empirical results hold for policymakers about dealing with war-torn countries? One major lesson relates to peacekeeping operations. In general, peacekeeping missions face constraints on their personnel and need to deploy forces in an economical and efficient manner. Earlier work on ethnic conflict often focused on how intermixed areas should be most prone to violence as their denizens are inherently vulnerable to actions of the other group causing fear and insecurity.[8] Conversely, my argument shows why intermixed areas may be less prone to extensive violence since residents can learn about individual non-coethnics through social intermixing, while homogenous enclaves are most prone to ethnic cleansing. A related peacekeeping lesson concerns the value of keeping combatants physically and geographically separated from each other. The two worst episodes of ethnic cleansing during the Lebanese civil war—the eviction of Muslims from East Beirut by Christian militias in 1975–1976 and the displacement of Christians by Druze in Mount Lebanon during 1983–1985—both resulted from instances where two sets of hostile militias contested the same geographic space. Armed groups ruling space with non-coethnics present does not necessarily result in violence, but efforts by hostile militias to mobilize those non-coethnics almost certainly will.

Another lesson involves postwar reconstruction, reconciliation, and return migration after non-separatist ethnic wars. Separatist wars may end with either the successful partition of a country by separatist rebels or some form of accommodation for minority claims to national recognition and self-determination by the government.[9] Non-separatist wars, in contrast, generally end with two or more ethnic groups coexisting in the aftermath of bloodshed. Since the former enemies must coexist by necessity, reconciliation takes on added urgency as lingering resentments could cause renewed political instability, violence, or war. However, while we know a tremendous amount about how violence, vicious elites, and other factors cause ethnic polarization and conflict, we know very little about how to deescalate tensions and conflict between different ethnic communities and heal the wounds and trauma of the past. Like so many proverbial devices, ethnic relations are easier to break apart than to put back together. One would imagine that efforts of transitional justice—including documenting abuse, prosecuting perpetrators, compensating victims, and issuing apologies—should facilitate reconciliation, but more research is needed to clarify the mechanisms involved and the relative importance of these different components of reconciliation processes. Lebanon demonstrably chose the opposite approach with its general amnesty law, which seems intended to sweep the war into collective amnesia. What are the costs and benefits of this approach? We do not know at present and have few means of systematically evaluating this path versus other conceivable approaches.

As for return migration, one important lesson is that it could actually be more difficult to induce victims of selective violence to return to their original homes than those who suffered ethnic cleansing. This counterintuitive expectation results whenever selective violence affected intermixed locations while ethnic cleansing targeted homogenous enclaves. The reason is that those who suffered selective violence know that they were targeted because of their individual characteristics, and they may be more likely to face returning to their original homes in intermixed locations where the non-coethnic perpetrators still live. Victims of ethnic cleansing, on the other hand, may be aware that their displacement had nothing to do with their person and may be more likely to hail from homogenous enclaves where they would not be living next to non-coethnics if they were to return. As a result, ethnic violence may exacerbate ethnic separation in society, not only by generating displacement but also by inhibiting return migration into intermixed areas. This outcome is deeply regrettable since most recent research suggests that multiethnic societies are more resilient to political conflict and tension when members of different ethnic groups mix in social, residential, and professional life.[10] Again, one would look to transitional justice efforts as the most logical starting point for increasing victims' willingness to return to intermixed areas, although more research is needed to better understand the effects of such programs and their relative importance compared to other factors such as economic reconstruction.

Finally, one major set of policy implications concerns the prospects for partition as a model for solving ethnic conflict, especially regarding the contemporary Arab world. There is a rich academic literature on partition as scholars have long contemplated the best institutional arrangements for promoting peaceful coexistence in multiethnic societies.[11] One school of thought promotes separation of different groups and partition as the main solution to ethnic wars on the assumption that different ethnic groups are animated with different and competing nationalist ideologies defining group membership and purpose.[12] Trying to merge two such ethnic groups into one coherent nation is a naive, futile, and even potentially dangerous exercise, according to this line of argument. The other school of thought emphasizes the instrumentality of ethnicity, rather than its ideological content, as a powerful tool for building and sustaining successful communities.[13] If intra-ethnic cooperation is driven more by shared language, preferences, culture, knowledge, or social capital than by ideology, then there is more scope for designing institutions that can include other groups. The horrid history of partition between India and Pakistan shows that the cure of partition is sometimes worse than the disease of ethnic tensions, while partitioning Ireland from the United Kingdom did not prevent "The Troubles" from erupting half a century later.

Lebanon offers several lessons in why partition may prove undesirable, if not disastrous, as a solution to many civil wars fought across ethnic divides. The most obvious lesson is that Lebanon experienced a non-separatist war, where neither party wanted to see the country divided into separate nation states, for reasons discussed above, including its small geographic size, demographic intermixing, and economic interdependence. Furthermore, while theories of partition typically assume conflict between two groups, Lebanon has numerous ethnoreligious communities and constantly evolving political fault lines. The natural division of Lebanon in 1975 might have seemed a partition between Christians and Muslims. Today, however, its central political conflict pits Sunni versus Shia Muslims, who under partition would constitute even larger blocs of an even smaller country. Such a demographic configuration would most likely have made the Sunni–Shia conflict more intense and more severe.[14] The Christian community today is largely divided politically between close allies of the Shia movement Hezbollah and the Sunni party Future Movement.

The Arab world is currently ravaged by persistent political instability and violence, affecting most of the territory from Libya to Iraq. One line of argument claims that political instability stems from how most Arab states are artificial entities created by European imperial planners in the aftermath of World War I, including through the infamous Sykes–Picot Agreement.[15] The solution, according to proponents of this argument, is to repartition Arab states like Syria and Iraq into smaller and more "natural" polities, each dominated by a single ethnic or sectarian group. Yet repartitioning Arab states today looks no more appealing than partitioning Lebanon in the 1970s. Such a project would run into all the same problems, including the non-separatist nature of intra-Arab conflicts, the realities of demographic intermixing, the economic interdependence of resultant units, and the presence of numerous ethnic and sectarian communities with ever-shifting political alliances. Furthermore, like the partitions of Greece and Turkey or India and Pakistan, repartitioning the Arab states would most likely generate new international conflicts. For instance, an independent Iraqi Kurdistan would face tensions with Turkey over its relations with Turkish Kurds. An independent Sunni country of present-day eastern Syria and western Iraq might become dominated by fundamentalist groups, such as the Islamic State. Iran would likely dominate an independent Shia Iraq, but Saudi Arabia and its Gulf Cooperation Council allies would not tolerate an Iranian client on their doorstep. These are just a few examples of the tensions and instability that would follow from creating new states. Repartitioning the Arab world would create far more problems than it solves.

This last point touches on an important problem bedeviling many attempts to end civil wars: the role of outside powers. All militias in Lebanon quickly acquired foreign sponsors, who were motivated primarily by regional security rivalries. As a result, no side could hope to score a decisive military victory.[16] The Christian militias were essentially a defeated military force by the late summer of 1976, and if not for outside intervention, the civil war may have ended at this point. However, Syrian president Hafez al-Assad intervened at that point to prevent Lebanon from becoming a de facto PLO-controlled state. Christian leaders initially greeted the Syrians as liberators before quickly turning against their erstwhile allies and courting Israeli intervention, which eventually materialized in 1982. Israeli involvement in turn caused Syria and Iran to increase their involvement by turning local proxy groups into major armies. No party desired partition of Lebanon, and with a considerable number of internal and external potential spoilers, it was difficult to reach a negotiated settlement. The role of outside powers is one major reason why this conflict became so intractable and lasted for a full fifteen years.

This situation has many parallels with Iraq and Syria today, where outside powers like Iran, Saudi Arabia, Turkey, and others fuel competing armed factions. One lesson from Lebanon for contemporary regional conflicts is that sometimes it takes a regional settlement to put an end to political instability and armed conflict. European powers tried—with varying levels of success—to end persistent instability with regional settlements such as the Congress of Vienna and the Treaty of Versailles. In Lebanon the civil war only ended with a regional settlement in 1991 because of an entirely unrelated event, the Gulf War against Saddam Hussein. The United States granted Syria hegemony over Lebanon in return for participation in its UN-sanctioned international coalition. It is difficult to predict what it would require today to bring all regional players together in a grand diplomatic bargain for regional stability, but it is also hard to see any other way in which the contemporary regional instability would subside.

Notes

Introduction

1. In these pages I use the terms "ethnic" and "sectarian" interchangeably, as the former is more common in the literature on conflict and violence while the latter is more common in discussions about the Arab world in general and Lebanon in particular. Both terms refer to social identities, perceived as ascriptive and descent-based categories, which individuals cannot easily manipulate or change (see Cammett 2014, chap. 1; Chandra 2006).
2. The United Nations (1994, para. 130) defines ethnic cleansing as "a purposeful policy designed by one ethnic or religious group to remove by violent and terror-inspiring means the civilian population of another ethnic or religious group from certain geographic territory." Among political scientists, Zeynep Bulutgil (2016, 1) defines the concept as "wholesale deportations and/or killings that target ethnic groups." I define ethnic cleansing as intentional forced displacement of one ethnic group by another. I consider this practice conceptually distinct from mass killings or genocide (see Mann 2004; Valentino 2004). While I study forced displacement during wars, it also happens in peacetime, as shown by Kelly Greenhill (2010).
3. Ministry of the Displaced 1996, 10.
4. Out of the dystopic rubble of Karantina, meanwhile, award-winning Lebanese architect Bernard Khoury designed the famous nightclub B 018 as an underground bunker with a drawbridge-style roof that opens up in the small

hours of the night to let revelers enjoy the moon and stars. See its website, http://www.b018.com/, for further information.
5. Birnir 2007; Chandra 2004; Horowitz 1985; Posner 2005.
6. Kaufmann 1996; Posen 1993.
7. Balcells and Steele 2016; Somer 2001; Steele 2009.
8. Cunningham 2014; Griffiths 2016; Petersen 2002, 2011; Toft 2003, 2012.
9. Goddard 2006; Hassner 2009; Johnson and Toft 2014; Kaufman 2001.
10. Bulutgil (2016) discusses the history of ethnic cleansing in Eastern Europe, an area of the world that has been particularly affected by this phenomenon.
11. Kumar 1997; Kuperman 2004.
12. Fearon and Laitin 1996; Gutierrez-Sanin and Wood 2014; Straus 2015; Thaler 2012.
13. Straus 2015.
14. Out of 136 civil wars since 1945, Monica Toft (2010) finds that 48 to 58 out of 84 identity-based civil wars involved claims to national self-determination, depending on coding rules.
15. Guevara 1961; Kalyvas 2006; Lawrence 1926; Lyall and Wilson 2009; Nagl 2005; Popkin 1979; Thompson 1966.
16. Balcells 2017; Hägerdal 2019; Kalyvas 2006; Lichtenheld 2020; Steele 2011, 2017; Zhukov 2015.
17. Bates 2011; Parkinson 2013; Petersen 2001; Staniland 2014; Wood 2003; Weinstein 2007.
18. Wood 2003.
19. Weinstein 2007.
20. Nagl 2005; Thompson 1966.
21. Posen 1993; van Evera 1994, 2001.
22. Kalyvas 2006; Kalyvas and Kocher 2007a.
23. Kalyvas and Kocher 2007a, 187; Picard 2002, 109–10.
24. Khalaf 2002; Makdisi 2000.
25. Cammett 2014; Corstange 2016.
26. Azevedo 1998; Driscoll 2015; Minter 1994; Nolutshungu 1996; Rubin 1993; Sayigh 1999.
27. The issue of ethnicity remains a deeply controversial topic in Lebanese politics. Sunni Muslims generally affirm their Arab identity, while many Christians reject such notions, and some argue that they are descendants of ancient Phoenicia. In general, most Lebanese are quite uncomfortable with the moniker "ethnic" altogether. Armenians and Kurds, however, speak other languages than Arabic and are not considered to be Arabs. Armenians divide further into distinct confessional groups, of which Armenian Orthodox is the largest; most Kurds are Sunni Muslims.
28. The Druze faith is an offshoot of Shia Islam.

29. Eid 2010; IFES 2009.
30. Lebanese Information Center 2013; Verdeil 2007.
31. There are at present over four hundred thousand registered Palestinian refugees in Lebanon, although detailed survey work, for instance, by Jad Chaaban and colleagues (2010), suggests that the true number is now below three hundred thousand as many have left in clandestine ways to seek economic and other opportunities elsewhere especially in Western Europe and the Persian Gulf.
32. With the Lebanese population currently estimated at about 4 million resident citizens, the refugees thus make up at least 20 percent of the total population and may be as many as one-third. The refugees are Syrian citizens and increasingly lack legal status in Lebanon; it remains unclear whether they will stay in Lebanon permanently or whether they will one day return to Syria (see Hägerdal 2018; Janmyr 2016; Mourad 2017). Lebanon also hosts a sizable community of foreign workers, largely from South and Southeast Asia, employed in domestic labor.
33. El-Khazen 2000; Hanf 1993; Salibi 1976; Traboulsi 2007.
34. See Norton (1987, 2007) on the rise of Shia political movements in Lebanon; Nasr (2006) for a regional perspective; and Hägerdal and Krause (2020) on Sunni-Shia violence in Lebanon during 2013–2014 connected to the Syrian civil war.
35. Many former militia leaders at this point had seats in parliament and thus effectively voted to pardon their own crimes.
36. Quilty 2007.
37. Most of the major TV stations that dominate viewership in Lebanon today are affiliated with political parties. Examples include LBC (Lebanese Forces), OTV (Free Patriotic Movement), Al-Manar (Hezbollah), NBN (Amal), and Future TV (Future Movement).
38. Fujii 2010; Sluka 2000.
39. The key works are Labaki and Abou Rjeily (1993) and Kasparian, Beaudoin, and Abou (1995). Nasr (2013) contains several academic articles, originally published in various outlets in French, collected into one volume, and translated into Arabic.

1. Ethnic Violence in Non-Separatist Wars

1. For a recent print edition, see Clausewitz 1976.
2. In international wars, states often target civilian populations and centers of economic production with enormous levels of violence (see Downes 2008; Pape 1996).

3. Balcells 2017; Ghodes 2020; Hägerdal 2019a; Kalyvas 2006; Lichtenheld 2020; Steele 2011, 2017; Zhukov 2015.
4. The literature on assassinations is very limited, but we have some evidence that high-profile assassinations can produce large political change including in wartime settings (see Jones and Olken 2009). Jenna Jordan (2009) argues that leadership decapitation rarely defeats armed groups but fails to deal with the selection issues that arise when the strategy is more commonly used against particularly powerful or persistent groups.
5. Kalyvas 2006; Lyall and Wilson 2009; Popkin 1979.
6. Stathis Kalyvas (2006) and Kalyvas and Matthew Kocher (2007b) argue, based on both theory and empirics, that collective punishment should be an inherently flawed strategy, while Jason Lyall (2009) makes the opposite argument. Yuri Zhukov (2014) points to a bounded answer: collective punishment can be successful but mostly in settings of asymmetric warfare where both the government and rebels are using brutal levels of violence to control a population and one side can simply dwarf the efforts of the other.
7. See Balcells and Steele 2016; Lichtenheld 2020; Steele 2011, 2017; Zhukov 2015.
8. Martin 1998; Zhukov 2015.
9. Balcells and Steele 2016; Steele 2011, 2017.
10. Kaufmann 1996; Posen 1993. The phrase about draining the sea is commonly attributed to Mao Zedong.
11. The basic dynamic of ascribing views or behaviors to individuals based on their ethnic group membership is not restricted to episodes of political violence but also pertains, for instance, to electoral politics (see Alesina, Baqir, and Easterly 1999; Birnir 2007; Chandra 2004; Habyarimana et al. 2007).
12. On cross-cutting cleavages based on economic interests, see Christia 2008; Kalyvas 2006; Mazur 2019. For discussion about the effects of left-wing and secular ideologies on inhibiting ethnic violence, see Thaler 2012; Bulutgil 2016.
13. Chandra 2004. However, correctly identifying ethnic identities is not always a trivial task; James Habyarimana and colleagues (2010) make this point and find experimental evidence in its support. Armed groups in various conflicts have devised numerous ways to deal with this challenge, such as by asking individuals to pronounce certain words or to recite nationalist songs or religious phrases.
14. Beath, Christia, and Enikolopov 2011; Berman, Shapiro, and Felter 2011; Friedman 2011; Lyall 2010.
15. Mobilization can be sudden, rapid, extensive, and unpredictable (see Granovetter 1978; Kuran 1995; Somer 2001).
16. Lyall 2009; Zhukov 2014.
17. See Bulutgil 2016, Cunningham 2014, Griffiths 2016, and Toft 2003, 2012. See also Cunningham, Bakke, and Seymour 2012.
18. Goddard 2006; Hassner 2009; Johnson and Toft 2014; Toft 2003.

19. Anderson 1983; Gellner 1983; Horowitz 1985; Petersen 2002.
20. Bulutgil 2010, 2016; Kumar 1997; Petersen 2002, 2011; Weidmann 2011.
21. This conceptual distinction is an analytical choice of mine. Others define ethnic cleansing in such a way that genocide becomes a subset thereof, such as Zeynep Bulutgil (2016, 1), who defines ethnic cleansing as "wholesale deportations and/or killings that target ethnic groups."
22. See Mann 2004; Montalvo and Reynal-Querol 2008; Valentino 2004. For models of how elites may stir up ethnic animosity for self-interested reasons, including increasing electoral support, see Fearon and Laitin 2000; Glaeser 2005; Kaufman 2001; Mansfield and Snyder 1995; Wilkinson 2004.
23. Gutierrez-Sanin and Wood 2014; Straus 2015.
24. Blaydes 2018; Tripp 2000.
25. The classic argument by Machiavelli dates back to 1532; see, for instance, Machiavelli (2003) for a recent version.
26. Fearon and Laitin 1996.
27. Freedman 1989; Schelling 1960.
28. Bates 2011; Weinstein 2007; Weinstein and Francisco 2005.
29. Weinstein and Humphreys 2006.
30. See Marx 1998; Patterson 1975; Sidanius and Pratto 1999. Manuel Vogt (2019) shows how economic stratification of ethnic groups may reduce the likelihood of violent conflict.
31. Olsson and Siba 2013.
32. Hoover Green 2016; Weinstein and Humphreys 2006; Wood 2009.
33. Bulutgil 2016; Cunningham 2014; Griffiths 2016; Toft 2003, 2012.
34. This is true of combatants in most influential studies of the micro-level dynamics of civil war violence, including Balcells (2010, 2017), Kalyvas (2006), Steele (2011, 2017).
35. This amendment removes one case in Asia (Indonesia, 1945–1949) and nine cases in sub-Saharan Africa.
36. Reno 2011.
37. Both resources are available online. See The World Factbook, https://www.cia.gov/library/publications/the-world-factbook/; and Ethnologue: Languages of the World, https://www.ethnologue.com/.
38. The only three cases recorded elsewhere are Cyprus (1963–1964), Afghanistan (1978–2001), and Tajikistan (1992–1997).
39. Duursma 2020; Englebert 2009; Herbst 2000; Michalopoulos and Papaioannou 2016; Reno 2011.
40. Kerr 1971; Seale 1965.
41. Balcells and Steele 2016; Bulutgil 2016; Downes 2008; Kaufmann 1996.
42. Roger Petersen (2001) discusses a ladder of qualitatively different levels of support that individuals may provide to armed groups. Sarah Parkinson (2013) and

Paul Staniland (2014) also emphasize the range of differentiated nonmilitary roles that individuals may serve in as part of the ecological support systems that sustain most armed groups.

43. Keegan 2003; Lowenthal 2008; O'Hanlon 2009.
44. Balcells 2017; Bateson 2017; Daly 2016; Kalyvas 2006; Popkin 1979.
45. Greitens 2016.
46. Balcells 2017; Kalyvas 2003, 2006.
47. See, for instance, Bates 2011; Staniland 2012, 2014; and Weinstein 2007. On the general topic of rebel governance, see Arjona 2016; Arjona, Kasfir, and Mampilly 2015; Mampilly 2012; on the role of socialization in sustaining terrorist groups, see Abrahms 2008.
48. Not all rebels create sufficiently powerful military forces to fight through conventional warfare. Insurgency warfare involves one weaker side eschewing conventional battles because they do not have sufficient military power to contest them, while symmetric nonconventional warfare involves two weak combatants typically unable to sustain regular front lines or systematic strategic campaigns (see Kalyvas and Balcells 2010).
49. Olsson and Siba 2013; Weinstein and Humphreys 2006.
50. Cohen 2016.
51. Finkel 2017; Parkinson 2013; Petersen 2001; Staniland 2014; Wood 2003, 2008.
52. Habyarimana et al. 2007; Varshney 2002. For classic treatments of the conditions favoring interethnic coexistence, see Horowitz 1985; Lijphart 1977.
53. Alexander and Christia 2011.
54. Varshney 2002.
55. Scholars in this tradition tend to be more optimistic about the possibilities of designing institutions that can mitigate the challenges of multiethnic societies and less sanguine about partition as a peacetime or postconflict solution. See, for instance, Sambanis 2000; Habyarimana et al. 2008.
56. Marx 1998; Patterson 1975; Sidanius and Pratto 1999.
57. Fujii 2008; Petersen 2002.
58. Varshney 2002.
59. For the former view, see Geertz (1963), Kaufmann (1996), Posen (1993), Van Evera (1994, 2001); for the latter, see Kalyvas (2003, 2006) and Kalyvas and Kocher (2007a).
60. Civilians often choose to flee conflict zones not only because of security concerns but also because of indirect war-related processes, such as economic decline. For more work on when individuals choose to flee, see Davenport, Moore, and Poe (2003), Engel and Ibáñez (2007), Serrano (2011), and Steele (2009).
61. It is well known in social science that cooperation can arise even among groups that act out of pure self-interest; my argument is that such patterns of

cooperation may sometimes survive from prewar politics into active warzones (see Axelrod 1981; Fehr and Gachter 2000). Evgeny Finkel (2017) and Oliver Kaplan (2017) discuss how civilians may organize during civil wars to prevent violence.

2. The Lebanese Civil War, 1975–1990

1. Saadeh, Brunnquell, and Couderc 2005. At least fifty-six Muslims were killed during this massacre, although the number may be as high as several hundred (see ICTJ 2013, 12–13).
2. ICTJ 2013.
3. Randal 1983, 112–16.
4. Schulhofer-Wohl (2020, 54–91) is a strong exception.
5. Khalaf 2002; Makdisi 2000. See also Haddad (2011) for an excellent discussion of the development of distinct Sunni and Shia sectarian identities in 1990s Iraq, a process with many parallels to Lebanese history despite occurring a century and a half later.
6. Traboulsi 2007. The Sublime Porte, used metaphorically to refer to the central government of the Ottoman Empire, literally refers to the outer gate of the Topkapi Palace in Istanbul.
7. Barr 2011; Cleveland 2004; Patel 2016; Rogan 2009, 2015; Traboulsi 2007.
8. Salibi 1988.
9. Suleiman 1967.
10. The party is fiercely secular but gathers its deepest support among Greek Orthodox Christians; coincidentally, the areas it wants to unify would constitute the largest concentration of Greek Orthodox in the Eastern Mediterranean.
11. Rougier 2015; Seale 2010.
12. Seale 1965. The King–Crane Commission that visited the Levant on behalf of U.S. president Woodrow Wilson in the aftermath of World War I documented this near-universal support during innumerable town halls, elite meetings, and popular petitions. See Rogan 2009.
13. Rougier 2015.
14. For a description of contemporary Shia politics in Lebanon, see Norton (1987). For the Druze, see Lapousterle 1982; Richani 1998.
15. Norton 2007.
16. Khoury 1983, 1987; Seale 2010.
17. The Fertile Crescent—literally a crescent-shaped band of arable land—stretches across the Levant (Syria, Lebanon, Jordan, and Mandate Palestine) and most of present-day Iraq. See Seale 1965.
18. Picard 2002, chap. 6.

19. See chapter 3 and especially figure 3.1 for an estimate of prewar sectarian settlement patterns.
20. See Gilmour (1983, chap. 3), for a discussion of the democratic system in postindependence Lebanon, including its shortcomings. Jeffrey Karam (2017) discusses the underappreciated ways in which the consociational model incentivizes cross-sectarian alliances. See also Lijphart 1977.
21. Karam 2020; Kerr 1971; Seale 1965; Traboulsi 2007, 133–37.
22. The UAR caused ripple waves across the entire Arab world. Only the intervention of thousands of British paratroopers prevented Jordanian Army officers from overthrowing the Hashemite Monarchy and merging their country with the UAR as well. Iraqi officers staged a coup in Baghdad ostensibly to merge their country as well, although they later had second thoughts when the UAR proved autocratic and unstable.
23. Lijphart 1977.
24. The most detailed, nuanced, and rigorous accounts of the outbreak of civil war in Lebanon are El-Khazen 2000; Hanf 1993; Salibi 1976; but see also Gilmour 1983; Khalaf 2002; Makdisi and Sadaka 2005; Picard 2002; Traboulsi 2007 for additional perspectives.
25. Hourani and Shehadi 1992.
26. Gilmour 1983, 42.
27. Fisk 1990; Gilmour 1983; Traboulsi 2007.
28. Among the tiny number of very wealthy Lebanese is a strong overrepresentation of Christians, although many are Greek Orthodox or Greek Catholic rather than Maronite. In general, the Christian and Sunni communities had relatively similar distributions of their members across different social classes (see Haley and Snider 1979). The Shia community had a noticeable concentration of both urban and rural poor, and significantly smaller shares of middle class, upper-middle class, and wealthy families than other communities.
29. Fawwaz Traboulsi (2007) argues that the prewar regime represents a strategic alliance between the Maronite community, who wanted to protect their sectarian privileges, and the wealthy business elites who wanted to preserve their economic privileges as socialist ideas swept populist leaders to power in other Arab countries like Egypt, Syria, and Iraq.
30. The history of Palestinian dispossession, refugees, and its movement for national self-determination is recounted in Cobban 1984; Khalidi 2005; Morris 1999; Sayigh 1999.
31. It did deploy locally to buffer between rival militias at various points during the 1970s, although some personnel defected outright to join civil war factions. In the mid-1980s the Army started to fracture entirely as various units came under informal control by whichever militia controlled the local area. In the

late 1980s Army general Michel Aoun made an unsuccessful gamble to reunite the Army and defeat the militias.

32. As noticed by Lewis Snider (1984, 6): "The rudimentary beginnings of this effort are suggested by the fact that wooden dummy rifles were used in the early stages of the program."
33. For organizational charts of both the LNM and PLO, see Salibi (1976, app. 2 and 3). For more background on this alliance and its membership, formation, and expansion, see Khalidi (1979). Michael Johnson (1986) describes the traditional Sunni elites.
34. Hanf 1993, 85; Lapousterle 1982; Richani 1998; Suleiman 1967.
35. Its constituent parties have periodically fought each other for power and influence (see Krause 2013, 2017).
36. While Israel would likely always have remained militarily stronger than the Palestinian movement, one key strategic tenet was to develop major artillery units hidden among the lush hills of south Lebanon within striking distance of Israeli territory. Interestingly, this is precisely the strategy that allowed Hezbollah to fight the Israeli military to a draw in the summer of 2006.
37. Randal 1983, 110.
38. Michael Suleiman (1967) provides an excellent overview of all major Lebanese political parties active in prewar politics. On the origins and history of Katayyib, see Entelis (1974) and Baun (2017). Pierre Gemayel (n.d.), Katayyib's founding president and long-time political leader, has written an exposition of party ideology.
39. In the decades between independence and civil war, the party membership may at times have climbed up to 5 percent Shia Muslim. Some Shia were attracted by its Lebanese nationalist ideology, which they preferred to various pan-Arab schemes that they perceived to be entirely Sunni-dominated (see Entelis 1974).
40. Of course, the self-image as a mass party belies the fact that in 1975 the party was still controlled by its 1932 founder, Pierre Gemayel, whose son Bashir would go on to become the most important Christian leader of the civil war.
41. Dölerud 2011; Snider 1984.
42. This process started in 1976 and was completed in 1980 (see Snider 1984).
43. Fisk 1990.
44. Note, however, that Christian forces ethnically cleansed several Lebanese Sunni and Shia neighborhoods. In addition, one Palestinian refugee camp in an area controlled by Christian forces (Dbayeh, northeast of Beirut) suffered violence but was not comprehensively cleansed.
45. Two of the most outspoken and widely disseminated proponents of this view are trade press accounts by Western observers: Gilmour 1983; Randal 1983.

46. Farid El-Khazen (2000) presents the most sophisticated and nuanced version of this argument.
47. Ajami 1978.
48. On the role of regional politics, see, for instance, Khalaf 2002.
49. Idean Salehyan (2009) and Salehyan and Kristian Skrede Gleditsch (2006) make general arguments about refugees and civil war onset.
50. Westad 2005.
51. See El-Khazen 2000; Salibi 1976.
52. Traboulsi (2007, 238) estimates that the war killed 71,328, injured 97,184, and caused 894,717 people—a third of the prewar population—to emigrate.
53. See ICTJ (2013) and Schulhofer-Wohl (2020, 83–85) for more extensive efforts at periodization.
54. For a history of Syria under Hafez al-Assad, see Seale (1988).
55. The history of Israeli foreign policy in general, including toward Lebanon and its other neighbors, is told by Benny Morris (1999) and Avi Shlaim (2000). On the invasion of Lebanon, see works by Jonathan Randal (1983) and Zeev Schiff and Ehud Yaari (1984).
56. Labaki and Abou Rjeily (1993, 55–59).
57. The data for this figure comes from a report by the Institut Libanais de Developpement Economique et Social (ILDES), a Lebanese research institute (see Abou Rjeily 2008; Camarena and Hägerdal 2020).
58. Traboulsi 2007, 204.
59. Andary 2012; De Clerck 2008; ICTJ 2013, 40–45.
60. Andary 2012; De Clerck 2008; Labaki and Abou Rjeily 1993; Randal 1983, 298–300; Traboulsi 2007, 224.
61. ICTJ 2013, 51–52.
62. Norton 2007.
63. Hanf 1993.
64. For accounts of postwar politics, see Blanford (2006), Leenders (2012), Rizkallah (2017), and Young (2010).
65. Kalyvas and Kocher 2007a.
66. Bulutgil 2016; Kumar 1997; Weidmann 2011.

3. Demographics, Migration, and Violence

1. For more on those and similar experiences, see Gibson (2004) and Nobles (2008).
2. Variations of the main results in this chapter appear in Hägerdal (2019). However, readers familiar with that article will still find novel material in this chapter, including the section on prewar electoral support for Christian parties.

3. Exceptions include a handful of tiny rural locations with fanciful names like "the gas station" (see Eid 2010).
4. For an introduction to the electoral system and districting, see IFES (2009).
5. The 1953 data comes from Hartmann (1980). Data for the 2009 election comes from Information International (2009) and Eid (2010).
6. The key works are Courbage and Fargues (1974), Kasparian, Beaudoin, and Abou (1995), Labaki and Abou Rjeily (1993), and Nasr (2013).
7. It would still have been preferable to use 1953 voter data, which is likely to be a more accurate picture of prewar demographics. However, the 1953 data presented in Hartmann (1980) only captures demographic data at the level of the twenty-eight electoral districts; for 2009 I can access data for over 1,400 cadastral zones. Given the nature of my project and the requirements of statistical analysis, I therefore use figures from the 2009 election as a starting point instead of the 1953 data that I otherwise would prefer.
8. See, for instance, IFES (2018, esp. 10–12). International election monitors consistently note and criticize this feature of Lebanese elections; see, for instance, the reports on the June 2009 election by the National Democratic Institute (NDI 2009) and the European Union Election Observation Mission (EUEOM 2009). Yehia El Amine (2016) describes the general role of the *mukhtar* figure, which helps explain the intricacies of the process. One exception is married women, who join the Civil Registry entry of their husband and vote in his ancestral village.
9. Cammett 2014; Corstange 2016.
10. Boutros Labaki and Khalil Abou Rjeily (1993, 55) describe the displacement of Christians in this area as "quasi-complete."
11. For extensive and detailed work on wartime displacement and postwar return among Christian in the Mount Lebanon region, see Abou Rjeily (2008). Note that many displaced Christians also maintain a social connection to this area through regular visits on weekends and summer holidays rather than as permanent residents (see Camarena and Hägerdal 2020).
12. Eid 2010.
13. Hartmann 1980.
14. UNDP 2006. See, in particular, chapter 1, which deals exclusively with Lebanese demographics.
15. The official administrative region of Beirut measures less than ten kilometers in either north–south or east–west dimensions.
16. Labaki and Abou Rjeily 1993; Nasr 2013.
17. These neighborhoods earned the nickname "the Misery Belt" (Hazaam Al-Bou'as; see Traboulsi 2007).
18. Labaki and Abou Rjeily 1993; Ministry of the Displaced 1996; Nasr 2013.
19. UNRWA makes this information available on its website, at http://www.unrwa.org/where-we-work/lebanon/. UNRWA also collaborates with academics and

NGOs to produce periodic reports, including for instance the highly informative Chaaban et al. 2010.
20. I also add data on the three camps that existed in 1975 but were permanently razed during the war; these cases are well documented by UNRWA and others.
21. Chaaban et al. 2010.
22. Chaaban et al. 2010.
23. I refer to locations as homogenous if they have zero recorded non-coethnics of the majority group in the data provided (Eid 2010). However, that data set does not report concentrations of less than fifty voters for any confessional group, and it is unclear how they round the numbers to arrive at this threshold. Consequently, locations that I code as homogenous could have token numbers of non-coethnics present.
24. About 10 percent of Palestinians globally are Christians, but the number of Christian Palestinians who support Lebanese Christian parties is infinitesimal.
25. Since the war was fought predominantly through conventional warfare with clear front lines, every village is coded as controlled by one of the two coalitions.
26. My empirical models employ region fixed effects and standard errors clustered on the district level, which should mitigate any bias resulting from shifting front lines in these two regions.
27. Balcells 2017; Balcells and Steele 2016; Steele 2011, 2017.
28. I obtained this data from the reference librarian at American University of Beirut.
29. While left-wing in ideology, the Progressive Socialist Party was also at all times a vehicle advancing the interests of the Druze community and its senior leadership, a fact reflected in its patterns of electoral success.
30. ICTJ 2013.
31. *Al-Nahar* is generally perceived to be more sympathetic to the Lebanese nationalist and pro-Western perspectives common in the Christian community. *Al-Safir* remains devoted to advancing left-wing, pro-Palestinian, and pan-Arab nationalist causes. Lebanon has a bewildering diversity of media sources, many of which are little but partisan mouthpieces; *Al-Nahar* and *Al-Safir* are generally regarded as two of the highest quality publication houses in the country, and were central to the political debate in 1975. Today the media landscape has changed somewhat, and new media sources run by the Shia party Hezbollah and the predominantly Sunni party Future Movement perhaps more forcefully represent the mounting Sunni–Shia tensions in the region.
32. During fieldwork, I interviewed the head of ICTJ's Beirut office, the leader of the team that compiled this particular report, their liaison at Université Saint-Joseph that cosponsored the report, and the one researcher who contributed

previously unpublished material to it. The report was commissioned by ICTJ after the Syrian withdrawal from Lebanon in 2005, at a time when many Lebanese hoped to chart a new course for their country and believed that Syrian withdrawal might finally enable a transparent debate on wartime abuse. However, by the time the report was published, the Syrian civil war had reached full intensity and the moment seemed to have passed.

33. The authors openly discuss these shortcomings in our interviews.
34. Lebanon in 1975 had the most extensive press freedom of any Arab country and therefore became a regional center for journalism and the publishing industry. All major factions had sympathetic media sources eager to tell their story. Violence in 1975–1976 would have had to occur in very remote, isolated, and poorly connected rural areas to remain unreported.
35. If a location experienced first selective violence and then subsequently ethnic cleansing at a later time, it will thus be coded as only experiencing ethnic cleansing. Ethnic cleansing proved surprisingly difficult to code; see below for more discussion of the different coding rules I employ as robustness checks. One downside of constructing a cross-sectional dataset is that I cannot study time effects, such as tit-for-tat attacks or other forms of retaliation.
36. I exclude events that relate to frontline combat or artillery bombardment.
37. If only some members of the civilian community left, then we could study the fate of the remaining ones to infer whether the militia planned to cleanse the location; for this reason I only include cases where an ethnic group in its entirety vacated a location.
38. IFES 2009.
39. It is difficult, even conceptually, to establish relative military strategic importance because different actors had different goals, beliefs, and strategies. Even Israeli political and military leaders at the highest level fiercely disagreed on the relative strategic value of different Lebanese territories, as detailed by Zeev Schiff and Ehud Yaari (1984) and Benny Morris (1999). I owe this point to Shai Feldman.
40. Melani Cammett (2014) relies on USAID land-use data as well as cell phone coverage as measures of relative local wealth. However, aside from the fact that this postwar data would introduce post-treatment bias in a study of wartime violence, neither data source consistently covers all regions of the country. Kara Ross Camarena and Nils Hägerdal (2020) use exogenous price fluctuations for agricultural products to assess economic opportunities across five electoral districts of Mount Lebanon and the south, but this data is not available for other regions.
41. Global positioning coordinates for each location were derived manually using Google Maps. The reference point is the balcony of my West Beirut apartment, located in Shatila Building on Labban Street of the Hamra district.

42. All quantitative results hold for both coding protocols, but the main coding has many data points that overlap in the figures and produce visual clutter.
43. All other—excluded—data points would have 100 percent coethnics, and thus fall along the right-most edge of the figure.
44. For explanations of forced displacement that focus on these variables, see Balcells (2017), Balcells and Steele (2016), and Steele (2011, 2017).
45. Arguably its most significant religious site, the Qadisha Valley, is a secluded area deep in the mountains that was already exclusively settled by Christians and did not play an important role in the civil war.
46. Kalyvas 2006.
47. Militias on both sides quickly grew to approximate the capabilities of conventional armies, and Lebanon is geographically small.
48. Militants could be using predation to sustain their combat operations, for private financial gain, or some combination thereof (see Mueller 2000; Weinstein 2007; Weinstein and Humphreys 2006). Samir Makdisi and Richard Sadaka (2005, 32) estimate that predation allowed militias in Lebanon to amass a combined total of $15 billion of wealth by the end of the war, contributing to its long duration. However, the profitability of nonviolent crimes, like smuggling drugs, dwarfed that of theft and robbery. For a history of narcotics production in Lebanon and its influence on the civil war, see Marshall (2012).
49. I have used block bootstrapped standard errors clustered at the district level as Lebanon has only twenty-eight electoral districts and conventions dictate that we should use at least forty clusters (see Angrist and Pischke 2008). All simulations use one thousand repetitions unless otherwise noted.
50. These tend to be some of the most sparsely populated rural locations in the sample and are too small to appear in Google Maps. There is no record of any of them experiencing violence or otherwise playing a strategic or noteworthy role in the war. As described above, rather than using the full sample of 1,453 locations, I subset the data to those 638 locations that had non-coethnic residents of the militia in military control.
51. All substantive effects are estimated using the Clarify software as introduced by Gary King, Michael Tomz, and Jason Wittenberg (2000) and Tomz, Wittenberg, and King (2003).
52. The number of variables in these interaction models proved too taxing to permit both probit models and block bootstrapped standard errors. I therefore used linear probability models instead of probit but kept the block bootstrapped standard errors throughout.
53. Palestinians who lived in Christian-controlled territory suffered the most extensive displacement of any group. Most members of this community were forcibly displaced. However, one Palestinian refugee camp in Christian-controlled territory, Dbayeh, northeast of Beirut, was not ethnically cleansed.

The camp was small relative to others, many of its inhabitants were Palestinian Christians, and the camp did experience certain episodes of selective violence and victimization; however, the larger point is that even Palestinians living in Christian-controlled territory did not suffer comprehensive ethnic cleansing.

54. The block bootstrap simulation technique proved extremely taxing on the data when also including region fixed effects, particularly in the second column, with only 122 observations, and typically fails often enough not to successfully complete 1,000 simulations. I therefore reduced the number of simulations to 100 for these specifications, and even with that number the simulations do not always compile successfully.
55. Admittedly, the correlation between share of coethnics and modality of violence in column 3 slips into marginal statistical significance at only the 10 percent confidence level. It may simply be too taxing to determine correlations in a multivariate regression with only sixty-four data points.
56. The one exception is when using both a linear probability model and the most conservative coding of violence, where the value of Christian members of Parliament narrowly slips into marginal significance at the 10 percent level.

4. Lebanon's Christian Militias

1. Zeev Schiff and Ehud Yaari (1984, chap. 1) recount the episodes that introduce this chapter.
2. Hanf 1993, 79.
3. Fisk 1990, 75.
4. Gilmour 1983, chap. 3.
5. Cammett 2014; Corstange 2016.
6. Traboulsi 2007.
7. Fisk 1990, 76; Salibi 1976, 48–50, 120–25.
8. A 1950s electoral challenge by the Douaihi family to the Frangieh clan in this district ended in a legendary shootout during requiem mass in a local church, leaving about twenty people dead (see Randal 1983, 157–59).
9. Suleiman 1967.
10. See Salibi 1976, 3–4; Snider 1984; Traboulsi 2007, 191–96.
11. Baun 2017; Entelis 1974; Salibi 1988; Suleiman 1967. *Qalat al-Katayyib* (Gemayel n.d.) is an exposition of party ideology written by its founder.
12. For background on Katayyib during the French mandate, see Baun 2017.
13. Suleiman 1967, 241. These membership figures are quite impressive given that Lebanon at that point in time had a population of less than two million people.

14. John Entelis (1974, 94–95) notes that the "section (*qism*) is the fundamental structural unit of the party organization. As such it groups members according to a definite geographical location such as a village (in the provinces) or city quarter (in Beirut). There are presently several hundred sections (*aqsam*) in Beirut and 356 regional sections distributed relatively evenly according to population density throughout the country's four administrative districts (*muhafazat*)."
15. Harik 1994, 8.
16. Snider 1984.
17. Interview, Broummana, April 2014.
18. Interview, Beirut, February 2014.
19. According to Jonathan Randal (1983, 166), the Christian-dominated Lebanese Forces militia had about two thousand fighters with full-time salaries by the late 1970s.
20. Interview, Beirut, March 2014.
21. Snider 1984, 13.
22. Interview, Beirut, February 2014.
23. Interview, Beirut, March 2014.
24. Interview, Louaize, April 2014.
25. Eggert 2018.
26. Snider 1984, 6.
27. Harik 1994, 17.
28. Interview, Broummana, April 2014.
29. For empirical evidence on the effects of mass communication on conflict processes, see Yanagizawa-Drott (2014).
30. Interview, Beirut, March 2014.
31. Randal 1983, 145, 219–20.
32. Cammett 2014, 39–41.
33. Randal 1983, 107–8, 219–20.
34. Interview, Broummana, April 2014.
35. Interview, Jdeideh, July 2014.
36. This relationship began with informal contacts between the Mossad and individual Maronite politicians but expanded into major arms consignments and personal meetings between Christian leaders and senior Israeli politicians, including Prime Minister Yitzhak Rabin. Israeli journalists estimate that Israel spent $150 million on aiding the Christian militias during the Rabin government alone (see Schiff and Yaari 1984).
37. Farid El-Khazen (2000, 299–304) lists all foreign sponsors of the major armed groups in 1975–1990. Note that Iran under the shah was a major U.S. ally in the Middle East until the revolution of 1979.
38. Dölerud 2011.

39. Snider 1984, 13–14.
40. Interview, Beirut, July 2014.
41. Interview, Jdeideh, April 2014.
42. Interview, Sid El-Bouchrieh, May 2014.
43. Interview, Beirut, February 2014.
44. Dölerud 2011.
45. The slogan originated with Christian warlord Bashir Gemayel as he vowed to continue armed struggle until all Lebanese territory was "liberated." In the 1990s Sunni prime minister Rafik Hariri appropriated the slogan to bolster his own Lebanese nationalist credentials. It has more recently been used by a local telecommunications firm boasting about how good reception is for their cell phone network.
46. Harik 1994, 13–18; Snider 1984, 17–28.
47. Harik 1994, 15.
48. Snider 1984, 23.
49. All major Lebanese militias made huge profits from the drug trade (see Marshall 2012). Yet the most spectacular smuggling operation of the civil war involved Lebanese Forces operatives smuggling toxic waste into Lebanon in close collaboration with the Italian Mafia in 1987, which reportedly paid the militia about $22 million to take this commodity off their hands and dump it inside Lebanon (see Hägerdal 2021).
50. Cammett 2014; Harik 1994; Snider 1984.
51. Interview, Beirut, March 2014.
52. El-Khazen 2000; Hanf 1993; Traboulsi 2007.
53. Some had Christian residents, although almost always Armenian or Palestinian; very few Lebanese Christians felt welcome in these neighborhoods.
54. Salibi 1976, 7–10; Traboulsi 2007, 161–62. Translations of the Arabic phrase vary, and some authors prefer to use "poverty belt."
55. Cammett 2014, 234.
56. Interview, Mkalles, December 2013.
57. Interview, Beirut, February 2014.
58. Interview, Louaize, April 2014.
59. El-Khazen 2000, 194–98.
60. Interview, Beirut, March 2014.
61. Labaki and Abou Rjeily 1993; Nasr 2013.
62. Interview with the president of the municipality, Jdeideh, February 2014.
63. The comprehensive report by the Ministry of the Displaced (1996, 18) confirms that both Muslims and Christians were forcibly displaced from Jdeideh during 1975–1976 and that displacement involved select individuals for political reasons rather than general targeting along sectarian lines.

64. Interview with a contemporary Communist party activist, Beirut, January 2014; interview with a contemporary member of the Syrian Social Nationalist Party, Beirut, March 2014.
65. Interview, Beirut, January 2014.
66. Picard 2002, 109.
67. Interview, Beirut, July 2014.
68. Interview, Sid El-Bouchrieh, May 2014.
69. See chapter 3 for an extensive discussion of the politics behind Lebanese voter registration.
70. Interview, Beirut, January 2014.
71. Interview, Beirut, March 2014.
72. Interview, Beirut, January 2014.
73. Interview with a contemporary Syrian Social Nationalist Party activist, Beirut, March 2014.
74. Christians cluster along the coast and in some mountainous villages. Shia Muslims constitute about 10 percent of the population in the town of Byblos but otherwise live mostly in a series of homogenous Shia villages that start just to the east of the town (see Eid 2010).
75. The National Bloc was not a mass party but a clientelist machine operated by the Edde family, who had for generations served as the local Maronite Catholic potentates of the area (see Suleiman 1967).
76. Interview, Beirut, January 2014.
77. Muslim and Christian elites in Jbeil even signed a written declaration, known as the Annaya Agreement after the location of its ceremonial signing, to specify certain principles of peaceful coexistence. The full story of the Annaya Agreement is a fascinating study in the desire for peace and intersectarian coexistence, although it falls outside of the scope of the present project and space considerations force me to exclude it.
78. Interview, Jbeil, May 2014.
79. Ministry of the Displaced 1996. That said, interviewees concur that some number of Shia left the district to go fight elsewhere in the country and that those who left would not have been welcome to return back to the district after they had made this decision.
80. El-Khazen 2000, 299; PFLP 1977; Salibi 1976, 149–52.
81. Interview, Beirut, February 2014.
82. Interview, Beirut, March 2014.
83. Randal 1983, 120–21.
84. Interview, Beirut, July 2014.
85. El-Khazen 2000, 191–92.
86. Interview, Sid El-Bouchrieh, May 2014.

87. Randal 1983, 120–21.
88. Salibi 1976, 153–55.
89. Interview with a Christian fighter who participated in the attack, Beirut, March 2014.
90. In the words of Randal (1983, 120): "It wasn't much of a fight. The Palestinians, according to Lebanese survivors, prevented the noncombatants from fleeing. The Palestinians themselves held out for three days in a furniture factory, called Sleep Comfort, until killed to the last man."
91. Fisk 1990, 98; Salibi 1976, 155.
92. Interview, Beirut, March 2014.
93. Kataeb.org 2019.

5. Palestinian, Muslim, and Left-Wing Armed Groups

1. Sluka 2000.
2. David Gilmour (1983, 34–51), describes the *"zuama"* culture in some detail. See also Hanf 1993, 79–81; Johnson 1986.
3. Seale 2010.
4. Lebanese capitalists saw how progressive left-wing governments in other Arab countries such as Egypt, Syria, and Iraq nationalized key industries and supported the sectarian Lebanese political regime as a bulwark against socialism. This calculation created a curious alliance between sectarian and economic elites that dominated prewar Lebanon (see Salibi 1976; Traboulsi 2007).
5. Suleiman 1967, 227.
6. For more background on the Progressive Socialist Party, see Lapousterle 1982; Richani 1998; Suleiman 1967.
7. Suleiman 1967, 217–18.
8. As Kamal Salibi (1976, chap. 1) describes, the crisis of 1958 significantly polarized politics in Lebanon along sectarian lines as the Christian community overwhelmingly rallied to defend Lebanese independence and sovereignty while Sunnis and Druze largely favored its inclusion in the United Arab Republic. See also Karam 2020, chap. 13.
9. Richani 1998; Suleiman 1967.
10. The Joumblatt family and its party had a dominant position but not sole command of the Druze community before the civil war as the Arslan family vied with the Joumblatts for community leadership and usually won at least one seat during elections.
11. Lapousterle 1982, 1.

12. Richani 1998, 90–94.
13. Picard 2002; Suleiman 1967.
14. Suleiman 1967, 74.
15. Harik 1994; Norton 1987.
16. While technically a secular political movement advocating for dispossessed from all communities, in practice it had strong Islamist undertones, leaders who were mostly Shia clerics, and little appeal outside of the Shia community.
17. The party is often referred to with its French name and acronym, Parti Populaire Syrien, or PPS.
18. See Suleiman 1967; Yamak 1966.
19. Interview, Beirut, March 2014.
20. Interview, Beirut, March 2014.
21. Interview, Beirut, March 2014.
22. Parkinson 2013.
23. Interview, Beirut, March 2014.
24. Cammett 2014; Harik 1994.
25. Hanf 1993, 187.
26. El-Khazen 2000, chap. 24.
27. Interview, Beirut, May 2014.
28. The helicopters never materialized because Druze leaders could not solve the taxing logistical issues involved, such as designing bases and guaranteeing adequate and continuous fuel supply. Interview with the former head of the armed wing of the Progressive Socialist Party, the Armée Populaire, Baaqline, June 2014.
29. Interview, Beirut, May 2014.
30. Eggert 2018; Parkinson 2013.
31. Khalidi 2005; Sayigh 1999.
32. Sayigh 1999, 244.
33. Krause 2017.
34. Traboulsi 2007, 154, 206.
35. Interview, Bourj el-Barajneh refugee camp, December 2013.
36. On the politics of oil in the Arab world during the 1970s, see, for instance, Rogan (2009, chap. 12).
37. Interview, Beirut, March 2014.
38. For a full exposition of this argument, see El-Khazen (2000, chap. 27).
39. Interview, Beirut, March 2014. Other Palestinian factions also had Lebanese recruits, but as they often had more narrow ideological platforms based on specific tenets of left-wing or pan-Arab creeds, they did not appeal to as wide of a cross-section of Lebanese society.
40. El-Khazen 2000; Hanf 1993, 187; Sayigh 1999, 370.

41. Some observers describe them more as akin to street gangs than militias, and they typically used their firmly entrenched position in certain neighborhoods to engage in racketeering and other forms of criminal activity. However, these groups did sometimes play a meaningful military role in particular military campaigns or stretches of the front lines.
42. Khalidi 1979.
43. Interview, summer 2018.
44. Cammett 2014, 46–49.
45. Harik 1994; Richani 1998.
46. Harik 1994, 40.
47. Harik 1994, 44.
48. Cammett 2014; Harik 1994; Norton 1987, 2007.
49. Norton 1987, 2007.
50. Interview, Beirut, July 2014.
51. Postwar prime minister Rafik Hariri spent the war years amassing a fortune as a construction magnate in Saudi Arabia and first emerged as a political actor in Lebanon by distributing aid and organizing humanitarian and reconstruction efforts in his native Saida during the 1980s. He subsequently used his money to exploit the leadership void in the Sunni community and propel himself to the premier executive position in the immediate postwar years (see Blanford 2006, chap. 2).
52. Harik 1994, 14.
53. Snider 1984, 20–21.
54. Interview with a former PLO military commander in West Beirut, Beirut, May 2014.
55. For a full list of operational ties between major Lebanese organizations and Palestinian factions, see Hanf 1993, 187.
56. Interview, summer 2018.
57. El-Khazen 2000, 191–92.
58. Interview, Beirut, March 2014.
59. Interview, summer 2018.
60. During interviews in Arabic, interviewees typically use the word "Katayyib."
61. Interview, Beirut, March 2014.
62. Interview, Beirut, March 2014.
63. Interviews, Jdeide, April and July 2014.
64. Interviews, Beirut, December 2013 and May 2014.
65. Randal 1983, 144–45; Salibi 1976, 83–84.
66. Interview, Jdeide, March 2014.
67. Interview, Beirut, April 2014.
68. Interview, summer 2018.

69. Interview, Beirut, May 2014.
70. Interview, Beirut, April 2014.
71. El-Khazen 2000, 325–27; Fisk 1990, 99; Salibi 1976, 153–54.
72. Gilmour 1983, 127.
73. See the account in Sayigh 1999, 375–76.
74. Fisk 1990, 99.
75. Salibi 1976, 158.
76. Fisk 1990, 98–102.
77. Randal 1983, 122.
78. Interview, Beirut, February 2014.
79. Interview, Beirut, March 2014.
80. Interview, Beirut, February 2014.

Conclusion

1. Of the 65 million displaced, about 22 million have crossed an international border and count as refugees under international legal conventions. The other 43 million are technically internally displaced persons rather than refugees. The UNHCR maintains updated statistics on its website: http://www.unhcr.org/.
2. The UNHCR (2017) contains data as of the end of 2015. Aside from the UNHCR definition of "Middle East and North Africa" I also add Iran, Turkey, and Sudan; however, I do not include stateless individuals of Palestinian origin, as this group falls under the UNRWA mandate, and the UNHCR does not provide statistics on this community. The member states of the Arab League, Iran, and Turkey have a combined population of about 460 million people in a world with about 7.8 billion inhabitants (as of March 2020).
3. Balcells 2017; Kalyvas 2006; Lichtenheld 2020; Steele 2017.
4. Hägerdal 2020; Kilcullen 2015; Nedal, Stewart, and Weintraub 2020.
5. Some recent examples include Cammett 2014; Eggert 2018; Parkinson 2013; Rizkallah 2017; and Schulhofer-Wohl 2020.
6. Harild, Christensen, and Zetter 2015.
7. See Camarena and Hägerdal 2020; Ibáñez, Arias, and Querubin 2014; Serrano 2011.
8. Kaufmann 1996.
9. Of course, they can also end with continued government repression of the minority.
10. Alexander and Christia 2011; Habyarimana et al. 2008; Varshney 2002.
11. Horowitz 1985; Lijphart 1977.
12. Kaufmann 1996.

13. Habyarimana et al. 2008.
14. Jose Montalvo and Marta Reynal-Querol (2008) show that this exact demographic configuration correlates with the onset of ethnic violence in general, and genocide in particular.
15. For a summary of the argument and wider debate, see Patel 2016.
16. Schulhofer-Wohl 2020.

References

Abou Rjeily, Khalil. 2008. *Movement de Retour des Déplacés a Leurs Localités d'Origine au Mont Liban Sud et dans les Cazas de Saida et de Jezzine de 1991 à 2007.* Jal El-Dib: Institut Libanais de Développement Economique et Social (ILDES).
Abrahms, Max. 2008. "What Terrorists Really Want: Terrorist Motives and Counterterrorism Strategy." *International Security* 32 (4): 78–105.
Ajami, Fouad. 1978. "The End of Pan-Arabism." *Foreign Affairs* 57 (2).
Alesina, Alberto, Reza Baqir, and William Easterly. 1999. "Public Goods and Ethnic Divisions." *Quarterly Journal of Economics* 114: 1234–84.
Alexander, Mark, and Fotini Christia. 2011. "Context Modularity of Human Altruism." *Science* 334 (6061): 1392–94.
Andary, Paul. 2012. *War of the Mountain: Israelis, Christians and Druze in the 1983 Mount Lebanon Conflict Through the Eyes of a Lebanese Forces Fighter.* Beirut: CreateSpace.
Anderson, Benedict. 1983. *Imagined Communities: Reflections on the Origin and Spread of Nationalism.* London: Verso.
Angrist, Joshua, and Jörn-Steffen Pischke. 2008. *Mostly Harmless Econometrics: An Empiricist's Companion.* Princeton, N.J.: Princeton University Press.
Arjona, Ana. 2016. *Rebelocracy.* Cambridge: Cambridge University Press.
Arjona, Ana, Nelson Kasfir, and Zachariah Mampilly. 2015. *Rebel Governance in Civil War.* Cambridge: Cambridge University Press.
Axelrod, Robert. 1981. "The Emergence of Cooperation Among Egoists." *American Political Science Review* 75 (2): 306–18.

Azevedo, Mario. 1998. *Roots of Violence: A History of War in Chad.* Amsterdam: Gordon and Breach.

Balcells, Laia. 2010. "Rivalry and Revenge: Violence Against Civilians in Conventional Civil Wars." *International Studies Quarterly* 54 (2): 291–313.

———. 2017. *Rivalry and Revenge: The Politics of Violence During Civil War.* Cambridge: Cambridge University Press.

Balcells, Laia, and Abbey Steele. 2016. "Warfare, Political Identities, and Displacement in Spain and Colombia." *Political Geography* 51: 15–29.

Barr, James. 2011. *A Line in the Sand: Britain, France and the Struggle for the Mastery of the Middle East.* London: Simon & Schuster.

Bates, Robert. 2011. "The Industrial Organization of Violence." Harvard University, unpublished research memorandum.

Bateson, Regina. 2017. "The Socialization of Civilians and Militia Members: Evidence from Guatemala." *Journal of Peace Research* 54 (5): 634–47.

Baun, Dylan. 2017. "The Gemmayzeh Incident of 1949: Conflict over Physical and Symbolic Space in Beirut." *Arab Studies Journal* 25 (1): 92–122.

Beath, Andrew, Fotini Christia, and Ruben Enikolopov. 2011. "Winning Hearts and Minds Through Development: Evidence from a Field Experiment in Afghanistan." MIT Political Science Department Research Paper No. 2011–14.

Berman, Eli, Jacob Shapiro, and Joseph Felter. 2011. "Can Hearts and Minds Be Bought? The Economics of Counterinsurgency in Iraq." *Journal of Political Economy* 119 (4): 766–819.

Birnir, Johanna Kristin. 2007. *Ethnicity and Electoral Politics.* Cambridge: Cambridge University Press.

Blanford, Nicholas. 2006. *Killing Mr. Lebanon: The Assassination of Rafik Hariri and Its Impact on the Middle East.* London: I. B. Tauris.

Blaydes, Lisa. 2018. *State of Repression: Iraq under Saddam Hussein.* Princeton, N.J.: Princeton University Press.

Bulutgil, H. Zeynep. 2010. "War, Collaboration, and Endogenous Ethnic Polarization: The Path to Ethnic Cleansing." In *Rethinking Violence: States and Non-State Actors in Conflict,* ed. by Erica Chenoweth and Adria Lawrence, 57–82. Cambridge, Mass.: Belfer Center for Science and International Affairs.

———. 2016. *The Roots of Ethnic Cleansing in Europe.* Cambridge: Cambridge University Press.

Camarena, Kara Ross, and Nils Hägerdal. 2020. "When Do Displaced Persons Return? Postwar Migration Among Christians in Mount Lebanon." *American Journal of Political Science* 64 (2): 223–39.

Cammett, Melani. 2014. *Compassionate Communalism: Welfare and Sectarianism in Lebanon.* Ithaca, N.Y.: Cornell University Press.

Chaaban, Jad, Hala Ghattas, Rima Habib, Sari Hanafi, Nadine Sahyoun, Nisreen Salti, Karin Seyfert, and Nadia Naamani. 2010. *Socio-Economic Survey of*

Palestinian Refugees in Lebanon. Beirut: Report published by the American University of Beirut (AUB) and the United Nations Relief and Works Agency for Palestine Refugees in the Near East (UNRWA).

Chandra, Kanchan. 2004. *Why Ethnic Parties Succeed: Patronage and Ethnic Head Counts in India.* Cambridge: Cambridge University Press.

———. 2006. "What Is Ethnic Identity and Does It Matter?" *Annual Review of Political Science* 9: 397–424.

Christia, Fotini. 2008. "Following the Money: Muslim on Muslim in Bosnia's Civil War." *Comparative Politics* 40 (4): 461–80.

Clausewitz, Carl von. 1976. *On War.* Princeton, N.J.: Princeton University Press.

Cleveland, William. 2004. *A History of the Modern Middle East.* Boulder, Colo.: Westview Press.

Cobban, Helena. 1984. *The Palestinian Liberation Organization: People, Power, and Politics.* Cambridge: Cambridge University Press.

Cohen, Dara Kay. 2016. *Rape During Civil War.* Ithaca, N.Y.: Cornell University Press.

Corstange, Daniel. 2016. *The Price of a Vote in the Middle East: Clientelism and Communal Politics in Lebanon and Yemen.* Cambridge: Cambridge University Press.

Courbage, Youssef, and Philippe Fargues. 1974. *La Situation Demographique au Liban.* Beirut: Lebanese University Press.

Cunningham, Kathleen Gallagher. 2014. *Inside the Politics of Self-Determination.* Oxford: Oxford University Press.

Cunningham, Kathleen Gallagher, Kristin Bakke, and Lee Seymour. 2012. "Shirts Today, Skins Tomorrow: Dual Contests and the Effects of Fragmentation in Self-Determination Disputes." *Journal of Conflict Resolution* 56 (1): 67–93.

Daly, Sarah. 2016. *Organized Violence After Civil War: The Geography of Recruitment in Latin America.* Cambridge: Cambridge University Press.

Davenport, Christian, Will Moore, and Steven Poe. 2003. "Sometimes You Just Have to Leave: Domestic Threats and Forced Migration, 1964–1989." *International Interactions* 29 (1): 27–55.

De Clerck, Dima. 2008. "La Montagne: Un Espace de Partages et de Ruptures." *Cahiers de l'IFPO*, 1.

Dölerud, Magnus. 2011. "In the Guise of Unity: The Lebanese Front and Christian Cooperation, 1975–1978." Master's thesis, University of Bergen, Bergen, Norway.

Downes, Alexander. 2008. *Targeting Civilians in War.* Ithaca, N.Y.: Cornell University Press.

Driscoll, Jesse. 2015. *Warlords and Coalition Politics in Post-Soviet States.* Cambridge: Cambridge University Press.

Duursma, Allard. 2020. "African Solutions to African Challenges: The Role of Legitimacy in Mediating Civil Wars in Africa," *International Organization* 74 (2): 295–330.

Eggert, Jennifer. 2018. "Female Fighters and Militants During the Lebanese Civil War: Individual Profiles, Pathways, and Motivations." *Studies in Conflict & Terrorism* (forthcoming). https://doi.org/10.1080/1057610X.2018.1529353.

Eid, Francois. 2010. *Le Liban-Mosaique: Interpretation Graphique des Listes des Électeurs 2010*. Beirut: Byblos Modern Printing Press.

El Amine, Yehia. 2016. "At a Glance: The Role of the Mukhtar." *An-Nahar*, May 7, 2016.

El-Khazen, Farid. 2000. *The Breakdown of the State in Lebanon, 1967–1976*. Cambridge, Mass.: Harvard University Press.

Engel, Stefanie, and Ana Maria Ibáñez. 2007. "Displacement Due to Violence in Colombia: A Household-Level Analysis." *Economic Development and Cultural Change* 55 (2): 335–65.

Englebert, Pierre. 2009. *Unity, Sovereignty, and Sorrow*. Boulder, Colo.: Lynne Rienner.

Entelis, John. 1974. *Pluralism and Party Transformation in Lebanon: Al-Kata'ib, 1936–1970*. Leiden: E. J. Brill.

European Union Election Observation Mission (EUEOM). 2009. "Lebanon, Final Report, Parliamentary Elections, 7 June 2009," European Union Election Observation Mission to Lebanon Report.

Fearon, James, and David Laitin. 1996. "Explaining Interethnic Cooperation." *American Political Science Review* 90 (4): 715–35.

——. 2000. "Violence and the Social Construction of Ethnic Identity." *International Organization* 54 (4): 845–77.

Fehr, Ernst, and Simon Gachter. 2000. "Cooperation and Punishment in Public Goods Experiments." *American Economic Review* 90 (3): 980–94.

Finkel, Evgeny. 2017. *Ordinary Jews: Choice and Survival during the Holocaust*. Princeton, N.J.: Princeton University Press.

Fisk, Robert. 1990. *Pity the Nation: The Abduction of Lebanon*. New York: Atheneum.

Freedman, Lawrence. 1989. *The Evolution of Nuclear Strategy*. London: Macmillan.

Friedman, Jeffrey. 2011. "Manpower and Counterinsurgency: Empirical Foundations for Theory and Doctrine." *Security Studies* 20 (4): 556–91.

Fujii, Lee Ann. 2008. "The Power of Local Ties: Popular Participation in the Rwandan Genocide." *Security Studies* 17 (3): 568–97.

——. 2010. "Shades of Truth and Lies: Interpreting Testimonies of War and Violence." *Journal of Peace Research* 47 (2): 231–41.

Geertz, Clifford. 1963. "The Integrative Revolution: Primordial Sentiments and Civil Politics in the New States." In *Old Societies and New States*, ed. by Clifford Geertz, 255–310. New York: Free Press.

Gellner, Ernst. 1983. *Nations and Nationalism*. Ithaca, N.Y.: Cornell University Press.

Gemayel, Pierre. N.d. *Qalat al-Katayyib*. Beirut: Manshurat al-Kata'ib al-Lubnaniyya.

Ghodes, Anita. 2020. "Repression Technology: Internet Accessibility and State Violence." *American Journal of Political Science* 64 (3): 488–503.

Gibson, James. 2004. *Overcoming Apartheid: Can Truth Reconcile a Divided Nation?* New York: Russell Sage Foundation.

Gilmour, David. 1983. *Lebanon: The Fractured Country*. New York: St. Martin's Press.

Glaeser, Edward. 2005. "The Political Economy of Hatred." *Quarterly Journal of Economics* 120 (1): 45–86.

Goddard, Stacie. 2006. "Uncommon Ground: Indivisible Territory and the Politics of Legitimacy." *International Organization* 60 (1): 35–68.

Granovetter, Mark. 1978. "Threshold Models of Collective Behaviour." *American Journal of Sociology* 83 (6): 1420–43.

Greenhill, Kelly. 2010. *Weapons of Mass Migration: Forced Displacement, Coercion and Foreign Policy*. Ithaca, N.Y.: Cornell University Press.

Greitens, Sheena. 2016. *Dictators and Their Secret Police: Coercive Institutions and State Violence*. Cambridge: Cambridge University Press.

Griffiths, Ryan. 2016. *Age of Secession: The International and Domestic Determinants of State Birth*. Cambridge: Cambridge University Press.

Guevara, Che. 1961. *Guerilla Warfare*. New York: Monthly Review Press.

Gutierrez-Sanin, Francisco, and Elisabeth Wood. 2014. "Ideology in Civil War." *Journal of Conflict Resolution* 51 (2): 213–26.

Habyarimana, James, Macarthan Humphreys, Daniel Posner, and Jeremy Weinstein. 2007. "Why Does Ethnic Diversity Undermine Public Goods Provision?" *American Political Science Review* 101 (4): 709–25.

———. 2008. "Better Institutions, Not Partition." *Foreign Affairs* 87 (4): 138–41.

———. 2010. "Placing and Passing: Evidence from Uganda on Ethnic Identification and Deception." Georgetown University working paper. http://www.columbia.edu/~mh2245/papers1/passing.pdf.

Haddad, Fanar. 2011. *Sectarianism in Iraq: Antagonistic Visions of Unity*. New York: Columbia University Press.

Hägerdal, Nils. 2018. "Lebanon's Hostility to Syrian Refugees." Crown Center for Middle East Studies *Middle East Brief* 116.

———. 2019. "Ethnic Cleansing and the Politics of Restraint: Violence and Coexistence in the Lebanese Civil War." *Journal of Conflict Resolution* 63 (1): 59–84. https://doi.org/10.1177/0022002717721612.

———. 2021. "Toxic Waste Dumping in Conflict Zones: Evidence from 1980s Lebanon." *Mediterranean Politics* 26 (2): 198-218. https://doi.org/10.1080/13629395.2019.1693124.

———. 2020. "Starvation as Siege Tactics: Urban Warfare in Syria." *Studies in Conflict & Terrorism* (forthcoming). https://doi.org/10.1080/1057610X.2020.1816682.

Hägerdal, Nils, and Peter Krause. 2020. "Blowback Operations as Rebel Strategy: How Sunni-Shia Violence Spread from Syria into Lebanon, 2013–14." Tufts University, Center for Strategic Studies working paper.

Haley, Edward, and Lewis Snider. 1979. *Lebanon in Crisis: Participants and Issues.* Syracuse, N.Y.: Syracuse University Press.

Hanf, Theodor. 1993. *Coexistence in Wartime Lebanon: Decline of a State and Rise of a Nation.* London: Centre for Lebanese Studies.

Harik, Judith. 1994. *The Public and Social Services of the Lebanese Militias.* Oxford: Center for Lebanese Studies.

Harild, Niels, Asger Christensen, and Roger Zetter. 2015. *Sustainable Refugee Return.* Washington, D.C.: World Bank Global Program on Forced Displacement Issue Note Series.

Hartmann, Klaus-Peter. 1980. *Untersuchungen zur Sozialgeographic Christlicher Minderheiten in Vorderen Orient.* Wiesbaden: Ludwig Reichert.

Herbst, Jeffrey. 2000. *States and Power in Africa: Comparative Lessons in Authority and Control.* Princeton, N.J.: Princeton University Press.

Hassner, Ron. 2009. *War on Sacred Grounds.* Ithaca, N.Y.: Cornell University Press.

Hoover Green, Amelia. 2016. "The Commander's Dilemma: Creating and Controlling Armed Group Violence." *Journal of Peace Research* 53 (6): 619–32.

———. 2018. *The Commander's Dilemma: Violence and Restraint in Wartime.* Ithaca, N.Y.: Cornell University Press.

Horowitz, Donald. 1985. *Ethnic Groups in Conflict.* Berkeley: University of California Press.

Hourani, Albert, and Nadim Shehadi, eds. 1992. *The Lebanese in the World: A Century of Emigration.* London: I. B. Tauris.

Ibáñez, Ana María, María Alejandra Arias, and Pablo Querubin. 2014. "The Desire to Return During Civil War: Evidence for Internally Displaced Populations in Colombia." *Peace Economics, Peace Science and Public Policy* 20 (1): 209–33.

Information International. 2009. *Al-Intakhabaat An-Niyabiya Al-Lubnaniyya 2009: Wafqan Lil-Aqlaam wa Al-Murashiheen wa At-Taouaaif.* Beirut: Kutub Ltd.

International Center for Transitional Justice (ICTJ). 2013. *Lebanon's Legacy of Political Violence: A Mapping of Serious Violations of International Human Rights and Humanitarian Law in Lebanon, 1975–2008.* Beirut: International Center for Transitional Justice.

International Foundation for Electoral Systems (IFES). 2009. *Lebanon's 2009 Parliamentary Elections, The Lebanese Electoral System.* Arlington, Va.: International Foundation for Electoral Systems, Lebanon Briefing Paper.

———. 2018. *Lebanon's 2017 Parliamentary Election Law.* Arlington, Va.: International Foundation for Electoral Systems, Lebanon Briefing Paper.

Janmyr, Maja. 2016. "Precarity in Exile: The Legal Status of Syrian Refugees in Lebanon," *Refugee Survey Quarterly* 35: 58–78.

Johnson, Dominic, and Monica Toft. 2014. "Grounds for War: The Evolution of Territorial Conflict." *International Security* 38 (3): 7–38.

Johnson, Michael. 1986. *Class and Client in Beirut: The Sunni Muslim Community and the Lebanese State 1840–1985.* London: Ithaca.

Jones, Benjamin, and Benjamin Olken. 2009. "Hit or Miss? The Effect of Assassinations on Institutions and War." *American Economic Journal: Macroeconomics* 1 (2): 55–87.

Jordan, Jenna. 2009. "When Heads Roll: Assessing the Effectiveness of Leadership Decapitation." *Security Studies* 18 (4): 719–55.

Kalyvas, Stathis. 2003. "The Ontology of 'Political Violence': Action and Identity in Civil Wars." *Perspectives on Politics* 1 (3): 475–94.

———. 2006. *The Logic of Violence in Civil War.* Cambridge: Cambridge University Press.

Kalyvas, Stathis, and Laia Balcells. 2010. "International System and Technologies of Rebellion: How the End of the Cold War Shaped Internal Conflict." *American Political Science Review* 104 (3): 415–29.

Kalyvas, Stathis, and Matthew Kocher. 2007a. "Ethnic Cleavages and Irregular War: Iraq and Vietnam." *Politics & Society* 35 (2): 183–223.

———. 2007b. "How Free Is 'Free Riding' in Civil Wars? Violence, Insurgency, and the Collective Action Problem." *World Politics* 59 (2): 177–216.

Kaplan, Oliver. 2017. *Resisting War: How Communities Protect Themselves.* Cambridge: Cambridge University Press.

Karam, Jeffrey. 2017. "Beyond Sectarianism: Understanding Lebanese Politics Through a Cross-Sectarian Lens." Crown Center for Middle East Studies *Middle East Brief* 107.

———, ed. 2020. *The Middle East in 1958: Reimagining a Revolutionary Year.* London: I. B. Tauris.

Kasparian, Robert, André Beaudoin, and Sélim Abou. 1995. *La population déplacée par la guerre au Liban.* Paris: Editions L'Harmattan.

Kataeb.org. 2019. "Kataeb Party Inaugurates Independence Museum." Online edition, April 12. https://kataeb.org/local/2019/04/12/kataeb-party-inaugurates-independence-museum.

Kaufman, Stuart. 2001. *Modern Hatreds: The Symbolic Power of Ethnic War.* Ithaca, N.Y.: Cornell University Press.

Kaufmann, Chaim. 1996. "Possible and Impossible Solutions to Ethnic Civil Wars." *International Security* 20 (4): 136–75.

Keegan, John. 2003. *Intelligence in War: Knowledge of the Enemy from Napoleon to Al-Qaeda*. New York: Knopf.

Kerr, Malcolm. 1971. *The Arab Cold War: Gamal 'Abd al-Nasir and his Rivals, 1958–1970*. Oxford: Oxford University Press.

Khalaf, Samir. 2002. *Civil and Uncivil Violence in Lebanon: A History of the Internationalization of Communal Conflict*. New York: Columbia University Press.

Khalidi, Rashid. 2005. *The Iron Cage: The Story of the Palestinian Struggle for Statehood*. Boston: Beacon.

Khalidi, Walid. 1979. *Conflict and Violence in Lebanon: Confrontation in the Middle East*. Cambridge, Mass.: Center for International Affairs, Harvard University.

Khoury, Philip. 1983. *Urban Notables and Arab Nationalism: The Politics of Damascus 1860–1920*. Cambridge: Cambridge University Press.

———. 1987. *Syria and the French Mandate: The Politics of Arab Nationalism, 1920–1945*. Princeton, N.J.: Princeton University Press.

Kilcullen, David. 2015. *Out of the Mountains: The Coming Age of the Urban Guerrilla*. Oxford: Oxford University Press.

King, Gary, Michael Tomz, and Jason Wittenberg. 2000. "Making the Most of Statistical Analyses: Improving Interpretation and Presentation." *American Journal of Political Science* 44 (2): 347–61.

Krause, Peter. 2013. "The Political Effectiveness of Non-State Violence: A Two-Level Framework to Transform a Deceptive Debate." *Security Studies* 22 (2): 259–94.

———. 2017. *Rebel Power: Why National Movements Compete, Fight, and Win*. Ithaca, N.Y.: Cornell University Press.

Kumar, Radha. 1997. "The Troubled History of Partition." *Foreign Affairs* 76 (1): 22–34.

Kuperman, Alan. 2004. "Is Partition Really the Only Hope? Reconciling Contradictory Findings About Ethnic Civil Wars." *Security Studies* 13 (4): 314–49.

Kuran, Timur. 1995. *Private Truths, Public Lies: The Social Consequences of Preference Falsification*. Cambridge, Mass.: Harvard University Press.

Labaki, Boutros, and Khalil Abou Rjeily. 1993. *Bilan des Guerres du Liban 1975–1990*. Paris: Éditions L'Harmattan.

Lapousterle, Philippe. 1982. *Kamal Joumblatt: I Speak for Lebanon*. London: Zed.

Lawrence, Thomas Edward. 1926. *Seven Pillars of Wisdom: A Triumph*. New York: Doubleday.

Lebanese Information Center. 2013. *The Lebanese Demographic Reality*. Beirut: PAPEC.

Leenders, Reinoud. 2012. *Spoils of Truce: Corruption and State-Building in Postwar Lebanon*. Ithaca, N.Y.: Cornell University Press.

Lichtenheld, Adam. 2020. "Explaining Population Displacement Strategies in Civil Wars: A Cross-National Analysis," *International Organization* 74 (2): 253–94.

Lijphart, Arend. 1977. *Democracy in Plural Societies: A Comparative Exploration*. New Haven, Conn.: Yale University Press.

Lowenthal, Mark. 2008. *Intelligence: From Secrets to Policy*. Washington, D.C.: CQ Press.

Lyall, Jason. 2009. "Does Indiscriminate Violence Incite Insurgent Attacks? Evidence from Chechnya." *Journal of Conflict Resolution* 53 (3): 331–62.

———. 2010. "Are Co-Ethnics More Effective Counter-Insurgents? Evidence from the Second Chechen War." *American Political Science Review* 104 (1): 1–20.

Lyall, Jason, and Isaiah Wilson. 2009. "Rage Against the Machines: Explaining Outcomes in Counterinsurgency Wars." *International Organization* 63 (1): 67–106.

Machiavelli, Niccolo. 2003. *The Prince*. Boston: Dante University of America Press.

Makdisi, Samir, and Richard Sadaka. 2005. "The Lebanese Civil War, 1975–90." In *Understanding Civil War: Evidence and Analysis*, Vol. 2: *Europe, Central Asia, & Other Regions*, ed. Paul Collier and Nicholas Sambanis, 59–86. Washington, D.C.: World Bank.

Makdisi, Ussama. 2000. *The Culture of Sectarianism: Community, History, and Violence in Nineteenth-Century Lebanon*. Berkeley: University of California Press.

Mampilly, Zachariah. 2012. *Rebel Rulers: Insurgent Governance and Civilian Life During War*. Ithaca, N.Y.: Cornell University Press.

Mann, Michael. 2004. *The Dark Side of Democracy: Explaining Ethnic Cleansing*. Cambridge: Cambridge University Press.

Mansfield, Edward, and Jack Snyder. 1995. "Democratization and War." *Foreign Affairs* 74 (3): 79–97.

Marshall, Jonathan. 2012. *The Lebanese Connection: Corruption, Civil War, and the International Drug Traffic*. Palo Alto, Calif.: Stanford University Press.

Martin, Terry. 1998. "The Origins of Soviet Ethnic Cleansing." *Journal of Modern History* 70 (4): 813–61.

Marx, Anthony. 1998. *Making Race and Nation: A Comparison of the United States, South Africa and Brazil*. Cambridge: Cambridge University Press.

Mazur, Kevin. 2019. "State Networks and Intra-Ethnic Group Variation in the 2011 Syrian Uprising." *Comparative Political Studies* 52 (7): 995–1027.

Michalopoulos, Stelios, and Elias Papaioannou. 2016. "The Long-Run Effects of the Scramble for Africa." *American Economic Review* 106 (7): 1802–48.

Ministry of the Displaced. 1996. *Qadayat At-Tahajir fi Lubnan 1975–1990: Thuruf At-Tahajir*. Beirut: Ministry publication.

Minter, William. 1994. *Apartheid's Contras: An Inquiry into the Roots of War in Angola and Mozambique*. London: Zed.

Montalvo, Jose, and Marta Reynal-Querol. 2008. "Discrete Polarisation with an Application to the Determinants of Genocides." *The Economic Journal* 118: 1835–65.

Morris, Benny. 1999. *Righteous Victims: A History of the Zionist-Arab Conflict, 1881–1998*. New York: Knopf.

Mourad, Lama. 2017. "'Standoffish' Policy-Making: Inaction and Change in the Lebanese Response to the Syrian Migrant Crisis." *Middle East Law and Governance* 9 (3): 249–66.

Mueller, John. 2000. "The Banality of 'Ethnic War.'" *International Security* 25 (1): 42–70.

Nagl, John. 2005. *Learning to Eat Soup with a Knife: Counterinsurgency Lessons from Malaya and Vietnam*. Chicago: University of Chicago Press.

Nasr, Selim. 2013. *Sociologia Al-Harb fi Lubnan: Atraf As-Seraea Al-Ijtimaaeaiy wa Al-Iqtisadiy 1970–1990*. Beirut: Dar Al-Nahar.

Nasr, Vali. 2006. *The Shia Awakening*. New York: Norton.

National Democratic Institute (NDI). 2009. *Final Report on the Lebanese Parliamentary Election*, June 7. National Democratic Institute for International Affairs Report. https://www.ndi.org/sites/default/files/Lebanese_Elections_Report_2009.pdf.

Nedal, Dani, Megan Stewart, and Michael Weintraub. 2020. "Urban Concentration and War." *Journal of Conflict Resolution* 64 (6): 1146–71.

Nobles, Melissa. 2008. *The Politics of Official Apologies*. Cambridge: Cambridge University Press.

Nolutshungu, Sam. 1996. *Limits of Anarchy: Intervention and State Formation in Chad*. Charlottesville: University of Virginia Press.

Norton, Augustus Richard. 1987. *Amal and the Shia*. Austin: University of Texas Press.

———. 2007. *Hezbollah: A Short History*. Princeton, N.J.: Princeton University Press.

O'Hanlon, Michael. 2009. *The Science of War*. Princeton, N.J.: Princeton University Press.

Olsson, Ola, and Eyerusalem Siba. 2013. "Ethnic Cleansing or Resource Struggle in Darfur? An Empirical Analysis." *Journal of Development Economics* 103 (2): 299–312.

Pape, Robert. 1996. *Bombing to Win: Air Power and Coercion in War*. Ithaca, N.Y.: Cornell University Press.

Parkinson, Sarah. 2013. "Organizing Rebellion: Rethinking High-Risk Mobilization and Social Networks in War." *American Political Science Review* 107 (3): 418–32.

Patel, David. 2016. "Repartitioning the Sykes-Picot Middle East? Debunking Three Myths." Crown Center for Middle East Studies *Middle East Brief* 103.

Patterson, Orlando. 1975. "Context and Choice in Ethnic Allegiance: A Theoretical Framework and Caribbean Case Study." In *Ethnicity: Theory and Experience*, ed. by Nathan Glazer and Daniel Moynihan, 305–49. Cambridge, Mass.: Harvard University Press.

Petersen, Roger. 2001. *Resistance and Rebellion: Lessons from Eastern Europe.* Cambridge: Cambridge University Press.

———. 2002. *Understanding Ethnic Conflict: Fear, Hatred and Resentment in Twentieth-Century Eastern Europe.* Cambridge: Cambridge University Press.

———. 2011. *Western Intervention in the Balkans: The Strategic Use of Emotion in Conflict.* Cambridge: Cambridge University Press.

Picard, Elizabeth. 2002. *Lebanon: A Shattered Country.* New York: Holmes & Meier.

Popkin, Samuel. 1979. *The Rational Peasant: The Political Economy of Rural Society in Vietnam.* Berkeley: University of California Press.

Popular Front for the Liberation of Palestine (PFLP). 1977. *Tel al-Zaatar: Al-Ramz wa al-Ustura.* Beirut: PFLP.

Posen, Barry. 1993. "The Security Dilemma and Ethnic Conflict." *Survival* 35 (1): 27–47.

Posner, Daniel. 2005. *Institutions and Ethnic Politics in Africa.* Cambridge: Cambridge University Press.

Quilty, Jim. 2007. "Separate Learning. Learning Separateness." *Daily Star,* February 19.

Randal, Jonathan. 1983. *Going All the Way: Christian Warlords, Israeli Adventurers, and the War in Lebanon.* New York: Viking.

Reno, William. 2011. *Warfare in Independent Africa.* Cambridge: Cambridge University Press.

Richani, Nazih. 1998. *Dilemmas of Democracy and Political Parties in Sectarian Societies: The Case of the Progressive Socialist Party of Lebanon 1949–1996.* New York: St Martin's.

Rizkallah, Amanda. 2017. "The Paradox of Power-Sharing: Stability and Fragility in Postwar Lebanon." *Ethnic and Racial Studies* 40 (12): 2058–76.

Rogan, Eugene. 2009. *The Arabs: A History.* London: Penguin.

———. 2015. *The Fall of the Ottomans: The Great War in the Middle East.* New York: Basic Books.

Rougier, Bernard. 2015. *The Sunni Tragedy in the Middle East: Northern Lebanon from Al-Qaeda to ISIS.* Princeton, N.J.: Princeton University Press.

Rubin, Barnett. 1993. "The Fragmentation of Tajikistan." *Survival* 35 (4): 71–91.

Saadeh, Joseph, Frédéric Brunnquell, and Frédéric Couderc. 2005. *Ana al-Dahiyya wal-Jallad Ana.* Beirut: Dar al-Jadid.

Salehyan, Idean. 2009. *Rebels Without Borders: Transnational Insurgencies in World Politics.* Ithaca, N.Y.: Cornell University Press.

Salehyan, Idean, and Kristian Skrede Gleditsch. 2006. "Refugees and the Spread of Civil War." *International Organization* 60 (2): 335–66.

Salibi, Kamal. 1976. *Crossroads to Civil War: Lebanon 1958–1976.* Delmar, N.Y.: Caravan.

———. 1988. *A House of Many Mansions: The History of Lebanon Reconsidered*. London: I. B. Tauris.

Sambanis, Nicholas. 2000. "Partition as a Solution to Ethnic War: An Empirical Critique of the Theoretical Literature." *World Politics* 52 (4): 437–83.

Sayigh, Yezid. 1999. *Armed Struggle and the Search for State: The Palestinian National Movement, 1949–1993*. Oxford: Oxford University Press.

Schelling, Thomas. 1960. *The Strategy of Conflict*. Cambridge, Mass.: Harvard University Press.

Schiff, Zeev, and Ehud Yaari. 1984. *Israel's Lebanon War*. New York: Simon & Schuster.

Schulhofer-Wohl, Jonah. 2020. *Quagmire in Civil War*. Cambridge: Cambridge University Press.

Seale, Patrick. 1965. *The Struggle for Syria: A Study of Post-War Arab Politics*. Oxford: Oxford University Press.

———. 1988. *Asad of Syria: The Struggle for the Middle East*. London: I. B. Tauris.

———. 2010. *The Struggle for Arab Independence: Riad el-Solh and the Makers of the Modern Middle East*. Cambridge: Cambridge University Press.

Serrano, Inmaculada. 2011. "Return After Violence: Rationality and Emotions in the Aftermath of Conflict." PhD diss., Juan March Institute, Madrid, Spain.

Sidanius, James, and Felicia Pratto. 1999. *Social Dominance: An Intergroup Theory of Social Hierarchy and Oppression*. Cambridge: Cambridge University Press.

Shlaim, Avi. 2000. *The Iron Wall: Israel and the Arab World*. New York: Norton.

Sluka, Jeffrey, ed. 2000. *Death Squad: The Anthropology of State Terror*. Philadelphia: University of Pennsylvania Press.

Snider, Lewis. 1984. "The Lebanese Forces: Their Origins and Role in Lebanon's Politics." *Middle East Journal* 38 (1): 1–33.

Somer, Murat. 2001. "Cascades of Ethnic Polarization: Lessons from Yugoslavia." *ANNALS of the American Academy of Political and Social Science* 573: 127–51.

Staniland, Paul. 2012. "Organizing Insurgency: Networks, Resources, and Rebellion in South Asia." *International Security* 37 (1): 142–77.

———. 2014. *Networks of Rebellion: Explaining Insurgent Cohesion and Collapse*. Ithaca, N.Y.: Cornell University Press.

Steele, Abbey. 2009. "Seeking Safety: Displacement and Targeting in Civil Wars." *Journal of Peace Research* 46 (3): 419–29.

———. 2011. "Electing Displacement: Political Cleansing in Apartado, Colombia." *Journal of Conflict Resolution* 55 (3): 423–55.

———. 2017. *Democracy and Displacement in Colombia's Civil War*. Ithaca, N.Y.: Cornell University Press.

Straus, Scott. 2015. *Making and Unmaking Nations: War, Leadership, and Genocide in Modern Africa*. Ithaca, N.Y.: Cornell University Press.

Suleiman, Michael. 1967. *Political Parties in Lebanon: The Challenge of a Fragmented Political Structure.* Ithaca, N.Y.: Cornell University Press.

Thaler, Kai. 2012. "Ideology and Violence in Civil Wars: Theory and Evidence from Mozambique and Angola." *Civil Wars* 14 (4): 546–67.

Thompson, Robert. 1966. *Defeating Communist Insurgency: Experiences from Malaya and Vietnam.* London: Chatto & Windus.

Toft, Monica. 2003. *The Geography of Ethnic Violence: Identity, Interests, and the Indivisibility of Territory.* Princeton, N.J.: Princeton University Press.

———. 2010. *Securing the Peace: The Durable Settlement of Civil Wars.* Princeton, N.J.: Princeton University Press.

———. 2012. "Self-Determination, Secession, and War." *Terrorism and Political Violence* 24 (4): 581–600.

Tomz, Michael, Jason Wittenberg, and Gary King. 2003. "CLARIFY: Software for Interpreting and Presenting Statistical Results. Version 2.1." Stanford University, University of Wisconsin, and Harvard University. Available at http://gking.harvard.edu/.

Traboulsi, Fawwaz. 2007. *A History of Modern Lebanon.* London: Pluto.

Tripp, Charles. 2000. *A History of Iraq.* Cambridge: Cambridge University Press.

United Nations. 1994. *Final Report of the Commission of Experts established pursuant to Security Council Resolution 780.* New York: United Nations.

United Nations Development Programme (UNDP). 2006. *Living Conditions of Households: The National Survey of Household Living Conditions, 2004.* Beirut: UNDP, Ministry of Social Affairs, and the Central Administration for Statistics.

United Nations High Commissioner for Refugees (UNHCR). 2017. *Statistical Yearbook 2015.* Geneva: UNHCR.

Valentino, Benjamin. 2004. *Final Solutions: Mass Killing and Genocide in the 20th Century.* Ithaca, N.Y.: Cornell University Press.

van Evera, Stephen. 1994. "Hypotheses on Nationalism and War." *International Security* 18 (4): 5–39.

———. 2001. "Primordialism Lives!" *APSA-CP: Newsletter of the Organized Section in Comparative Politics of the American Political Science Association* 12 (1): 20–22.

Varshney, Ashutosh. 2002. *Ethnic Conflict and Civic Life: Hindus and Muslims in India.* New Haven, Conn.: Yale University Press.

Verdeil, Eric. 2007. *Atlas du Liban: Territoires et Société.* Beirut: Institut francais du Proche-Orient.

Vogt, Manuel. 2019. *Mobilization and Conflict in Multiethnic States.* Oxford: Oxford University Press.

Weidmann, Nils. 2011. "Violence 'from above' or 'from below'?: The Role of Ethnicity in Bosnia's Civil War." *Journal of Politics* 73 (4): 1178–90.

Weinstein, Jeremy. 2007. *Inside Rebellion: The Politics of Insurgent Violence*. Cambridge: Cambridge University Press.

Weinstein, Jeremy, and Laudemiro Francisco. 2005. "The Civil War in Mozambique: The Balance Between Internal and External Influences." In *Understanding Civil War: Evidence and Analysis*. Vol. 1: *Africa*, ed. by Paul Collier and Nicholas Sambanis, 157–92. Washington, D.C.: World Bank.

Weinstein, Jeremy, and Macartan Humphreys. 2006. "Handling and Manhandling Civilians in Civil War." *American Political Science Review* 100 (3): 429–47.

Westad, Odd Arne. 2005. *The Global Cold War: Third World Interventions and the Making of Our Times*. Cambridge: Cambridge University Press.

Wilkinson, Steven. 2004. *Votes and Violence: Electoral Competition and Ethnic Riots in India*. Cambridge: Cambridge University Press.

Wood, Elisabeth. 2003. *Insurgent Collective Action and Civil War in El Salvador*. Cambridge: Cambridge University Press.

———. 2008. "The Social Processes of Civil War: The Wartime Transformation of Social Networks." *Annual Review of Political Science* 11: 539–61.

———. 2009. "Armed Groups and Sexual Violence: When Is Wartime Rape Rare?" *Politics & Society* 37 (1): 131–62.

Yamak, Labib Zuwiyya. 1966. *The Syrian Social Nationalist Party: An Ideological Analysis*. Cambridge, Mass.: Center for Middle Eastern Studies.

Yanagizawa-Drott, David. 2014. "Propaganda and Conflict: Theory and Evidence from the Rwandan Genocide." *Quarterly Journal of Economics* 129 (4): 1947–94.

Young, Michael. 2010. *The Ghosts of Martyrs Square: An Eyewitness Account of Lebanon's Life Struggle*. New York: Simon & Schuster.

Zhukov, Yuri. 2014. "A Theory of Indiscriminate Violence." PhD diss., Harvard University, Cambridge, Mass.

———. 2015. "Population Resettlement in War: Theory and Evidence from Soviet Archives." *Journal of Conflict Resolution* 59 (7): 1155–85.

Index

Africa, 24, 24(t), 25, 151. *See also* Middle East and North Africa; *and specific countries*
Ain el-Rummaneh, Beirut, 58, 108
Akkar, 79
Al-Amal (newspaper), 99, 143
Alawi sect, 8
Aley (district), 69, 79, 126
Algeria, 17, 133
Al-Khatib, Ahmed, 130
Allon, Yigal, 93
Al-Mourabitoun, 135, 151, 183n41
Al-Nahar (newspaper), 76, 174n31
Al-Rahi, Patriarch Bechara, 120
al-Sadr, Imam Moussa. *See also* Amal Movement
Al-Safir (newspaper), 76, 174n31
Amal Movement, 45, 63, 76, 127, 130, 137–38, 182n16
American University of Beirut, 9, 11, 65, 66, 138
Amnesty International, 76
amnesty law, 10–11, 65, 121, 155, 159, 165n35

Angola, 3, 8, 25
Annaya Agreement, 170n77
Aoun, Michel, 63, 171n31
Arab League, 25–26, 49
Arab world: aid for Christian militias, 104; Arab–Israeli conflict and Lebanon's domestic conflicts, 13, 42, 49–50, 57–58 (*see also* Palestinian movement; Palestinian refugees); Arab unity and pan-Arab nationalism, 25–26, 45, 57, 125, 134, 151, 174n31 (*see also* Greater Syria; United Arab Republic); displaced persons in, 153, 184nn1–2; non-separatist ethnic conflicts in, 24(t), 25–26, 151; and the Palestinian movement, 132–33; partition in, 159–61; political instability, 160–62; population, 184n2; regional conflicts blamed for Lebanese civil war, 57–58; World War I and European occupation of, 43. *See also* Middle East and North Africa; Ottoman Empire; *and specific countries and groups*

[201]

Arafat, Yasser, 1, 49, 52, 59, 118, 132–36. *See also* Fatah; PLO
Armenians, 8–9, 72, 126, 164n27, 179n53
arms: Christian militias, 50, 56, 93, 94, 97, 99, 102–4, 107, 145; from foreign donors, 57–58, 93, 104, 130, 131, 133; Hezbollah, 63, 138; Lebanese Muslim and left-wing militias, 130, 135, 138; ownership as proof of "active" membership, 113, 115; Palestinian factions, 57, 110, 117, 130, 131, 171n36; presence considered a threat, 15, 36, 116, 117–18; smuggling, 93, 107; surrendered under Taif Agreement, 63
Arslan family, 181n10
Asia, civil wars in, 24–25, 24(t). *See also specific countries*
Assad, Bashar al-, 16, 45
Assad, Hafez al-, 49, 57, 59, 161
assassinations, 58, 60, 64, 77, 115, 142, 166n4

Baabda (district), 69, 75
Baath parties, 52
Bangladesh, 24–25
Bashoura, 53, 82(t)
Baydoun, East Beirut, 1–2, 40
Beirut: as administrative region, 71, 173n15; Black Saturday massacre and ID card killings, 40, 169n2; distance to, and likelihood of violence (1975–1976), 80–81, 81(f), 85, 85(t), 176n50; distance to, as control variable, 78–79, 175n41; as electoral district, 89; front lines (Green Line), 73, 82, 83(f), 108; golden era, 47; Lebanese Communist Party in, 126; media sources based in, 76; Palestinian–Lebanese clashes in, 50; sectarian demographics, 79; sectarian divide, 49; shantytowns surrounding (Misery Belt), 71, 108–9, 132, 149, 173n17; Shia migration to South Beirut, 137; Sunni elites in, 124; Two Years' War in, 58–59, 73, 78–79, 82–83, 83(f) (*see also* Two Years' War); urbanization, 70, 108–9; violence in leadup to civil war, 58. *See also* American University of Beirut; East Beirut; Greater Beirut; West Beirut
Bekaa Valley, 70(t), 71, 79
Black Saturday massacre, 40, 169n1
block bootstrap simulation technique, 88–89, 176nn49,52, 177n54. *See also* methodology
Bosnian civil war, 3, 20, 35, 64, 122, 150
Boustany, Fouad, 105
Britain. *See* Great Britain
Bulutgil, Zeynep, 163n2, 167n21
businesses and owners: in Beirut, 49, 109, 118; Beirut's business elites, 49; business elites and Lebanese politics, 124–25, 170n29, 181n4; Christian militias supported, 101, 102, 103–4; interethnic contact in business life, 34, 37

cadastral zones, 68, 173n3
Cairo Agreement, 110, 132
Camarena, Kara Ross, 175n40
Cammett, Melani, 175n40
causal identification, 156
Center for Arab and Middle Eastern Studies, 9. *See also* American University of Beirut
Central Administration for Statistics, 69
Central Political Council, 135–36. *See also* Lebanese National Movement
Chaaban, Jad, 165n31
Chad, 3, 8, 25, 154–55

Chamoun, Camille, 97; additional term sought, 47; and Christian militias, 96, 97, 99, 104, 145–47; clientelism, 97, 145; family and political dynasty, 150; Lebanese nationalism defended, 54; and Rabin, 93–94; stronghold attacked, 145–48. *See also* National Liberal Party

Chamoun, Dany, 97

Chehab, Fouad, 47

Chekka, 82(t)

China, 131

Chouf (district), 69, 75, 79, 124, 126

Christian militias (Christian forces), 93–120; about, 9, 41, 53–55; arms and equipment, 50, 56, 93, 94, 97, 99, 102–4, 107, 145; Black Saturday massacre, 40, 169n1; community support for, 14, 53, 94–95, 99–104, 151; demobilization, 63; displacement/ethnic cleansing of Lebanese Muslims by, 1–2, 14, 67, 78, 82, 83(f), 84, 85(t), 86–87, 112, 115–19, 149, 158, 171n44, 179n63; displacement/ethnic cleansing of Palestinians by, 14, 55, 60, 67, 78, 86–88, 147, 149, 171n44, 176–77n53; female fighters, 101; foreign aid, 93–94, 104, 161, 178nn36–37; funding, 103, 107, 176n48, 179n4; goals, 55, 105–6, 179n4; ill prepared in 1976, 94; intelligence capabilities, 14, 15, 108–20, 151; interviews (about), 10 (*see also* interviews); Israeli invasion and War of the Mountain, 60–62; Israeli relationship with, 65, 93–94, 104, 178n36; Karantina attacked, 1–2, 111–12, 117–19, 146, 147 (*see also* Karantina); Lebanese Communist Party's intelligence capabilities seen as threat, 139; Lebanese Front as political command for, 54–55; likelihood of violence/ethnic cleansing in areas controlled by, 13, 85–88, 85(t), 152; logistical support, 102–4; Marada Brigade, 97; merged into Lebanese Forces (1980), 106; military control data (1975–1976), 73–74, 174nn25–26; military stalemate to Taif Agreement, 63; moderation toward Muslims, 105, 114–16, 152; Palestinian-led forces' strength against, 54, 59; and partition, 151; pay, 100–101, 178n19; political leadership and governance, 104–7 (*see also* Lebanese Front); political parties and, 13, 14, 50, 74, 92, 94–96, 97, 99–100, 104–5, 107; recruitment and training, 62, 100–102, 101, 113; "restraint" defined, 122; rise of, 13, 50, 56, 74, 99–100, 171n32; selective violence by, 78, 111–15; violence more likely against Palestinians, 152. *See also* Christian political parties; Katayyib; Lebanese civil war; Lebanese Forces; Lebanese Front; South Lebanon Army

Christian political parties: affiliated media, 165n37, 174n31; and Christian militias, 13, 14, 50, 74, 92, 94–96, 97, 99–100, 104–5, 107; clientelism and patronage, 96–97, 116, 145, 180n75; and Lebanese youth, 98, 99, 113, 141–42; membership as indicator of allegiance, 141–44; political and strategic goals, during war, 105–6, 179n45; prewar electoral returns as proxy for political loyalty, 74–75, 90–92, 91(f); in prewar Lebanon, 74–75, 90–92, 91(f), 95–99, 177nn8,11,13. *See also* elections;

Christian political parties (*continued*)
Katayyib; National Liberal Party; political parties
Christians (Lebanese): chauvinist views of Muslims, Palestinians, 56; Christian leadership blamed for civil war, 55; community homogeneity and likelihood of ethnic violence against, 13, 79–85, 81(f), 83(f), 86, 145–48; *dhimma* status, 142–43; displacement/ethnic cleansing of, 13, 14–15, 60–62, 61(f), 67, 69–70, 78, 82–84, 83(f), 86, 87, 118, 140–41, 145–48, 150, 173nn10–11; extremist groups' violence against, 53; intelligence provided by community members, 110–14; Lebanese nationalism of, 9, 44, 54, 55, 74, 97, 171n39, 179n45, 181n8; Lebanon recognized as part of Arab world, 57; and Lebanon's creation and independence, 43–44, 45–46; left-wing and Communist Christians, 9, 41, 44, 109, 114–15, 126, 141–42, 150, 179n63; and the LNM, 51; non-Arab origins claimed, 43, 54; Palestinian/Muslim intelligence capabilities and, 140–48; political divisions today, 160; population share, by geographical location, 79, 80(f), 83(f); population share and political power, 44, 48; presence of armed Palestinian factions opposed, 41, 50, 54, 109, 142; prewar electoral returns and likelihood of violence against, 90–92, 91(f); prewar support for Christian parties, 74–75, 90–92, 91(f); and the PSP, 126; remaining in Muslim-dominated areas, 13, 14, 123; sectarian diversity, 8–9, 164n27; selective violence against, 141–44; standard of living (class), 49, 170n28; support for Christian militias, 53, 94–95, 99–104; support for Palestinian factions, 14, 86, 152; traditional elites (prewar), 96–97; violence leading to outbreak of civil war (1975), 58. *See also* Christian militias; Christian political parties; Greek Catholics; Greek Orthodox; Maronite Catholics; *and specific individuals*

Christians (Palestinian). *See under* Palestinian refugees

civilians: cooperation with armed groups, 157; distinguishing militants from, 6–7, 17, 19–20, 28, 31, 39, 147–48 (*see also* intelligence; militia intelligence capabilities); Karantina survivors known to be, 118–19; potential threat of individuals, 28, 167–68n42; tax base, 22; voluntary flight by, 77. *See also* coethnics; community members; ethnic cleansing (generally); ethnic cleansing in Lebanon; forced displacement; non-coethnics; selective violence; *and specific ethnicities and political groups*

civil wars: changes in ethnic violence over time, 38–39; complicated by civilian/militant comingling, 17 (*see also* civilians; intelligence); creating an effective fighting force, 30–31; debates over role of ethnicity in, 7, 36, 152–53; forced displacement generated by, 153 (*see also* ethnic cleansing; forced displacement); insurgency warfare, 168n48; local (community) support and, 5–6, 30–33, 39 (*see also* community members); nationalist ideologies and, 20–21, 164n14 (*see also* nationalist ideologies); peacekeeping missions, 158; recent scholarship on, 152–53; role of outside powers, 161–62; selective vs. indiscriminate violence in, 19–20, 166nn4,6 (*see also* ethnic cleansing; selective violence); symmetric nonconventional warfare, 168n48; threat identification in, 28 (*see also* intelligence); types of, 23–26, 24(t), 151. *See also* conflict studies; intelligence; Lebanese civil war; non-separatist ethnic conflicts; partition; separatist wars; violence; *and specific other countries and conflicts*

Clausewitz, Carl von, 16

coethnics: coding for coethnic presence, 73–74; correctly identifying, 166n13; identifying disloyal coethnics, 32–33; militia control, share of coethnics, and likelihood/type of violence, 13, 67, 84–86, 85(t), 88, 91–92, 177n55; as source of intelligence, 5–7, 28–33, 34–36, 38, 84, 111–15. *See also* community members; intermixed communities; *and specific ethnic/sectarian groups*

Cold War, 57–58, 130. *See also* arms: from foreign donors

collective punishment, 166n6

Colombia, 19–20

commander's dilemma, 22–23

communists. *See* Lebanese Communist Party; leftist movements and left-wing groups

communities. *See* civilians; community members; homogenous non-coethnic enclaves; intermixed communities

community members: distinguishing civilians from militants, 6–7, 17, 19–20, 28, 31, 39, 147–48 (*see also* intelligence; non-coethnics); false denunciations, 30, 32; indiscriminate violence against, 19 (*see also* ethnic cleansing; forced displacement); intelligence provided by, 4, 5–6, 12, 17–18, 28–36, 38–39, 110–11, 139, 151; military service by, 31; selective violence against (*see* selective violence); support for military organizations, 5–6, 14, 17–18, 30–33, 39, 99–104, 128–31, 139, 151 (*see also* Christian militias; Muslim militias); violence as joint production of militant groups and, 4. *See also* civilians; coethnics; intermixed communities; non-coethnics; *and specific communities and ethnic/sectarian groups*

conditional logit model, 84–86, 85(t), 90–91, 91(f). *See also* methodology

conflict studies, 3; author's argument and approach, 3–7 (*see also* methodology); debates over role of ethnicity in civil wars, 7, 36, 152–53; implications for further research, 154–57. *See also* civil wars; non-separatist conflicts; separatist wars; war

Congress of Vienna, 161

conscription, 30–31

consociational governance model, 13, 46, 170n20

cooperation, interethnic: designing institutions for, 168n55; vs. intra-ethnic cooperation, 34; Lebanon's National Pact, 46–47, 56, 106; survival of prewar patterns of, 37, 151, 168–69n61. *See also* intermixed communities; tolerance

corruption, 69, 96, 125. *See also* crime; political parties: clientelism

Cote d'Ivoire, 3
counterinsurgency operations (generally), 17, 19–20, 119. *See also* ethnic cleansing; forced displacement; selective violence
crime: arms smuggling, 93, 107; drug trade, 107, 176n48, 179n49; kidnappings, 41, 109, 110; looting, 84, 147; by Palestinian and allied militants, 57, 95, 109–10, 186n41; racketeering and extortion, 95, 109, 183n41

Damour, 140–41, 145–48, 150. *See also* Tel al-Zaatar refugee camp
Darfur. *See* Janjaweed militias
data. *See* methodology
Dbayeh refugee camp, 176–77n53
Democratic Front for the Liberation of Palestine, 52, 135
demographics and ethnic/sectarian diversity: diversity as cornerstone of Lebanon's success, 47
demographics and ethnic/sectarian diversity (Lebanon), 8–9, 149; Christian share of population, by location, 79, 80(f), 83(f); Palestinian refugee population, 165nn31–32; and political power, 48 (*see also* elections); population of Lebanon, 165n32, 177n13; voter registration rolls as measure of, 68–72 (*see also* voter registration rolls). *See also* intermixed communities; methodology; *and specific ethnic and sectarian groups*
dhimma status, 142
displacement of ethnic/sectarian groups. *See* ethnic cleansing; forced displacement; *and specific groups*
drug trade, 107, 176n48, 179n49

Druze forces: arms and equipment, 130, 182n28; ethnic cleansing/displacement by, 60–62, 61(f), 69, 158; governance initiatives, 137; intelligence capabilities, 151. *See also* Druze sect; Palestinian-led alliance
Druze sect (Lebanon), 8–9, 164n28; and the 1958 civil war, 47; in Chouf district, 79; and the creation of Lebanon, 45; Druze–Maronite civil war (1860), 43; gun ownership, 130; included in "Muslims" for statistical analysis, 72; and the Lebanese civil war, 9; Palestinian-led alliance supported, 14, 41, 50, 151; pan-Arab nationalism among, 181n8; political leadership, 50, 51–52, 125–26, 181n10; and the PSP, 51–52, 126, 128–31, 137, 174n29 (*see also* Progressive Socialist Party); Syrian Social Nationalist Party support among, 128; traditional elites, 123–25, 134, 181n10 (*see also* Joumblatt family); and the War of the Mountain, 60–62. *See also* Druze forces

East Beirut: Baydoun neighborhood, 1–2, 40; Christian militias' intelligence about, 110–11; crime/lawlessness by Palestinian factions, 95, 109–11; displacement/ethnic cleansing of Muslims in, 1–2, 82, 83(f), 111–12, 114, 117–19, 149, 158 (*see also* Karantina); intermixed communities and selective violence, 111–15; Karantina attack, 1–2, 108, 111–12, 117–19, 146, 147, 163–64n4; as part of Christian heartlands, 79; prewar opposition in, 95; prewar social and economic change, 108; Tel

[206] INDEX

al-Zaatar as threat to, 116–17;
urbanization, 108. *See also* Beirut
economic incentives against ethnic
cleansing, 22, 35
Edde family, 180n75
Egypt, 26, 47, 57, 131, 181n4
Eisenhower, Dwight, 47
El Amine, Yehia, 173n9
elections (Lebanon): clientelist nature
of, 49, 96–97, 116, 124–25;
corruption, 69, 125; electoral
districts, 78, 176n49; in Jbeil district,
116; prewar election data and coding,
74–75; sectarian power sharing, 124;
voting and voter registration rolls,
11–12, 66, 67–72, 70(t), 155, 173nn7,9.
See also Parliament; political parties
elites: business elites, 49, 124–25,
170n29, 181n4; Communists in
leadership positions, 126–27;
Palestinians' ties with Lebanese
elites, 124, 134; traditional sectarian
elites, 96–97, 123–25, 128, 134.
See also businesses and owners;
political parties; *and specific families
and individuals*
El-Khazen, Farid, 42, 172n46, 178n37
El Salvador, 5, 24
Entelis, John, 178n14
ethnic (term defined), 163n1
ethnic cleansing (generally): Bosnian
model, 3, 20, 35, 64, 122, 150;
conflicting political and military
incentives, 3–4, 7–8, 16–17, 21–22,
26–28, 27(f); defined, 20, 77,
163nn1–2, 167n21; as dependent
variable, 67; effects of social
intermixing on, 33–38; vs. genocide,
21, 167n21; homogenous non-
coethnic enclaves more prone to, 7,
13, 36, 38, 66, 82–83, 158 (*see also*
homogenous non-coethnic enclaves);
increase in, 153; international norms
against, 22; as last resort, 4; local
intelligence capabilities and
likelihood of, 5–8, 20, 26–27, 27(f),
36–37, 84, 148, 158 (*see also* coethnics;
intelligence; militia intelligence
capabilities); as military strategy, 2–3,
6–7, 20–21, 118–19, 153–54; in
nationalist/separatist wars, 2–3, 23,
122–23, 150; return migration, 62–63,
69, 159; strategic incentives for/
against, 3–4, 6–8, 16–17, 19–23,
118–19, 145–46, 149–50, 152–53.
See also ethnic cleansing in Lebanon;
forced displacement; *and specific groups*
ethnic cleansing in Lebanon: by both
sides, 41, 64; Christian denial of, 105;
by Christian forces, 1–2, 55, 60, 78,
82, 83(f), 84, 85(t), 86–87, 112,
117–19, 149, 171n44 (*see also*
Karantina); controlling militia, local
share of coethnics, and, 79–81, 81(f);
data sources and coding, 75–78,
175nn35–37; by Druze forces, 60–62,
61(f), 69, 158; implications for further
research, 153–54; lessons from,
150–52; likelihood, in PLO-
controlled vs. Christian-controlled
locations, 85–86, 85(t); motivations
for, 84; by Palestinian factions and
allies, 69, 82–84, 83(f), 140–41,
145–48, 150; prior explanations for, 7,
84; restraint (moderation) shown,
122–23, 150, 152; during the Two
Years' War, 59, 80–84, 81(f), 83(f);
during the War of the Mountain,
60–63, 61(f), 69, 173nn10–11. *See also*
ethnic cleansing (generally); forced
displacement; Lebanese civil war; *and
specific ethnic/sectarian groups*

ethnic conflicts. *See* ethnic cleansing (generally); forced displacement; Lebanese civil war; non-separatist ethnic conflicts; partition; separatist wars; *and specific locations, conflicts, and groups*

ethnicity (ethnic identity): building/sustaining multiethnic societies, 160; ethnic diversity in Lebanon, 8–9, 164n27, 165nn31–32 (*see also* demographics; *and specific groups*); ID card killings (Lebanon), 40, 169n1; identifying ethnic identities, 166n13; as informational cue (heuristic device; proxy), 2, 6, 7, 17, 18, 20, 26, 27, 37, 39, 148, 152; political loyalties not consistent with, 39; political mobilization and, 2; role in civil war violence debated, 7, 36, 152–53; self-segregation vs. intermixing, 33–34 (*see also* homogenous non-coethnic enclaves; intermixed communities); use of term, 163n1. *See also* coethnics; ethnic cleansing (generally); non-coethnics; non-separatist ethnic conflicts; *and specific groups and locations*

Eurasia, civil wars in, 24, 24(t). *See also specific countries*

extortion, 95, 109

false denunciations, 30, 32

Fatah, 49, 52, 131, 133–36, 139, 146. *See also* Arafat, Yasser; Palestinian armed factions; PLO

federalism, 106

Feldman, Shai, 175n39

Finkel, Evgeny, 169n61

forced displacement: 1996 Ministry of the Displaced report, 12; in Angola, Chad, and Tajikistan, 8; behavior of refugees, 15, 156–57; to create homogenous nation states, 3; data sources and coding, 75–78, 175nn35–37; from Jdeideh, for political reasons, 113–15, 179n63; in Lebanon, as shown by data, 67; during Lebanon's military stalemate, 63; as military strategy, 19, 118–19; return migration, 62–63, 69, 159; during Two Years' War (1975–1976), 80–86, 81(f), 83(f), 85(t), 115, 176n53; voluntary flight, 77, 156; worldwide, 153, 184nn1–2. *See also* ethnic cleansing (generally); ethnic cleansing in Lebanon; Karantina; *and specific groups*

foreign powers: arms supplied by, 57–58, 93, 104, 130, 131, 133; role in ending civil wars, 161–62. *See also specific countries*

Frangieh, Suleiman, 54, 96–97

Frangieh, Tony, 97

Frangieh family, 96–97, 124, 177n8

French mandate, 43–44

Future Movement (party), 160, 174n31

Gemayel, Bashir, 60, 93, 115, 171n40, 179n45

Gemayel, Pierre, 98, 104, 114, 171nn38,40

gender equality, 130–31. *See also* women

genocide, 21, 167n21

geospatial intelligence, 29

Gleditsch, Kristian Skrede, 172n49

governance by non-state actors, 106–7, 135–38, 183n5; refugee camps, 63, 132–33

Great Britain, 17, 43, 170n22

Greater Beirut: shantytowns and Misery Belt, 71, 108–9, 132, 149, 173n17; Shia migration to South Beirut, 137;

urbanization, 70; voter registration rolls, 70, 70(t)
Greater Syria, 45, 46
Greece, 3, 20, 64, 122, 161
Greek Catholics, 8–9, 14, 44, 54, 99, 170n28. *See also* Lebanese Christians
Greek Orthodox, 8–9, 44; business elites (Beirut), 49; economic conditions, 170n28; and the LNM, 51; and the Syrian Social Nationalist Party, 44, 127–28, 169n10; in West Beirut, 141. *See also* Lebanese Christians
Green, Amelia Hoover, 22–23
Guardians of the Cedars, 99
Guevara, Che, 131
Gulf War (1991), 63, 162

Habyarimana, James, 166n13
Haddad, Father Gregoire, 109
Hägerdal, Nils, 175n40
Hamat, 82(t)
Hanf, Theodor, 42
Haret el-Ghawarneh, 108
Hariri, Rafik, 64, 179n45, 183n51
health care, 102, 107, 129, 132
Hezbollah: atrocities (human rights abuses), 76; Christian allies, 160; governance by, 138; insurgency against Israeli forces, 63, 65; Iran's sponsorship, 41, 45, 63, 138; media sources, 174n31
Ho Chi Minh, 131
homogenous non-coethnic enclaves: in the dataset, 72, 174n23; ethnic cleansing of, 1–2, 82–84, 83(f), 85(t), 86, 111–12, 115–19, 140–41, 145–48; intelligence gathering in/about, 6–7, 14, 18, 33, 36, 66, 111–12, 115–19, 140–41, 145–48; more prone to ethnic cleansing, 7, 13, 36, 38, 66, 82–83, 158; return migration to, 69,

159; rural villages more likely to be, 70; shantytowns as, 71; Shia villages in Jbeil nonthreatening, 116, 180nn74,77,79. *See also* non-coethnics; *and specific communities*
human intelligence, 29. *See also* intelligence; militia intelligence capabilities
human rights abuses. *See* ethnic cleansing (generally); forced displacement; selective violence
Hussein (King of Jordan), 49
Hussein, Saddam, 21, 25, 63, 162. *See also* Iraq

ICTJ report. *See* International Center for Transitional Justice report
ID card killings, 40, 169n1
India, 3, 20, 24–25, 64, 122, 160, 161
indiscriminate violence, 4, 15, 17, 19–20, 153, 154, 166n6. *See also* ethnic cleansing (generally); ethnic cleansing in Lebanon; forced displacement
Indonesia, 24–25
information. *See* intelligence
Institut français du Proche-Orient, 11
intelligence: breakdowns in, over time, 38–39; coethnics as source of, 5–7, 28–33, 34–36, 38, 84, 111–15; distinguishing civilians from militants, 6–7, 17, 19–20, 28, 31, 39, 147–48; false denunciations, 30, 32; forms of, 28–29; identifying disloyal coethnics, 32–33; in/about homogenous non-coethnic enclaves, 6–7, 14, 18, 33, 36, 66, 111–12, 115–19, 140–41, 145–48; in/about intermixed communities, 5–7, 12, 18, 33–38, 111–15, 140–44, 154; local intelligence capabilities and

intelligence (*continued*)
likelihood of ethnic violence, 5–8, 17–18, 20, 26–27, 27(f), 31–32, 36–39, 84, 111, 148, 154, 158 (*see also* ethnic cleansing in Lebanon); party membership as indicator of allegiance, 111–15, 140–44, 148; problems solved by local support, 31–33; provided by community members, 4, 5–6, 12, 18, 28–36, 38–39, 110–11, 151 (*see also* community members); soliciting local collaboration, 29–30; trustworthiness of intelligence, 32; and urban warfare, 154–55; use of selective or indiscriminate violence determined by, 13, 15, 19–20, 26–27, 29, 31–32, 38–39, 62, 66, 85, 143–44. *See also* coethnics; militia intelligence capabilities; non-coethnics

intermixed communities: Beirut as, 79; in the dataset, 72; effects of social intermixing, 12, 33–38, 154, 158, 168–69n61; intelligence gathering in/about, 5–7, 14, 18, 33–37, 111–15, 140–44, 154 (*see also* intelligence); likelihood of violence in, 86, 89–90, 158; more often urban, wealthier, 89–90; regional vs. local intermixing, 37–38; return migration to, 159; selective violence in, 7, 13, 38, 66, 82–84, 83(f), 111–15, 141–44 (*see also* selective violence); voter roll data as indicator of, 70. *See also* coethnics; non-coethnics; *and specific communities*; *and specific locations*

International Center for Transitional Justice (ICTJ) report (2013), 12, 42, 75–77, 174–75n32

interviews, use of, 9–11, 94, 121–22. *See also specific individuals and topics*

Iran, 41, 45, 104, 127, 138, 161, 178n37
Iraq: aid for Christian militias, 104; American forces in, 17; Baath party, 52; ethnic divisions in, 45, 161; ethnic violence in, 21; Gulf War, 63; industries nationalized, 181n4; and the Lebanese civil war (generally), 57, 136; and the Palestinian movement, 133; Shia in, 25, 127; and the UAR, 170n22
Ireland, 160. *See also* Northern Ireland
Islam, 142–43, 164n28. *See also* Shia Muslims (Iraqi); Shia Muslims (Lebanese); Sunni Muslims (Syrian)
Israel: Arab–Israeli conflict and Lebanon's domestic conflicts, 13, 42, 49–50, 57–58; Hezbollah's insurgency against, 63, 65; and the Lebanese civil war (generally), 41, 56, 57; Lebanon invaded, 56, 57, 59–60; Palestinian struggle against (*see* Palestinian movement); PLO threat to, 52, 171n36; relationship with Lebanese Christian groups, 93–94, 104, 161, 178n36; strategic value of Lebanese territories debated, 175n39; use of torture, 17. *See also* Arab world: Arab-Israeli conflict
Italian Mafia, 179n49

Janjaweed militias (Darfur), 22, 122–23
Jbeil, 116, 180nn74,77,79
Jdeideh, 111–15, 119, 179n63
Jezzine (district), 60, 69, 75
Jiyeh, 140–41, 145–47, 150
Jordan: aid for Christian militias, 104; civil war, 57, 157; and Greater Syria, 45; non-separatist ethnic conflicts, 3, 25; Palestinian refugees/movement in, 49, 52, 131–32, 134, 157; and the UAR, 170n22

Jordan, Jenna, 166n4
Joumblatt, Kamal, 51–52, 60, 125–26, 130. *See also* Progressive Socialist Party
Joumblatt family, 124, 130, 181n10
justice, postwar, 158–59. *See also* amnesty law

Kab Elias, 82(t)
Kalyvas, Stathis, 166n6
Kaplan, Oliver, 169n61
Karam, Jeffrey, 170n20
Karame family, 124
Karantina, 1–2, 108, 111–12, 117–19, 146, 147, 163–64n4
Kaslik University, 103
Katayyib (party): and Christian militias, 54–55, 96, 102, 119–20; ethnic makeup, 54, 98, 171n39; intelligence section, 108; members/sympathizers in West Beirut, 142–44; origins and ideology, 54, 97–99, 177n11; PPS presence in Katayyib strongholds, 139; prewar support for, 74–75, 99, 177n13; strategic goals in civil war, 105; use of term, by opponents, 140. *See also* Gemayel, Pierre
Khoury, Bernard, 163n4
kidnappings, 41, 109, 110
King, Gary, 176n51
King–Crane Commission, 169n12
Knights of Ali, 53
Kocher, Matthew, 166n6
Kosovo, 3
Koura region, 73
Kurds, 8–9, 21, 24, 126, 161, 164n27

Labaki, Boutros, 173n10
Latin America, 24, 24(t), 151. *See also* Colombia; El Salvador
LBC channel, 102

Lebanese Arab Army (Sunni splinter faction), 129–30
Lebanese Armed Forces (army): and the attack on Jiyeh, 146; Cairo Agreement, 110, 132; and Christian militias, 99, 101–2, 108; defectors to Druze and Muslim militias, 129–30; fracturing of (1980s), 63, 170–71n31; and Palestinian forces, 50, 57, 110, 111; and refugee camps, 132; soldiers from Damour, Jiyeh, and Saadiyat, 145; weakness (1970s), 50. *See also* Christian militias
Lebanese Christians. *See* Christians (Lebanese)
Lebanese civil war (1975–1990): apportioning blame, 55–58; Black Saturday and ID card killings, 40, 169n1; as case study (empirical evidence), 8–12 (*see also* methodology); casualties, 172n52; data difficult to obtain, 11, 65; data sources, 11–12, 65–66, 69–70; differing narratives, 10, 55–58, 64; end of, 63, 162; ethnic violence widespread, 41; evolving political fault lines, 160; as example of urban warfare, 154–55; global geopolitics and, 104; intelligence during (*see* militia intelligence capabilities); Israeli invasion and, 59–60; largest body counts (1975–1976), 81–82; media coverage, 76, 174n31, 175n34; military control data (1975–1976), 73, 174nn25–26; Muslim–Christian cleavage, 9, 13; as non-separatist conflict, 15, 55, 64, 122–23, 151, 160; outbreak and major phases, 58–64; Palestinian movement and (generally), 51–53, 157; parties and militias of, 50–58 (*see also specific*

INDEX [211]

Lebanese civil war (*continued*)
groups); postwar amnesty law, 10–11, 65, 121, 155, 159, 165n35; roots of, 13, 41, 43–47, 48–50; sectarian politics and Lebanese nationalism in, 7–8; stalemate and Taif Agreement (1986–1990), 63–64; strategic value of locations during, 78–79, 175n39; violence not always rational/organized, 121–22; War of the Mountain (1983–1985), 59–63, 61(f), 69, 137, 158, 173nn10–11. *See also* Christian militias; Druze forces; ethnic cleansing in Lebanon; Muslim militias; Palestinian armed factions; Palestinian-led alliance; Two Years' War; War of the Mountain

Lebanese Communist Party: Christian supporters, 44, 114–15; intelligence capabilities, 139–40; military commander interviewed, 11; militia, 128–29; newspaper, 113; Palestinian factions' ties to, 134–35, 151 (*see also* Palestinian-led alliance); and the Popular Front for the Liberation of Palestine, 134; prewar influence/support, 14, 74, 126–27, 130; Shia membership, 130; in the slums around Beirut, 109; supporters in Jdeideh and Karantina, 111, 112–15. *See also* leftist movements and left-wing groups

Lebanese Forces (Christian militias), 55, 102, 105–7, 178n19, 179n49. *See also* Christian militias

Lebanese Front, 42, 54–55, 104–5, 106–7. *See also* Christian militias

Lebanese Muslims. *See* Muslims (Lebanese)

Lebanese nationalism: Christian version, 9, 44, 54, 55, 74, 97, 105–6, 171n39,

179n45, 181n8 (*see also* Christian militias; Katayyib; National Liberal Party); differing views of, 8, 54; Muslim and left-wing version of (*see* Lebanese National Movement; leftist movements and left-wing groups; Muslim militias)

Lebanese National Movement (LNM), 42, 51, 53, 135–36, 151. *See also* Muslim militias; Palestinian-led alliance

Lebanese Phalange Party. *See* Katayyib

Lebanon: 1932 census, 11, 48, 65; 1958 civil war, 47; archives and records, 11–12, 65–66, 69–70, 155 (*see also* voter registration rolls); cadastral zones, 68, 173n3; creation and independence, 43–47; Druze–Maronite civil war (1860), 43; economic status of various groups/locations, 49, 78–79, 170n28, 175n40; economy, 48–49; electoral districts and administrative regions, 78, 176n49, 178n14 (*see also* elections; *and specific locales*); ethnicity as controversial topic in, 164n27; French mandate, 43–44, 97; general amnesty law, 10–11, 65, 121, 155, 159, 165n35; golden era (1960s), 47; Israel's use of torture in, 17; media sources (*see* media); militia takeover of governance, 106–7, 135–38, 183n5; National Pact, 46–47, 56, 106; police, 110; size, 46; social diversity (ethnic, sectarian), 8–9, 47 (*see also specific groups*); Sunni–Shia divide, 9, 160, 185n14; Taif Agreement, 63–64; voting and voter registration rolls, 11–12, 66, 67–72, 70(t), 155, 173nn7,9. *See also* demographics and ethnic/sectarian diversity; Lebanese civil war; political parties; *and specific*

[212] INDEX

locations, organizations, and ethnic/ sectarian groups
leftist movements and left-wing groups (Lebanon): *Al-Safir* and, 174n31; attack on Jiyeh, 146; business elites' resistance to, 170n29; community support for left-wing militias, 128–31; female fighters, 130; intelligence capabilities, 139–40; in Jdeideh and Karantina, 111; and Lebanese nationalism, 54; left-wing Christians, 9, 41, 44, 109, 114–15, 126, 141–42, 150; LNM and, 51, 53; Muslim–left-wing coalition, 50, 51–53, 54, 59, 63 (*see also* Progressive Socialist Party); Palestinian factions' ties to, 134–35, 151; Palestinian groups, 52, 134–35; political leadership and governance, 135–36; prewar presence in East Beirut, 95; prewar support for, 48, 49, 74; recruitment and training of left-wing militias, 128–30, 135; sectarian regime derided, 96; in the slums around Beirut, 109. *See also* elections; Lebanese Communist Party; political parties

left-wing insurgencies (elsewhere), 23–24, 24(t). *See also specific locales and insurgent groups*

Libya, 104, 133, 136
linguistic diversity, 25
LNM. *See* Lebanese National Movement
local residents. *See* coethnics; community members; non-coethnics
looting, 84, 147
L'Orient-Le Jour (newspaper), 76
Lyall, Jason, 166n6

Makdisi, Samir, 42
Malaysia, 5
Malek, Charles, 104

Mali, 3
Marada Brigade, 97
Maronite Catholics, 8–9; Christian militias supported, 14, 53, 94–95, 103, 151 (*see also* Christian militias); in Damour, 145 (*see also* Damour); Druze–Maronite civil war (1860), 43; in intermixed neighborhoods of West Beirut, 141–42; and Katayyib, 54, 98, 99 (*see also* Katayyib); and Lebanese nationalism, 44, 54, 97; likelihood of ethnic cleansing of, 87; Palestinian civilians massacred, 60; Palestinian factions deemed foreign occupation, 41; population share and political power, 48; sectarian privileges, 46, 52, 170n29; standard of living, 49, 170n28; traditional elites (prewar), 96–97, 124, 177n8 (*see also* Frangieh family). *See also* Chamoun, Camille; Gemayel, Bashir; Lebanese Christians

Maronite Church, 103, 119–20
Mazraa, 141
media: coverage of Lebanon's civil war, 76, 175n34; militia-affiliated radio and television stations, 102, 137; political leanings/affiliations, 10, 113, 143, 165n37, 174n31

MENA. *See* Middle East and North Africa

methodology, 89–90; conditional logit model, 84–86, 85(t), 90–91, 91(f); control variables, 78–79, 175nn39–41; data collection and sources, 11–12, 65–66, 69–70; demographic data and sources, 67–72 (*see also* voter registration rolls); descriptive statistics, 79–84, 80(f), 81(f), 82(t), 83(f), 176nn42–43; interviews, 9–11, 94, 121–22 (*see also specific individuals*);

INDEX [213]

methodology (*continued*)
military control data and coding, 73–74; mixed-methods research designs, 155–56; model choice, specifications, and results, 13, 84–90, 85(t), 176nn49–52, 176–77n53, 177n54; nationwide dataset, 13, 66–67, 72, 149, 155; objections to empirical evidence, 121–22; prewar election data and coding, 74–75; prewar electoral returns as proxy for political loyalty, 90–92, 91(f); quantitative data collection (overview), 11–12, 65–66, 69–70, 155; selective violence and forced displacement data and coding, 75–78, 174–75n32, 175nn34–35, 37; structured case comparisons, 111–19, 140–48 (*see also* Karantina); Two Years' War chosen for study, 42, 66–67; variables, 67

Metn, 75, 128, 139

Middle East and North Africa (MENA): forced displacement in, 153, 184n2; types of civil wars in, 24, 24(t), 25–26, 151. *See also* Arab world; *and specific countries*

military organizations (generally): commander's dilemma, 22–23; community support for, 5–6, 17–18, 30–33, 39 (*see also* community members; *and specific forces*); creating an effective fighting force, 30–31. *See also* intelligence; militia intelligence capabilities; *and specific groups, organizations, and countries*

militia intelligence capabilities: Christian militias, 14, 15, 108–20, 151; distinguishing civilians from militants, 6–7, 17, 19–20, 28, 31, 39, 147–48 (*see also* civilians); Druze forces, 151; in/about homogenous non-coethnic enclaves, 6–7, 14, 18, 33, 36, 66, 111–12, 115–19, 140–41, 145–48; in/about intermixed communities, 5–7, 14, 18, 33–37, 111–15, 140–44; intelligence problems solved by local support, 31–33; local capabilities and likelihood of ethnic violence, 5–8, 17–18, 20, 26–27, 27(f), 31–32, 36–39, 84, 111, 148, 154, 158 (*see also* coethnics; ethnic cleansing in Lebanon); media consumption as source, 113; Palestinian factions and allies, 14–15, 139–48, 151; party membership as indicator of allegiance, 111–15, 140–44, 148; research on, 154; soliciting local collaboration, 29–30. *See also* coethnics; intelligence; non-coethnics

Minet el Hosn, 82(t), 141

Ministry of Interior and Municipalities (Lebanon), 11, 67, 68. *See also* voter registration rolls

Ministry of Social Affairs, 69

Ministry of the Displaced report (1996), 12, 75, 179n63

mixed-methods research designs, 155–56. *See also* methodology

moderation (term defined), 122–23. *See also under* non-coethnics; non-separatist ethnic conflicts

Montalvo, Jose, 185n14

Morris, Benny, 175n39

Mosaitbe, 140–44

Mossad, 178n36

Mount Lebanon: Christian militias in, 60–62, 102; Christians/Maronites in, 44, 49, 60–62, 173nn10–11 (*see also* Christians; Maronite Catholics); and

the creation of Lebanon, 43–44;
Druze community in, 51, 60–62, 137,
158; PSP in, 129, 137; urbanization,
70–71; voter registration rolls, 69–70,
70(t); War of the Mountain and
displacement of Christians, 59–63,
61(f), 69–70, 137, 158, 173nn10–11.
See also Jdeideh
Mouvement Social, 109
Movement of the Dispossessed, 127,
182n16. *See also* Amal Movement
Mtein, 82(t)
mukhtar, 68, 173n9
Multinational Force, 59
Muslim Bosniaks, 3, 122, 150. *See also*
Bosnian civil war
Muslim militias, 9; anti-Christian
violence by extremist groups, 53;
arms, 135, 138; community support
for, 128–31, 139 (*see also* Palestinian
armed factions); demobilization, 63;
dominated by Palestinian factions,
136; ethnic cleansing by, 60;
Fatah-sponsored militias, 135,
183n41; funding, 179n49; ID card
killings, 40; intelligence capabilities,
139–48; political leadership and
governance, 135–38; recruitment and
training, 128–30, 135. *See also*
Lebanese civil war; Lebanese
National Movement; Muslims
(Lebanese); Palestinian-led alliance;
and specific groups
Muslim political parties: affiliated
media, 165n37, 174n31; clientelism
and patronage, 124–25; and the
Lebanese National Movement,
135–36; and Lebanese youth, 113,
141–42; before the war, 123–28.
See also elections; political
parties

Muslims (Lebanese): Alawi sect, 8; appeal
of left-wing and Palestinian
movements, 109; Black Saturday
massacre of, 40, 169n1; Christian
forces' intentions toward, 105; and
Christian-style Lebanese nationalism,
9; community homogeneity and
likelihood of ethnic violence against,
79–86, 81(f), 83(f); displacement/
ethnic cleansing of, from Christian-
controlled territories, 1–2, 14, 67, 78,
82, 83(f), 84, 85(t), 86–87, 112, 115–16,
117–19, 149, 158, 171n44, 179n63
(*see also* Karantina); ethnic and sectarian
diversity, 8–9, 164n27; institutional
reforms demanded, 13; in intermixed
Jdeideh, 111–15; population share and
political power, 48; prewar political
parties and movements, 123–28 (*see also*
political parties); remaining in
Christian-dominated areas, 2, 13; in
the slums around Beirut, 108–9
(*see also* shantytowns). *See also* Muslim
militias; Muslim political parties; Shia
Muslims (Lebanese); Sunni Muslims
(Lebanese); *and specific individuals*

Naa'man, Abbott Boulos, 104
Nabatieh, 70(t), 71
Nasser, Gamal Abdel, 45, 151. *See also*
Arab world: Arab unity and
pan-Arab nationalism
National Appeal, 125
National Bloc, 116, 170n75, 180n75
National Democratic Institute report,
173n9
nationalist ideologies, 3, 20–21, 122–23,
164n14. *See also* Arab world: Arab
unity and pan-Arab nationalism;
Lebanese nationalism; Palestinian
movement

National Liberal Party, 74–75, 96, 97, 142, 143, 145. *See also* Chamoun, Camille
National Pact, 46–47, 56, 106
National Survey of Household Living Conditions 2004, 69–70, 70(t)
non-coethnics: choice to relocate or remain, 2, 13, 37, 123, 168n60, 168–69n61; coding for non-coethnic presence, 73–74; correctly identifying, 166n13; economic value of, 22; effects of social intermixing, 33–38, 154, 168–69n61; ethnic cleansing of (*see* ethnic cleansing); identifying hostile non-coethnics, 12, 31–32, 34, 36, 62, 66, 111–17, 140–48, 151 (*see also* Karantina); identifying nonthreatening non-coethnics, 3–4, 5–6, 12, 17–18, 26–28, 33, 35, 38, 39, 66, 151; mobilization of, 2, 20, 38–39, 62, 166n15; moderation toward, 3–4, 8, 17, 21–22, 26–28, 27(f), 33, 35, 105, 122–23, 152; postwar reconciliation with, 158–59; potential threat of individuals, 28, 167–68n42; relationships key to survival in territory controlled by, 142–44; threat posed by non-militants, 28. *See also* cooperation; homogenous non-coethnic enclaves; intelligence; intermixed communities; militia intelligence capabilities; non-separatist ethnic conflicts; *and specific ethnic/sectarian groups*
non-separatist conflicts. *See* civil wars; nationalist ideologies; non-separatist ethnic conflicts
non-separatist ethnic conflicts, 16–39; about, 23–26; changes in ethnic violence over time, 38–39; coethnics as source of intelligence, 28–33 (*see also* coethnics); conflicting political and military incentives, 3–4, 7–8, 16–17, 21–22; end results, 158–59; further research needed, 154; geographic clustering, 25–26, 151, 167n38; intelligence problems solved by local support, 31–33; Lebanese civil war as, 15, 55, 64, 122–23, 151, 160 (*see also* Lebanese civil war); local intelligence capabilities and likelihood of ethnic violence, 5–8, 17–18, 20, 26–27, 27(f), 31–32, 36–39, 158; moderation in, 3–4, 8, 17, 21–22, 26–28, 27(f), 33, 35, 122–23, 152; policy implications, 15, 158–61; understudied, 12. *See also and specific countries, conflicts, and groups*; civil wars; coethnics; community members; ethnic cleansing (generally); ethnic cleansing in Lebanon; intelligence; intermixed communities; Lebanese civil war; military organizations; nationalist ideologies; non-coethnics
Northern Ireland, 17
North Lebanon, voter rolls in, 70, 70(t)

open-source intelligence, 29
Organization for Communist Action, 109, 111, 135, 151. *See also* leftist movements and left-wing groups
"original inhabitants," 114–15
Ottoman Empire, 43, 46, 124, 142, 169n6

Pakistan, 3, 20, 24–25, 64, 122, 160, 161
Palestine Liberation Organization (PLO). *See* PLO
Palestinian armed factions: arms and equipment, 57, 110, 117, 131, 133,

171n36; buildup of, 49–50, 128; Christian support for, 14, 86, 152; community support for, 128–31, 151; criminal activity, 57, 95, 109–10, 147; deemed foreign occupation by Lebanese Christians, 105; demobilization, 63; ethnic cleansing by factions/allies, 82–84, 83(f), 86–87, 140–41, 145–48, 150 (see also under Palestinian-led alliance); intelligence capabilities and likelihood of violence, 139–48; and the Israeli invasion and War of the Mountain, 59, 69, 171n36; Lebanese allies trained and equipped, 56, 110, 129, 135; Lebanese recruits, 14, 151; and Lebanon's domestic conflicts, 49–50, 56–57; "moderation defined, 122; and the outbreak of the Lebanese civil war, 58; recruitment of Lebanese citizens, 134, 182n39; seen as foreign occupation by Lebanese Christians, 41, 54; strength, experience, and capabilities, 133, 136; ties with Lebanese groups/communities, 128, 129, 134–35, 151; and the Two Years' War (1975–1976), 59, 78 (see also Two Years' War). See also Palestinian-led alliance; Palestinian movement; Palestinian refugees; PLO

Palestinian-led alliance: Christian community not seen as enemy, 140; community support for, 128–31, 151; displacement/ethnic cleansing of Christians in territory of, 13, 14–15, 60–62, 61(f), 67, 69–70, 78, 82–84, 83(f), 86, 87, 118, 140–41, 145–48, 150; dominated by Palestinian factions, 136; goals, 150; intelligence capabilities, 14–15, 139–48, 151; Lebanese National Movement and, 42; likelihood of violence in areas controlled by, 13, 85, 86–88, 90–92, 91(f), 139–48; logistical support, 129; military control data (1975–1976), 73–74, 75–76, 174nn25–26; political leadership and governance, 135–38. See also Druze forces; leftist movements and left-wing groups; Muslim militias; Palestinian armed factions; PLO

Palestinian movement: appeal among poor Lebanese, 109; foreign concern for Palestinian cause, 26, 45; in Jordan, 25, 131–32; and the Lebanese civil war (generally), 51–53, 157; Lebanese militias sponsored, 135, 183n41 (see also Muslim militias); and the Lebanese National Movement, 42; in Lebanon, before civil war, 13, 132–35; and Lebanon's domestic conflicts, 49–50, 56–57; left-wing Christians and, 41, 141–42, 150, 152; main goal in Lebanon, 52–53; Muslim supporters in Jdeideh and Karantina, 111; rise of, 49, 131; strategy in Lebanon, 133–35; ties to Lebanese population, 151. See also Palestinian armed factions; Palestinian-led alliance; Palestinian refugees; PLO

Palestinian National Fund, 133

Palestinian refugees (Lebanon): about, 9, 13, 49, 165n31; Christian attitudes toward, 55, 110–11; Christian Palestinians, 9, 72, 174n24, 176–77n53, 179n53; data on, in camps, 71–72, 173–74n19, 174n20; ethnic cleansing and violence toward, by Christian forces, 55, 60, 67, 86–88, 116–17, 149, 171n44, 176–77n53;

Palestinian refugees (Lebanon) (*continued*)
    included in "Muslims" for statistical analysis, 72; in Karantina, 1, 117 (*see also* Karantina); militancy and crime in/near refugee camps, 57, 95, 109–10; in the "Misery Belt," 108–9; not covered by voting register, 11–12; not "original inhabitants," 115; prewar presence in East Beirut, 95; statistics, 72. *See also* Palestinian armed factions; Palestinian movement; PLO; refugee camps
pan-Arab nationalism. *See under* Arab world
Parkinson, Sarah, 167–68n42
Parliament (Lebanon): amnesty law passed, 10, 65, 121, 155, 159, 165n35; function, 48; Katayyib in, 54; party support in 1972 election, 67; sectarian quotas, 8, 46; traditional sectarian elites and, 96 (*see also* elites). *See also* elections; political parties; *and specific parties*
partition, 3, 20, 64, 122, 151, 158, 159–61. *See also* Greece; India; Pakistan; Turkey
peacekeeping missions, 158
Petersen, Roger, 167n42
Phalangists. *See* Katayyib
Philippines, 24–25
PLO, 52, 171n35; Cairo Agreement, 110, 132; Christian community not seen as enemy, 140, 150; Christian forces committed to fighting, 94, 104, 105; as de facto state, 132–33; and exiled residents of Karantina, 1, 118; intelligence capabilities, 139; leadership evacuated to Tunisia, 60, 65; leadership not always heeded, 110; and the Lebanese civil war (generally), 51–53; prewar support for, 74; Rabin's interest in thwarting, 93–94; rise of, 49; strategies against Israel, 52, 171n36; strategy in Lebanon, 133–34, 150; Sunni and Druze leaders and, 50; Tel al-Zaatar survivors relocated, 147. *See also* Arafat, Yasser; Palestinian armed factions; Palestinian-led alliance; Palestinian movement; Palestinian refugees; refugee camps
pluralism, 3, 21. *See also* cooperation; non-coethnics; non-separatist conflicts; tolerance
police (Lebanese), 57, 68, 95, 109–10, 116, 132, 143
policy implications, 15, 158–62
political parties: affiliated media, 10, 113, 165n37, 174n31; clientelism and patronage, 49, 96–97, 116, 124–25, 145, 180n75; and the Lebanese National Movement, 135–36; and Lebanese youth, 98, 99, 113, 141–42; militias formed by, 50, 74, 92, 94–96, 97, 99–100 (*see also* Christian militias; Muslim militias); party membership as indicator of allegiance, 111–15, 140–44, 148; party structure (organization), 178n14; prewar electoral returns as proxy for political loyalty, 74–75, 90–92, 91(f); services provided by, 107 (*see also* governance by non-state actors). *See also* Christian political parties; elections; leftist movements and left-wing groups; Muslim political parties; Parliament; *and specific parties*
Popular Front for the Liberation of Palestine, 52, 131, 134. *See also* Palestinian armed factions; Palestinian movement

Popular Nasserist Organization, 135, 183n41
PPS. *See* Syrian Social Nationalist Party
predation, 84, 147, 176n48. *See also* crime
Progressive Socialist Party (PSP), 14, 51–52, 125–26; electoral returns, 74, 174n29; and gender roles, 131; intelligence capabilities, 144; militia, 128, 130, 137; services and governance, 129, 137. *See also* Druze forces; Joumblatt, Kamal
public services, 106–7, 132, 137. *See also* governance by non-state actors

Qadisha Valley, 176n45

Rabin, Yitzhak, 93, 178n36
racketeering, 109, 183n41
radio stations, 102, 137. *See also* media
Rahba, 82(t)
Randal, Jonathan, 178n19
reconciliation, 158–59
Red Cross, 118, 132
refugee camps, 9, 49; criminal activity in/around, 57, 95, 109–10; ethnic cleansing by Christian forces, 149, 171n44, 176–77n53; governance and control over, 63, 132–33, 138; as haven for Palestinian armed factions, 57, 116–17, 129, 134, 157; Israeli-organized incursion into, 60; in Jordan, 131, 157; Lebanese army clashes with militants in, 50; in the "Misery Belt," 108–9; PLO/Fatah intelligence operations in, 139; sovereignty under Cairo Agreement, 132; Tel al-Zaatar camp, 116–17, 147; UNRWA and, 9, 12, 49, 71–72, 132, 173–74n19, 174n20. *See also* Palestinian refugees

refugees (generally), 15, 153, 156–57, 184nn1–2. *See also* ethnic cleansing (generally); forced displacement; Palestinian refugees; refugee camps; Syrian refugees
residence, official, 68. *See also* voter registration rolls
return migration, 62–63, 69, 159
Reynal-Querol, Marta, 185n14
right-wing forces. *See* Christian militias; Katayyib
Rjeily, Khalil Abou, 173n10
Russia, 17, 154. *See also* Soviet Union
Rwanda, 35

Saadeh, Anton, 127–28
Saadiyat, 140–41, 145, 147, 150
Sadaka, Richard, 42
Saida: Christians displaced from, 60, 61(f), 69; as electoral district, 69, 89; Hariri in, 183n5; Palestinian proxy militia in, 135, 183n41; Palestinian stronghold in, 146; Sunni Muslims in, 79; Sunni politician killed, 58; traditional elites in, 124, 125; urban dummy variable, 78
Salam family, 124
Salehyan, Idean, 172n49
Salibi, Kamal, 42, 181n8
Salima, 82(t)
Saudi Arabia, 57, 63, 161
Sayyidat Al-Bir conclave (1977), 106
Schiff, Zeev, 175n39
schools. *See* youth
sectarianism (generally), 7–8, 9, 25–26, 163n1. *See also* Lebanese civil war; *and specific sectarian groups*
selective violence: assassinations, 60, 64, 77, 115, 142, 166n4; data sources and coding, 75–77, 175nn34–35; as dependent variable, 67; geographic

selective violence (*continued*)
  distribution of, in Lebanon (1975–1976), 79–84, 81(f), 82(t), 83(f); ID card killings, 40, 169n1; information key to, 15, 19–20, 26–27, 29, 31–32, 38–39, 62, 66, 85, 143–44 (*see also* intelligence; militia intelligence capabilities); in intermixed communities, 38, 111–15, 141–44 (*see also* intermixed communities); largest body counts (1975–1976), 82(t); militia control, share of coethnics, and, 13, 79–81, 81(f), 84–86, 85(f); party membership as indicator of allegiance, 111–15, 140–44, 148; return migration following, 159
Senegal, 3
separatist wars: based on identity cleavages, 23, 24–25, 24(t) (*see also* nationalist ideologies); end results, 158, 184n9 (*see also* partition); and ethnic cleansing, 2–3, 23, 122–23, 150 (*see also* ethnic cleansing); policy implications, 158–61. *See also specific countries, conflicts, and groups*; civil wars
Serbia, 3
Serbs, Bosnian, 3, 122, 150. *See also* Bosnian civil war
shantytowns, 71, 108–9, 109–11, 132, 149, 173n17. *See also* East Beirut; Karantina
Sharon, Ariel, 60
Sherman, William Tecumseh, 16
Shia Muslims (Iraqi), 21, 25
Shia Muslims (Lebanese), 8–9; Amal Movement, 45, 63, 76, 127, 130, 137–38, 182n16; Christian forces' treatment of, in East Beirut, 1–2; in Damour, 145 (*see also* Damour); economic conditions, 49, 170n28;

ethnic cleansing of Shia neighborhoods, 171n44; geographic clustering, 79 (*see also* Bekaa Valley); and Hezbollah, 45, 138 (*see also* Hezbollah); in intermixed Jdeideh, 111–15; in Jbeil district, 116, 180nn74,77,79; and Katayyib, 171n39; Knights of Ali, 53; and the Lebanese Communist Party, 126 (*see also* Lebanese Communist Party); and Lebanon's creation and independence, 45–46; in poor urban neighborhoods, 108; sectarian Shia movements, 109; Sunni–Shia conflict, 9, 160, 185n14; Syrian Social Nationalist Party support among, 128; traditional views on gender, 130; urban migration and shantytowns, 71; in West Beirut, 141. *See also* Hezbollah; Muslim political parties; Muslims (Lebanese)
signal intelligence, 29
smuggling: arms, 93, 107; drugs, 107, 176n48, 179n49
Snider, Lewis, 171n32
snipers, 41
social intermixing. *See* intermixed communities
socialist movements. *See* leftist movements and left-wing groups; left-wing insurgencies; Syrian Social Nationalist Party (PPS)
social services. *See* governance; health care; public services
Solh family, 124, 125
South Lebanon (district), 70(t), 71, 146
South Lebanon Army, 65
Soviet Union: counterinsurgency operations, 19, 154; implosion of, 24, 150; influence and arms donations,

57, 59, 130, 133, 182n28; and the Middle East, 57–58. *See also* Russia
Staniland, Paul, 168n42
Sudanese civil war, 22, 122–23
Suleiman, Michael, 171n38
Sunni Muslims (Lebanese), 8–9; and the 1958 civil war, 47; in Baydoun, 1–2, 40; business elites (Beirut), 49; community support for Muslim and Palestinian forces, 41, 151; ethnic cleansing/forced displacement of, 60, 171n44 (*see also* Karantina); Future Movement, 174n31; geographic clustering, 79; and Greater Syria, 45–46, 169n12; and the Lebanese National Movement, 42 (*see also* Lebanese National Movement); and Lebanon's creation and independence, 45–46; and the LNM, 51 (*see also* Lebanese National Movement); and the Ottoman Empire, 46; and Palestinian community/factions, 14, 41, 134, 151; Palestinian-sponsored militias, 135, 183n41; and pan-Arab nationalism, 45, 47, 53, 57, 125, 181n8; and the PLO, 49, 151; Sunni–Shia divide, 9, 160, 185n14; traditional elites, 123–25, 128, 134; wartime leadership and governance, 138, 183n5; in West Beirut, 141 (*see also* West Beirut). *See also* Muslim militias; Muslim political parties; Muslims (Lebanese); Palestinian-led alliance; Palestinian refugees
Sunni Muslims (Syrian), 16, 45, 161
Sykes–Picot Agreement, 43, 160
Syria: aid for Christian militias, 104, 161; Baath party, 52; civil war, 16, 45, 161; and Egypt, 26, 47, 57; human rights abuses in Lebanon, 76; industries nationalized, 181n4; and the Lebanese civil war (generally), 41, 56, 59, 161–62; and Lebanese political/military groups, 127, 136, 138 (*see also* Amal Movement; Hezbollah; Syrian Social Nationalist Party); Palestinian factions in, 49; and the Palestinian movement, 131, 133; as part of Greater Syria, 45 (*see also* Greater Syria); presence in and hegemony over Lebanon, 56, 57, 59, 63–64, 162; Saadeh on, 127; Sunni Syrians, 16, 45, 161
Syrian refugees, 9, 157, 165n32
Syrian Social Nationalist Party (PPS), 44, 111, 127–29, 139, 169n10, 182n17

Taalabaya, 82(t)
Taif Agreement, 63–64
Tajikistan, 3, 8, 167n38
Tal Abbas, 82(t)
Tanzim, 99
Tanzimat reforms, 43
Tawheed (Islamist movement), 142–43
taxes, 22, 107
Tel al-Zaatar refugee camp, 116–17, 147
"10,452" slogan, 106, 179n45
territory, military-strategic value of (generally), 27–28
Toft, Monica, 23, 24(t), 164n14
tolerance, 35–36, 46, 116, 154, 170n77. *See also* cooperation; intermixed communities
Tomz, Michael, 176n51
torture, 17
Traboulsi, Fawwaz, 170n29, 172n52
transitional justice, 158–59
Treaty of Versailles, 161
Tripoli, 45, 78, 79, 89, 124
Turkey, 3, 20, 64, 122, 161
24 October Movement, 151

Two Years' War (1975–1976), 9, 58–59; in Beirut, 58–59, 73, 78–79, 81(f), 82–83, 83(f); controlling militia, local share of coethnics, and violence, 79–81, 81(f); distance to Beirut, and likelihood of violence (1975–1976), 80–81, 81(f), 85, 85(t), 176n50; economic motivations during, 84, 176n48; ethnic cleansing during, 78; as focus of study, 42, 66–67 (see also methodology); geographic distribution of violence, 79–84, 81(f), 82(t), 83(f); military capabilities, 84, 176n47. See also Lebanese civil war; and specific ethnic, sectarian, and militant groups

UAR. See United Arab Republic
Uganda, 5
UNHCR, 153, 184nn1–2
United Arab Republic (UAR), 26, 47, 57, 170n22, 181n8. See also Arab world: Arab unity and pan-Arab nationalism
United Nations: Development Programme, 69; ethnic cleansing defined, 163n2; High Commissioner for Refugees (UNHCR), 153, 184nn1–2; Relief and Works Agency (UNRWA), 9, 12, 49, 71–72, 132, 173–74n19, 174n20, 184n2
United States: and the 1958 Lebanese civil war, 47; and the 1975–1990 Lebanese civil war, 63, 104, 162; Civil War, 16; Cold War, 57–58; forces in Iraq, 17; King–Crane Commission, 169n12
Université Saint-Joseph, 11, 66
UNRWA. See under United Nations

urbanization, 70–71, 89–90, 108–9, 154. See also Beirut; Saida; Tripoli
urban warfare, 154–55. See also Beirut; East Beirut; Karantina; West Beirut

Vietnam, 5, 131
violence: anthropology of, 10; coding modalities of, 76–78, 175nn35–37 (see also methodology); geographic distribution of, in Lebanon (1975–1976), 79–84, 81(f), 82(t), 83(f); as joint production of militant organizations and civilians, 4; model choice, specifications, and results, 84–90, 176nn49–52, 176–77n53, 177n54 (see also methodology); mutual escalation of, 21–22; not always rational/organized, 121–22; selective vs. indiscriminate violence, 4, 15, 17, 19–20, 26–27, 153, 154, 166nn4, 6. See also ethnic cleansing (generally); ethnic cleansing in Lebanon; forced displacement; non-separatist ethnic conflicts; selective violence; separatist wars; war
Voice of Lebanon (radio station), 102
Voice of the Free (*Sawt Al-Ahrar*; newspaper), 97
Voice of the Mountain (Sawt Al-Jabal; radio station), 137
voter registration rolls, 11–12, 66, 67–72, 70(t), 155, 173n7

war: categories of, 23–26, 24(t); Clausewitz on, 16; military-strategic value of territory in, 27–28; peacekeeping missions, 158; urban warfare, 154–55. See also civil wars; conflict studies; ethnic cleansing (generally); ethnic cleansing in

Lebanon; intelligence; military organizations; non-separatist ethnic conflicts; separatist wars; violence
War of the Camps, 63
War of the Mountain (1983–1985), 59–63, 61(f), 69, 137, 158, 173nn10–11
wealth. *See* economic status
West Bank, 17, 52
West Beirut, 141; Amal Movement in, 138 (*see also* Amal Movement); divided from East Beirut, 108; factional rivalries and wartime governance, 138; ID card killings, 40; Karantina exiles resettled in, 118, 147; Knights of Ali based in, 53; Mosaitbe (intermixed neighborhood), 140–44; Palestinian proxy militia in, 135, 183n41; selective violence in (1975–1976), 83, 83(f); Syrian Social Nationalist Party activists in, 128. *See also* Beirut
Wittenberg, Jason, 176n51
women, 101, 130–31, 173n9. *See also* community members

Yaari, Ehud, 175n39
youth: education about civil war, 10; militias and, 100–101, 107, 113, 129; political parties and, 98, 99, 113, 141–42

Zahle region, 73
Zghorta district, 96–97, 124, 177n8
Zhukov, Yuri, 166n6
zuama, 124–25

GPSR Authorized Representative: Easy Access System Europe, Mustamäe tee
50, 10621 Tallinn, Estonia, gpsr.requests@easproject.com

www.ingramcontent.com/pod-product-compliance
Lightning Source LLC
Chambersburg PA
CBHW021943290426
44108CB00012B/944